From Paragraphs to Plots

From Paragraphs to Plots
Architecture of the Novel

Matthew Clark

Louisiana State University Press
Baton Rouge

Published by Louisiana State University Press
lsupress.org

Copyright © 2024 by Louisiana State University Press
All rights reserved. Except in the case of brief quotations used in articles or reviews, no part of this publication may be reproduced or transmitted in any format or by any means without written permission of Louisiana State University Press.

Designer: Andrew Shurtz
Typeface: Martina Plantijn

Library of Congress Cataloging-in-Publication Data
Names: Clark, Matthew, 1948– author.
Title: From paragraphs to plots : architecture of the novel / Matthew Clark.
Description: Baton Rouge : Louisiana State University Press, 2024. | Includes bibliographical references and index.
Identifiers: LCCN 2024009654 (print) | LCCN 2024009655 (ebook) | ISBN 978-0-8071-8251-2 (cloth) | ISBN 978-0-8071-8332-8 (paperback) | ISBN 978-0-8071-8330-4 (epub) | ISBN 978-0-8071-8331-1 (pdf)
Subjects: LCSH: Fiction—Technique. | Narration (Rhetoric) | Plots (Drama, novel, etc.) | Fiction—History and criticism.
Classification: LCC PN3355 .C54 2024 (print) | LCC PN3355 (ebook) | DDC 808.3—dc23/eng/20240419
LC record available at https://lccn.loc.gov/2024009654
LC ebook record available at https://lccn.loc.gov/2024009655

This book is for Paul and Bayla

Contents

Acknowledgments ix

Introduction 1
1. The Composition of *Emma* and *Mrs. Dalloway* 3
2. Ring Composition 29
3. The Composition of *The Good Soldier* and *Catch-22* 50
4. Simple Plot Forms 90
5. Complex Plot Forms, Part I 112
6. Complex Plot Forms, Part II 130
7. Viet Thanh Nguyen's *The Sympathizer* 153
   Coda 190

Notes 193
References 197
Index 205

Acknowledgments

Much of my method of literary analysis and interpretation derives from lessons learned from teachers of music and philology; among these I owe a special debt to Michael Kelly, Don Doughty, Sophocles Papas, Boyanna Toyich, Roman Toi, Sister Mechtilde O'Mara, Malcolm Wallace, Alexander Dalzell, Michael O'Brien, Joan Bigwood, Christopher Jones, Richard Tarrant, Richard Thomas, Gregory Nagy, and Calvert Watkins.

I would also like to thank the Faculty of Liberal Arts and Professional Studies of York University, Toronto, for the financial support it provided for this volume and its companion, *How to Reread a Novel*.

From Paragraphs to Plots

Introduction

The novel has often been characterized as the art form without a form. According to G. K. Chesterton (1911, 114), the novel is "essentially formless," and therefore, unlike other modes of literature, such as tragedy or epic, it has no generic rules. Thomas Pavel (2013, 7) notes that "one reason why the novel's early development was not always understood is that for so long there were no written rules meant to govern prose narrative." E. M. Forster (1927, 42) remarks that "principles and systems may suit other forms of art, but they cannot be applicable here."

I don't suppose there are rules for writing a novel, but I'm convinced that a good novel is as well-formed in its way as a good poem is in its. In this volume and its companion, *How to Reread a Novel,* I describe some important common practices of narrative construction. *How to Reread a Novel* is primarily concerned with two topics: the narrative situation, that is, the interaction between authors and readers, and style. This volume is concerned with large narrative structures—the architecture of the novel. The scope of my investigation is deliberately broad and covers long narratives of all genres—realistic novels, fantasies, allegories, satires, and even long narratives in verse, such as the Homeric epics. The only exceptions I have found are certain unnatural or postmodern narratives, and even these may achieve their effects through deliberate opposition to assumed conventions.

Critics have made many insightful comments about the composition of individual works, but these comments have not been brought together into a comprehensive account of composition. This project aims toward such a comprehensive account but doesn't claim to have achieved it. Eventually it may be possible to sketch out something like a theory of composition, or perhaps a set of theories about different aspects of composition, but analysis of examples must come first.

In this volume, as in *How to Reread a Novel,* theory takes a backseat to practical questions of analysis and interpretation. It's fair to say, however, that I am guided by a pretheoretical inclination to look for beauty and the sources of beauty. The aesthetic experience of literature often has what may seem to be a paradoxical duality: on the one hand, the aesthetic experience is a goal in itself; on the other hand, it leads to something more, which for convenience we may call meaning. In literature, the aesthetic and the thematic are simultaneous and inextricable, though as an analytical convenience description usually precedes interpretation.

Chapter 1 begins with the division of a narrative into parts, from sentences to paragraphs to chapters and episodes up to complete plots, and then moves on to discuss the composition of Jane Austen's *Emma* and Virginia Woolf's *Mrs. Dalloway.* Chapter 2 focuses on an important but neglected feature of narrative structure, ring composition. Chapter 3 presents a detailed analysis of two novels, Ford Madox Ford's *The Good Soldier* and Joseph Heller's *Catch-22.* Chapter 4 examines some aspects of simple plot forms—plots that begin with a specific initiating event and proceed in a more or less regular chronological progression from beginning to middle to end. This chapter outlines a number of common beginnings (Arrival, Departure, Meeting, Need, Birth, and Death) and endings (Departures, Returns, Marriages, Need Satisfied, and Death) and also includes a short account of some less common beginnings. Chapters 5 and 6 examine some devices of complex plot forms, including Beginning with the Ending, Second Chapter Retrospects, Ghosts from the Past, Multiple Retrospects, One-Day Novels, One-Year Novels, Mirror Plots, Alternating Chapters, Simultaneous Narration, Unnatural Chronology, and Non-Narrative Elements in Narrative. Chapter 7 draws on the discussion in both volumes to analyze at length and in detail a recent novel, Viet Thanh Nguyen's *The Sympathizer.*

I

The Composition of *Emma* and *Mrs. Dalloway*

Segmentation

The traditional marks of punctuation—comma, colon, semicolon, dash, period, question mark, exclamation mark—operate within or at the boundary of a sentence. Capitalization should also be counted as a marker of a sentence boundary, although we don't think of it as a punctuation mark. These graphic marks of punctuation are a kind of representation of breathing and pausing and intonation in speech as well as the divisions of meaning in a sentence. The use of these marks has changed over time; these days, for example, we seem to be cutting down on commas.

Indentation to mark a new paragraph operates somewhat like a higher level of punctuation. The paragraph is a modern invention. The word "paragraphos" itself is old, but originally it meant a mark in the margin of a document (from the Greek "para," beside, and "graphô," to write); in ancient dramatic scripts, for instance, a paragraphos was used to show a change in speaker, whereas today we would indicate each speaker's name. In modern usage, a paragraph is not a mark, but a unit of text and a unit of meaning. All the sentences in a paragraph are supposed to go together in some way, and the indentation of a new paragraph suggests that there is some kind of break in the meaning and also some kind of pause or break in the rhythm—the rhythm of language or the rhythm of thought.

Paragraphs are complex and various, and they do not obey any simple rules or principles. We need to examine length, internal structure, and the connection of a paragraph to the larger text. Paragraphs in expository nonfiction are often straightforward, though by no means do they all work the same way. A nonfiction paragraph may be formed with a combination of topic sentences, subordinate sentences expanding or explaining the topic sentence, links from sentence to sentence within the paragraph, and perhaps a link or transition from one paragraph to the next. This kind of construction is hypotactic—organized in a hierarchy of main and subordinate elements. Fiction, however, is not usually organized by the logic of argument; fiction has its own kind of narrative logic, which can be based on the association of ideas or images or by the temporal or spatial organization of events or scenes, in parataxis rather than hypotaxis. But whatever logic is used, a paragraph should somehow feel on some rationale to be a whole.

Long paragraphs can be very long indeed. The first paragraph of Arnold Bennett's *The Old Wives' Tale* is thirty printed lines; the first paragraph of Virginia Woolf's *The Years* is forty-two; the first paragraph of George Eliot's *Silas Marner* is forty-five; the first paragraph of chapter 6 of Henry James's *The Portrait of a Lady* is 105 lines. I select for brief analysis the beginning of Elizabeth Gaskell's *North and South:*

> "Edith!" said Margaret gently, "Edith!"
>
> But as Margaret half suspected, Edith had fallen asleep. She lay curled up on the sofa in the back drawing-room in Harley Street, looking very lovely in her white muslin and blue ribbons. If Titania had ever been dressed in white muslin and blue ribbons, and had fallen asleep on a crimson damask sofa in a back drawing-room, Edith might have been taken for her. Margaret was struck afresh by her cousin's beauty. They had grown up together from childhood, and all along Edith had been remarked upon by everyone, except Margaret, for her prettiness; but Margaret had never thought about it until the last few days, when the prospect of soon losing her companion seemed to give force to every sweet quality and charm which Edith possessed. They had been talking about wedding dresses, and wedding ceremonies; and Captain Lennox, and what he had told Edith about her future life at Corfu, where his regiment was stationed; and the difficulty of keeping a piano in good tune (a difficulty which Edith seemed to consider as one of the most formidable that could befall her in her married life), and what gowns she should want in the visits to Scotland, which would immediately succeed her marriage; but the whispered tone had latterly become more drowsy; and Margaret, after a pause of a few minutes, found, as she fancied, that, in spite of the buzz in the next room, Edith had rolled herself

up into a ball of muslin and ribbon, and silken curls, and gone off into a peaceful little after-dinner nap. (1970, 35)

The initial short sentence of (unanswered) dialogue is set as its own paragraph by typographical convention, but it is closely linked to the following long paragraph by the repetition of the names. This long paragraph begins with the adversative conjunction "but," which connects by difference. The next sentence is immediately linked by the initial pronoun "she," which refers to Edith. The next sentence seems to strike out in a new direction, with the introduction of Titania—the Queen of the Fairies from *A Midsummer Night's Dream*—but the end of the sentence returns us to Edith. As we read through the paragraph we notice that each new sentence, sometimes each new clause, assumes what has already been said and then adds to it, but not necessarily with any logical connection. The paragraph is both progressive and cyclic: the ending repeats the words *muslin* and *ribbon,* and the last word of the paragraph, *nap,* recapitulates the last word of the first sentence, *asleep,* to form a ring. At the end of the paragraph we know that Margaret and Edith have been very close since childhood, we know that Edith is considered a beauty, and we know that Edith is about to marry Captain Lennox and move to Corfu, and we can guess something about the social status and the attitudes of the characters, but none of this in any way is implied by the beginning. This kind of paratactic and progressive composition, where one thing leads to another which leads to another, is quite different from hypotactic expository composition with a topic sentence and supporting material.

The following paragraph then tells us what Margaret would have said to Edith if Edith had been awake, in a variation of the traditional rhetorical figure *praeteritio*—"Margaret had been on the point of telling her cousin. . . ." At the beginning of the next sentence we note once again the adversative conjunction: "But in default of a listener, she had to brood over the change in her life silently as heretofore." A verbal repetition then links this sentence to the next: "It was a happy brooding . . ." (35–36).

As an example of composition in short paragraphs, here is the beginning of Kurt Vonnegut's early novel *Player Piano:*

>Ilium, New York, is divided into three parts.
>In the northwest are the managers and engineers and civil servants

and a few professional people; in the northeast are the machines; and in the south, across the Iroquois River, is the area known locally as Homestead, where almost all the people live.

If the bridge across the Iroquois were dynamited, few daily routines would be disturbed. Not many people on either side have reasons other than curiosity for crossing.

During the war, in hundreds of Iliums over America, managers and engineers learned to get along without their men and women, who went to fight. It was the miracle that won the war—production with almost no manpower. In the patois of the north side of the river, it was the know-how that won the war. Democracy owed its life to know-how.

Ten years after the war—after the men and women had come home, after the riots had been put down, after thousands had been jailed under the antisabotage laws—Doctor Paul Proteus was petting a cat in his office. He was the most important, brilliant person in Ilium, the manager of the Ilium Works, though only thirty-five. He was tall, thin, nervous, and dark, with the gentle good looks of his long face distorted by dark-rimmed glasses.

He didn't feel important or brilliant at the moment, nor had he for some time. His principle [sic] concern just then was that the black cat be contented in its new surroundings. (1980, 1)

In Vonnegut's later novels short paragraphs are something of a mannerism, but the tendency is present from the beginning of his career. In a different style, all of this passage could have been combined into a single paragraph. As the passage is written, each paragraph seems to be almost a new little beginning; the breaks foreground the separation of ideas, but pronoun reference and verbal repetition create links. The first paragraph situates the story in Ilium (an allusion to the *Iliad,* accompanied by an allusion to the first sentence of Caesar's *Gallic Wars*); there is no explicit link from the first paragraph to the second, but the reader easily supplies something like "In the northwest [of Ilium]." The next paragraph is linked by the name of the river, but the bridge across the river is new information. The next paragraph uses Ilium as the foundation for a generalization; this paragraph introduces further new information, the war and the know-how that won the war. The following paragraph puts the story in a specific time and introduces a specific character. The second sentence of the paragraph is linked to the first by pronoun reference: "Doctor Paul Proteus was petting a cat in his office. He was the most important, brilliant person in Ilium," and the following paragraph is also linked by pronoun reference: "He didn't feel important or brilliant at the moment." And the paragraphs in the whole passage are linked with repeated words: *people, Iroquois, men and women, war, brilliant,* and *cat.*

Contiguous narrative units—sentences, paragraphs, episodes, sections, chapters—can be part of a continuous narrative stream or not; they can also be linked or not linked. In more technical terms, roughly speaking, continuity refers to the events of the story, while linkage refers to the discourse, the way the story is told. The narrative stream can be continuous (or not continuous) in time, in space, or in the connection between ideas. Linkage is some kind of manifest connection, such as the repetition of a word. A narrative stream may be continuous and linked, continuous but not linked, linked but not continuous, or not linked and not continuous.

Examples of all these can be found in Hemingway's *A Farewell to Arms*. The sentences in the first paragraph of this novel are continuous and linked:

> In the late summer of that year we lived in a house in a village that looked across the river and the plain to the mountains. In the bed of the river there were pebbles and boulders, dry and white in the sun, and the water was clear and swiftly moving and blue in the channels. Troops went by the house and down the road and the dust they raised powdered the leaves of the trees. The trunks of the trees too were dusty and the leaves fell early that year and we saw the troops marching along the road and the dust rising and leaves, stirred by the breeze, falling, and the soldiers marching and afterward the road bare and white except for the leaves. (1997, 9)

The narration is continuous; everything in the paragraph refers to the same narrative situation, and there are no temporal or spatial discontinuities. In addition, a web of repeated words links the sentences to each other, until the final sentence draws them all together: (1) house, river; (2) river; (3) troops, house, road, dust, leaves, trees; (4) trees, leaves, troops marching, road, dust, leaves, soldiers marching, road, leaves. These links clearly indicate that the paragraph is a unified segment. The first sentence of the next paragraph is then linked to the first sentence of the first paragraph: "The plain was rich with crops; there were many orchards of fruit trees and beyond the plain the mountains were brown and bare."

The first and second chapters of *A Farewell to Arms* are linked but not continuous. The whole of the first chapter is a segment—at a level of segmentation above that of its constituent paragraphs. The chapter begins "In the late summer of that year . . ." and it ends, "At the start of the winter came the permanent rain and with the rain came the cholera. But it was checked and in the end only seven thousand died of it in the army" (10). The next chapter begins, "The next year there were many victories" (11). There is clearly some temporal gap between the chapters and a change in the military situation, but the phrases "In the late summer of that year" and "The next year" provide a clear link. The link is strengthened by the second sentence of the second chapter: "The mountain that was beyond the valley and the hillside where the chestnut forest grew was captured and there were victories beyond the plain on the plateau to the south and we crossed the river in August and lived in a house in Gorizia that had a fountain and many thick shady trees in a walled garden and a wisteria vine purple on the side of the house" (11). Many of the words in this sentence repeat words from the first paragraph of the first chapter: mountain, plain, river, house, trees.

Two events may be continuous in the narrative stream without any manifest link. In chapter 4, the narrator, Frederic Henry, returns from leave: "I was very dusty and dirty and went up to my room to wash. Rinaldi was sitting on the bed with a copy of Hugo's English grammar" (22). These are not two unrelated facts, as if one were to say, for instance, "I went up to my room. The rain in Kansas delayed the harvest." The reader is expected to make the connection: Henry went up to his room and saw Rinaldi sitting and reading. The narration is continuous but the sentences are not linked.

In this early part of the novel, Henry begins to spend time with a British nurse, Catherine Barkley. One night, after he has kissed her for the first time, he returns to the villa where he lives, and Rinaldi teases him. Henry knocks over their candle and gets into bed. "Rinaldi picked up the candle, lit it and went on reading" (31). This last sentence of chapter 5 gives a kind of closure at the end of the day. Chapter 6 begins: "I was away for two days at the posts" (32). The space between the chapters is a gap in the temporal flow of the story, and there is no explicit link to bridge that gap. The narrative stream is thus neither continuous nor linked. The next sentence, however, places this new chapter in the narrative stream: "When I got home it was too late and I did not see Miss Barkley until the next evening" (32). The reader knows that Miss Barkley has not dropped out of the story.

This tidy schema I think is a good basis for further analysis, but its tidiness may obscure some complications. We need to have a better idea of what constitutes a narrative stream; we need to know how large a gap is consistent with continuity; we need to ask if the continuity of the description of an object or a landscape is really comparable to the description of events unfolding in time. But these questions would take us too far afield; some answers may be suggested as we look at more passages.

Divisions of the Whole Narrative

Almost all novel-length narratives are divided into chapters or what may as well be thought of as chapters. Short stories and even some novellas may be presented without divisions. Gertrude Stein's *The Good Anna*—fifty-some printed pages—is divided into three parts, of which the first and third are quite short; but *Melanctha*—a little over one hundred printed pages—has no indication of internal divisions, and the story is constructed to avoid sharp breaks in the sequence of events. Toni Morrison's *Jazz* does not have numbered chapters, but the text is divided into ten sections, which may as well be chapters. Virginia Woolf's *Mrs Dalloway* has no chapter divisions, but in a few spots the text is printed with extra spacing, and twice the text is divided with an asterisk.[1] I have not been able to see any particular reason for these breaks; they don't seem to mark what I would call chapters. Instead, the narrative is segmented by shifting focalization, as I will discuss further on.[2]

Most novels are simply divided into numbered chapters, perhaps titled, perhaps not; sometimes chapters will be titled without numbers. Titles may be more or less elaborate. The titles in Henry Fielding's *Tom Jones* are moderately full: the title of book 1 is "Containing as much of the Birth of the Foundling as is necessary or proper to Acquaint the Reader with in the Beginning of this History"; the title of the first chapter is "The Introduction to the Work, or the Bill of Fare to the Feast," the title of the second chapter is "A Short Description of Squire Allworthy, and a Fuller Account of Miss Bridget Allworthy, his Sister," and the title of the third is "An Odd Accident which befell Mr. Allworthy at his Return Home. The Decent Behavior of Mrs. Deborah Wilkins, with some proper animadversions on

Bastards." Long chapter titles are often to be read as the voice of the implied author, as in Robert Montgomery Bird's satirical novel *Sheppard Lee: Written by Himself,* first published in 1836; the title of book 1 is "Containing Instructions How to Spend and How to Retrieve a Fortune"; the title of chapter 1 is "The Author's Preface;—which the reader, if in a great hurry, or if it is his practice to read against time, can skip"; the title of chapter 3 is "The pleasures of having nothing to do—Some thoughts on Matrimony." Long chapter titles fell out of favor in the later nineteenth century, but they have been revived from time to time. John Barth's *The Sot-Weed Factor,* published in 1960, is written as an imitation of an eighteenth-century novel. The first chapter is titled "The Poet is Introduced, and Differentiated from his fellows," the second is titled "The Remarkable Manner in which Ebenezer was Educated, and the no less Remarkable Results of that Education," and the third is "Ebenezer is rescued, and Hears a Diverting Tale involving Isaac Newton and Other Notables."

In some novels each chapter is provided with an epigraph; the first chapter of George Eliot's *Middlemarch* begins with two lines from Beaumont and Fletcher's *The Maid's Tragedy;* the second with a passage from Cervantes' *Don Quixote;* and so on. In *Sirens of Titan,* Kurt Vonnegut takes advantage of this convention to make jokes. His epigraphs are ascribed to characters within the story, rather than to canonical authors; the epigraph to chapter 1 is "I guess somebody up here likes me," and it is ascribed to Malachi Constant, the hero of the story; the epigraph to chapter 2 is "Sometimes I think it is a great mistake to have matter than can think and feel. It complains so. By the same token, though, I suppose that boulders and mountains and moons could be accused of being a little too phlegmatic"; this is ascribed to Winston Niles Rumfoord, who is also a character in the story. And so on.

Many novels are simply divided into a series of chapters, but sometimes chapters are grouped into books or parts, and they can be subdivided into smaller segments; thus there can be a hierarchy of nested narrative segments, from paragraphs to subsections, to chapters, to episodes, to books or parts. There is no canonical number of parts. A narrative can be divided into two books (*A Lost Lady,* Willa Cather); three books (*A Tale of Two Cities,* Charles Dickens); four books (*The Good Soldier,* Ford Madox Ford); five books (*One of Ours,* Willa Cather); six books (*Jude the Obscure,* Thomas Hardy); seven books (*The Mill on the Floss,* George Eliot); eight books

(*Daniel Deronda,* George Eliot); or even twelve books (*The Ambassadors,* Henry James).

A novel can consist of one well-integrated progression of events or of several episodes. An episode, according to Gerald Prince, is "a series of related events standing apart from surrounding (series of) events because of one or more distinctive features and achieving a unity" (Prince 1987, 27). The boundaries of an episode may be determined by the kinds of events which begin and end whole narratives, especially by Arrivals and Meetings. (For further discussion, see chapter 4.) An episode can take up a whole chapter, or it may be smaller or larger. In the *Odyssey,* for example, the episode of the hero's visit to the Land of the Dead takes up the whole of book 11 (where the books of the Homeric epics correspond to what we would call chapters).[3] The episode of the Lotus Eaters, however, takes up only part of book 9 (9.82–104). These two episodes are part of a larger episode, Odysseus's tales of his travels, along with other episodes, such as the story of Polyphemus, all told to the Phaiakians (books 9 through 12). This, in turn, is part of a larger episode, Odysseus's sojourn in the land of the Phaiakians (books 6 through the beginning of book 13). Most long narratives include episodes. Some narratives—such as Fielding's *Tom Jones*—include a number of well-demarcated episodes, and some novels—such as Nabokov's *Pnin*—consist of a series of independent stories. Even novels that are not considered episodic may include a few episodes, such as the Box Hill episode in Austen's *Emma* or the Pemberley episode in *Pride and Prejudice.*

These examples and many others suggest that writers often have a clear sense of the segmentation of the story, and that the divisions of a story may have something to do with its larger meaning. However, practices of publication can determine somewhat arbitrary divisions; many Victorian novels appeared in three volumes just as a publishing convenience. Dickens often published his novels in serial form, in monthly or weekly installments; some modern editions mark the serial divisions, and he clearly took care with crafting the ends of the installments; shorter installments required more cliffhangers.

Arnold Bennett's *The Old Wives' Tale* is divided into four books: book 1 is titled "Mrs. Baines," with seven titled chapters; book 2 is titled "Constance," with eight titled chapters; book 3 is titled "Sophia," with seven titled chapters; book 4 is titled "What Life Is," with five titled chapters. Each of the chapters is further divided into numbered sections without titles; in book 1, chapter 1, which is titled "The Square," for instance, there are three numbered sections; in book 2, chapter 2, there are four sections; and so on. Thus the narrative is organized in strata: paragraphs form sections; sections form chapters; chapters form books; and books form the novel as a whole. The books themselves are clearly organized: the first book presents Mr. and Mrs. Baines and their two daughters, Constance and Sophia, as well as Mr. Povey, who will marry Constance, and Gerald Scales, who will marry Sophia. Mr. Baines is an invalid, who dies in section 3 of chapter 4; Mrs. Baines is the matriarch of the family, but during this book her position is gradually eroded. By the end of the book Mr. Povey has proposed to Constance (the wedding takes place in the gap between book 1 and book 2), Sophia has run off with Gerald Scales, and Mrs. Baines has declared that her life is over. Book 2 follows Constance from her marriage to Mr. Povey, through the birth of her son, Cyril, to the death of her husband. Book 3 picks up with Sophia's elopement and marriage. She and Gerald Scales move to Paris, where he squanders all his money and leaves Sophia. She manages to set herself up as the owner of a lodging house, where she prospers. In book 4, Sophia sells her business and moves back to live with Constance. The novel ends with the deaths of the sisters: chapter 4 of book 4 is titled "End of Sophia," and chapter 5 is titled "End of Constance." It is clear from even this brief and superficial summary that the narrative is highly organized. A detailed analysis would show this careful organization throughout.

The divisions of a narrative—chapters, episodes, books, parts—may be more or less equal or quite unequal. Katherine Anne Porter's *Ship of Fools* is divided into three unequal parts (each of which has an epigraph): Part I: Embarkation (pages 1–68); Part II: High Sea (pages 69–360); and Part III: The Harbors (pages 361–497); each part is divided into sections, but there are no chapter divisions.

The elegant organization of J. R. R. Tolkien's *The Lord of the Rings* impressed me greatly when I first read the book. The story as a whole is divided into three parts, and the original edition was published in three volumes, one volume for each part. Each part is titled (I: "The Fellowship of the Ring"; II: "The Two Towers"; III: "The Return of the King") and each part is divided into two untitled books, for a total of six books. Each book is further divided into titled chapters—twelve, ten, eleven, ten, ten, and nine—with enough variation to prevent a feeling that the material is being artificially squeezed into preformed boxes.

A detailed analysis, which I will not present here, shows the careful organization of the novel, including the divisions into episodes, the transitions and links, and the overall shape of the plot. The first-time reader may not notice this careful organization, but on rereading the elegance of the construction is clear. The organization of the plot is aesthetically satisfying and also functional: without some controlling shape, a story involving so many characters in so many situations might fall into a jumble. Moreover, the orderliness of the narration is thematically consistent with the restoration of organic order as the goal of the story.

Segments and Links in *Emma*

This section will examine the various ways Jane Austen links narrative segments in *Emma*. I begin with links at roughly the level of a sentence and move on to larger links.

A strong link of one sentence to the next is anadiplosis, where the last word or phrase of a clause or sentence is the first word of the next sentence, as in "You were mentioning May. May is the very month . . ." (213). And another: Harriet Smith is introduced in Volume I, chapter 3. Emma finds that Harriet is not particularly clever, but she is engaging; neither too shy nor too pushing: "she must have good sense and deserve encouragement. Encouragement should be given" (18). In the strict form of anadiplosis, the repetition is immediate and exact, last word to first word, but more relaxed forms are common, with variation in form or a little distance between the repeated words: "Emma allowed her father to talk—but supplied her visitors in a much more satisfactory style; and on the present evening had particular pleasure in sending them away happy. The happiness of Miss Smith was quite equal to her intentions" (19): here "happy" is repeated in polyptoton as "happiness" and the two words are separated by the definite article.

Clauses and sentences can also be linked by initial repetition, that is, anaphora. Here Emma is comparing Mrs. Weston and Harriet: "Such a friend as Mrs. Weston was out of the question. Two such could never be granted. Two such she did not want" (20), with anaphora of "Two such," following "Such" in the first sentence. Final repetition, epistrophe, also occurs; during the scene where Mr. Elton proposes to Emma, he tells her, "I never thought of Miss Smith in the whole course of existence—never paid her any attentions, but as your friend; never cared whether she were dead or alive, but as your friend" (93).

Austen sometimes uses similar forms of repetition at the level of the paragraph or chapter. In paragraph anadiplosis the last word or phrase of a paragraph is repeated as the first word or phrase of the next paragraph. Austen often repeats a word in a kind of cluster within a paragraph or within a few paragraphs. In the following passage the word "letter" is repeated five times in the leading paragraph and then picked up, I think in an ironic tone, in the first sentence of the following paragraph:

> For a few days every morning visit in Highbury included some mention of the handsome letter Mrs. Weston had received. "I suppose you have heard of the handsome letter Mr. Frank Churchill had written to Mrs. Weston? I understand it was a very handsome letter, indeed. Mr. Woodhouse told me of it. Mr. Woodhouse saw the letter, and he says he never saw such a handsome letter in his life."
>
> It was, indeed, a highly prized letter. (14)

Paragraph anadiplosis, like sentence anadiplosis, can be more or less strict; Austen tends to use less strict forms. In the following passage, in which Emma is comparing Mrs. Weston to Harriet, the word "useful" in the leading paragraph is repeated in polyptoton by "usefulness" in the following paragraph:

> Mrs. Weston was the object of a regard which had its basis in gratitude and esteem. Harriet would be loved as one to whom she could be useful. For Mrs. Weston there was nothing to be done. For Harriet everything.
>
> Her first attempts at usefulness were in an endeavour to find out who were the parents.... (20)

In the following passage, Mr. Knightly and Emma have argued after Emma has convinced Harriet to reject Robert Martin's proposal to Harriet; Mr. Knightly cuts off the conversation; the link is "vexed" and "vexation":

> "Good morning to you,"—said he, rising and walking off abruptly. He was very much vexed. He felt the disappointment of the young man, and

was mortified to have been the means of promoting it, by the sanction he had given; and the part which he was persuaded Emma had taken in the affair, was provoking him exceedingly.

Emma remained in a state of vexation too. (49)

Paragraph anaphora occurs when the beginning of one paragraph is repeated at the beginning of the following paragraph:

Frank Churchill came back again; and if he kept his father's dinner waiting, it was not known at Hartfield; for Mrs. Weston was too anxious for his being a favourite with Mr. Woodhouse, to betray any imperfection which could be concealed.

He came back, had had his hair cut, and laughed at himself. . . . (146–47)

Austen often uses links between chapters, often in the form of chapter anadiplosis, more or less strict, in which the end of one chapter is repeated at the beginning of the next. There is, however, no link between the first two chapters of the novel. Volume I, chapter 1 ends with a discussion between Emma and Mr. Knightly about Mr. Elton; the last sentence is Mr. Knightly's comment, "Depend upon it, a man of six or seven-and-twenty can take care of himself" (11). Chapter 2 begins, "Mr. Weston was a native of Highbury, and born of a respectable family . . ." (12); the narration is neither continuous nor linked. But chapters 2 and 3 are linked by a reference to Emma's father, Mr. Woodhouse. Chapter 2 ends: "There was a strange rumour in Highbury of all the little Perrys being seen with a slice of Mrs. Weston's wedding-cake in their hands, but Mr. Woodhouse would never believe it." Chapter 3 begins: "Mr. Woodhouse was fond of society in his own way" (15). This new chapter introduces new material; it is not a continuation of the previous chapter; but the repetition of "Mr. Woodhouse" makes for a smooth transition. The chapters are linked but not continuous.

Chapter 3 then links to chapter 4 through Harriet Smith, who is introduced in the middle of the chapter; Emma (at the request of Mrs. Goddard, the schoolteacher) invites Harriet for a visit. Chapter 3 ends: "The humble, grateful little girl went off with highly gratified feelings, delighted with the affability with which Miss Woodhouse had treated her all the evening, and actually shaken hands with her at last" (19). Chapter 4 begins: "Harriet Smith's intimacy at Hartfield was soon a settled thing" (20). Again the chapters are linked but not continuous.

Chapter 4 ends with Emma's thought about the possibility of matching Harriet and Mr. Elton: "He was reckoned very handsome; his person much admired in general, though not by her, there being a want of elegance of feature which she could not dispense with:—but the girl who could be gratified by a Robert Martin's riding about the country to get walnuts for her, might very well be conquered by Mr. Elton's admiration" (27). And here is the first sentence of chapter 5: "I do not know what your opinion may be, Mrs. Weston," said Mr. Knightly, "of this great intimacy between Emma and Harriet Smith, but I think it is a bad thing." The whole chapter continues as a conversation between Mr. Knightly and Mrs. Weston about Emma. Evidently the two chapters are neither linked nor continuous. But here is the beginning of chapter 6: "Emma could not feel a doubt of having given Harriet's fancy a proper direction and raised the gratitude of her young vanity to a very good purpose, for she found her decidedly more sensible than before of Mr. Elton's being a remarkably handsome man, with most agreeable manners..." (31). The end of chapter 4 is thus continuous with and linked to the beginning of chapter 6; the chapters are linked over a gap. Chapter 5 is an intercalated digression and marked as such by the explicit linking of chapter 4 to chapter 6.

Chapter 6 then links to chapter 7, but the repetition is not immediate. The third paragraph before the end of chapter 6 begins "Mr. Elton was to take the drawing to London..." and chapter 7 begins "The very day of Mr. Elton's going to London..." (36). The last sentence of chapter 7 is "Harriet smiled again, and her smiles grew stronger" (41) and the first sentence of chapter 8 is "Harriet slept at Hartfield that night" (42).

Many of the chapters in *Emma* are linked, but many are not. In Volume I, there are no links between chapters 8 and 9 or 9 and 10. Chapter 10 ends with Emma's thoughts on her matchmaking, and chapter 11 begins "Mr. Elton must now be left to himself" (66); this is a sort of negative link—Austen could have simply moved the story forward without comment; the two chapters are linked but not continuous. I find no link between chapter 11 and chapter 12, nor between chapter 12 and chapter 13. The end of chapter 13 is continuous with the beginning of chapter 14, since they are two successive moments in the same action, but there is no verbal link between them; likewise chapter 14 and chapter 15 are continuous but not linked; likewise chapter 15 and chapter 16. Chapter 16 and chapter 17 are neither continuous nor linked; and so on.

The form of linkage, when it occurs, is various. Chapters 7 and 8 of Volume II link beginning to beginning rather than end to beginning, in what could be called chapter anaphora: "Emma's good opinion of Frank Churchill was a little shaken the following day, by hearing that he was gone off to London" (142); "Frank Churchill came back again . . ." (146); and this sentence, as we have noted above, then links to the beginning of the next paragraph.

Many of these links don't stand out, and I expect most readers don't notice them or pay them much attention, but I would suggest that they help create smooth transitions and coherence in the narrative stream. Other links, however, can be foregrounded for emphasis. At the end of Volume II, chapter 2, Emma has been talking with Jane Fairfax, who has returned to Highbury. Emma has been trying hard to get Jane to gossip, but Jane has been reserved in her responses to Emma's prying questions. The chapter ends with a series of questions about Frank Churchill and evasive answers by Jane. The last sentence of the chapter is "Emma could not forgive her." The first sentence of chapter 3 is "Emma could not forgive her." Verbatim repetition of the whole sentence is emphatic.

At the end of Volume III, chapter 2, at the ball, Mr. Knightly asks to dance with Emma:

> "Whom are you going to dance with?" asked Mr. Knightly.
> She hesitated a moment, and then replied, "With you, if you will ask me."
> "Indeed I will. You have shown that you can dance, and you know we are not really so much brother and sister as to make it at all improper."
> "Brother and sister! no indeed."

Then the new chapter begins: "This little explanation with Mr. Knightly gave Emma considerable pleasure" (228). The chapter break thus comes between an action and the narrator's comment on that action, with the phrase "this little explanation" forming the link.

These emphatic links may be noticeable, in some sense, on first reading, though the reader may not see them as instances of a particular technique of narrative construction. Less emphatic links might never be noticed unless they are a specific topic of analysis. But Austen clearly paid attention to the transitions between chapters, and these transitions are part of the reading experience and contribute to the even flow of the narrative, even when they are not foregrounded.

Repetition and Focalization in *Mrs. Dalloway*

Virginia Woolf's *Mrs. Dalloway* is concerned with large themes of life and death, with sanity and madness, with love and loss, and also with questions of class and gender. These themes have been exhaustively studied by the critics. The story also includes several sensitive and moving character studies: of Clarissa and her counterpart in the story, Septimus Warren Smith; of Clarissa's husband, Richard; of her former suitor Peter Walsh; of her old friend Sally Seaton; of her daughter, Elizabeth; of Elizabeth's teacher, Doris Kilman. Though the novel is titled after a single character, it is really a gallery of portraits. My focus, however, is not so much the themes or the character studies, but it is the way Woolf constructs and organizes the narrative stream of the story. Of course the construction of the story is what creates the characters and communicates the themes.

The book is moderately repetitive—more repetitive than *Emma,* but less repetitive than *The Good Soldier* (which I will discuss in chapter 3). Some of these repetitions occur within a sentence—"and with the wine and the coffee (not paid for) rise jocund visions before musing eyes; gently speculative eyes; eyes to whom life appears musical, mysterious; eyes now kindled to observe genially the beauty of the red carnations..." (116–17)—but many operate above the level of the sentence.

Some paragraphs are organized around repetitions, verbal and semantic:

> Quiet descended on her, calm, content, as her needle, drawing the silk smoothly to its gentle pause, **collected** the green folds together and attached them, very lightly, to the belt. So on a summer's day **waves collect,** overbalance, and **fall; collect and fall;** and the whole world seems to be saying **'that is all'** more and more ponderously, until even the **heart** in the **body** which lies in the sun on the **beach** says too, **That is all, Fear no more, says the heart, Fear no more, says the heart,** committing its burden to some **sea,** which sighs **collectively** for all sorrows, and renews, begins, **collects,** lets **fall.** And the **body** alone listens to the

passing bee; the **wave** breaking; the dog **barking**, far away **barking**, and **barking**. (42–43)

Other repetitions cluster in a page or so—"look" is repeated six times on 26 and 27 and "queer" five times on 27. Other repetitions have an effect over an episode: the word "proportion" is repeated during Septimus Warren Smith's medical appointment with Sir William Bradshaw: "he called it not having proportion" (107); "health we must have; and health is proportion" (110); "proportion, divine proportion" (110); "shared his sense of proportion" (111); "in fact his sense of proportion" (111); "But Proportion has a sister" (111); "what Sir William frankly admitted was a difficult art—a sense of proportion" (113). The point here is the superficiality of Sir William's attitudes and treatment and his failure to understand the gravity of Septimus Warren Smith's mental distress. Septimus Smith's mental distress is also emphasized by another set of repetitions: "but something failed him; he could not feel" (97); "but he could not taste, he could not feel" (98); "it must be the fault of the world then—that he could not feel" (98); "but he felt nothing" (100); "his wife was crying, and he felt nothing" (100).[4]

There are no chapter divisions in *Mrs. Dalloway;* the time of the story is marked by the ringing of Big Ben and other clocks, but this regular mechanical measure of time by clocks runs parallel to a more organic human time which ebbs and flows and mixes the past and the present. Segmentation moreover is to some extent marked by focalization. Focalization can change quickly; some of these focalized segments are very short, certainly not the length of a chapter, but others form the major blocks of the narrative. The beginning of the story is focalized on and through Clarissa:

> Mrs. Dalloway said she would buy the flowers herself.
> For Lucy had her work cut out for her. The doors would be taken off their hinges; Rumpelmayer's men were coming. And then, thought Clarissa Dalloway, what a morning—fresh as if issued to children on a beach. (1)

Focalization through Clarissa continues for the rest of this first page, as she recalls her youth at her family home and her friend and suitor of the time, Peter Walsh, who is now about to return from India. Then there is a quick change of focalization, just for a moment: "A charming woman, Scrope Purvis thought her (knowing her as one does know people who live next door to one in Westminster); a touch of the bird about her . . ." (2). This is still about Clarissa, but seen through the consciousness of Scrope Purvis. The next paragraph returns to Clarissa's thoughts. A little later she runs into her old friend Hugh Whitbread, but the narrative remains focalized on Clarissa. When Clarissa gets to the flower shop, the narrative briefly focalizes through Miss Pym, "who thought her kind, for kind she had been years ago; very kind, but she looked older, this year" (12). Then Mrs. Dalloway and Miss Pym hear a sudden noise from a motor car outside, and the focalization shifts to the general impressions of people in the street.

In this segment we first meet Septimus Warren Smith and his wife, Lucrezia—Rezia—who are among those who hear the motor car. The focalization overlaps here, moving from Septimus to Mrs. Dalloway and back to Septimus in the space of a few sentences. "Septimus Warren Smith, aged about thirty . . ."; then "Mrs. Dalloway, coming to the window with her arms full of sweet peas . . . ," and then back to Septimus: "Everyone looked at the motor car. Septimus looked . . ." (14). The focalization returns to Mrs. Dalloway (16), and then to several people in the street, some of whom are named (Sarah Bletchley, Emily Coates, Mr. Bowley) but who play no further role in the story (19–21), and then back to Septimus. A sensitive reader of the novel will note these shifts in focalization, perhaps unconsciously. Although the novel is named after Mrs. Dalloway, most of the narrative is focalized through other people. The shorter segments are focalized through minor characters who flash into view for just a moment—Masie Johnson (27–28), Mrs. Dempster (28–29), and so on—but longer segments are focalized through Septimus Warren Smith or through his wife, Rezia, or through Peter Walsh or Richard Dalloway.

Overlapping focalization may take the place of chapter links, which of course cannot occur in a story with no chapters. Overlapping may occur when two characters are in the same situation or perceive the same moment. We have already seen overlapping focalization of Mrs. Dalloway and Septimus Warren Smith, as they both hear the noise of the motor car. Overlapping also occurs when Peter Walsh sees Septimus and Rezia in Regent Park. The initial transition is abrupt; one paragraph ends "Peter Walsh laughed out" and the next begins "But Lucrezia Warren Smith was saying to herself, It's wicked, why should I suffer" (71). After some pages focalized through Septimus and Rezia there is another transition, as Peter Walsh sees them arguing: "And that is being young, Peter Walsh thought as he passed them" (78). Another form of overlapping occurs at the end of the novel, when Sir William Bradshaw, Septimus's doctor, attends Clarissa's party and tells her about Septimus's suicide.[5]

Although there are no chapter links in the novel, there are some paragraph links: "cared not a straw for either of them" and "Not a straw" (10); "Now where was her dress?" and "Her evening dresses hung in the cupboard" (40); "And it was an offering; to combine, to create; but to whom?" and "An offering for the sake of offering, perhaps" (137); "Now she did not envy women like Clarissa Dalloway; she pitied them" and "She pitied and despised them from the bottom of her heart" (139).[6]

Verbal repetitions are common throughout the story. Perhaps the most persistent repetition in the novel is the word "flowers," along with semantically related terms, such as the names of particular kinds of flowers. Here I will note just a few of many instances. The very first sentence of the novel introduces the theme: "Mrs. Dalloway said she would buy the flowers herself" (1). She goes out to "a shop where they kept flowers for her when she gave a party" (10). The shop is kept by Miss Pym, "whose hands were always bright red, as if they had been stood in cold water with the flowers" (12). This sentence links to the beginning of the next paragraph: "There were flowers: delphiniums, sweet peas, bunches of lilac; and carnations, masses of carnations. There were roses; there were irises" (12). The rest of this paragraph is largely taken up with the sensory effect of the various flowers. When Mrs. Dalloway is recalling Sally Seaton's effect on her, years ago when they were young, she notes Sally's "way with flowers.... Sally went out, picked hollyhocks, dahlias—all sorts of flowers that had never been seen together—cut their heads off, and make them swim on the top of water in bowls" (36). At the party at the end of the story Sally Seaton (now Lady Rosseter) thinks of her earlier friendship with Clarissa: "They had been friends, not acquaintances, and she still saw Clarissa all in white going about the house with her hands full of flowers" (213). When Peter Walsh thinks of Clarissa, he thinks of flowers: "And behind it all was that network of visiting, leaving cards, being kind to people, rushing about with bunches of flowers" (85–86).

But flowers are not associated exclusively with Clarissa. Clarissa's Aunt Helena objects to Sally Seaton's flower arrangements (36); but Aunt Helena was herself an avid botanist, and she was kind to Peter Walsh, because he had found a rare flower for her (67); she had gathered flowers in Burma and had written a book about orchids (202). When Hugh Whitbread goes to lunch with Lady Bruton, he brings carnations, which are mentioned several times during the episode.[7]

Flowers are also associated with Septimus Warren Smith and his wife, Rezia. Septimus first met Rezia after the armistice: "When peace came he was in Milan, billeted in the house of an innkeeper with a courtyard, flowers in tubs, little tables in the open, daughters making hats" (96). Later on, in London, when Septimus and Rezia go for a bus ride and have a moment of happiness, they see flowers: "They went to Hampton Court on top of a bus, and they were perfectly happy. All the little red and yellow flowers were out on the grass, like floating lamps, he said" (73). When they sit in Regent's Park he has a vision: "Red flowers grew through his flesh; their stiff leaves rustled by his head" (75). Later on, Septimus in their flat has a vision: "And Rezia came in, with her flowers" (104).

Flowers, of course, are not simply flowers, as we see in this important passage where Richard Dalloway uses them as a nonverbal sign of the affection for Clarissa he has so much trouble articulating in words. After his lunch with Lady Bruton he is eager to see Clarissa: "eager, yes, very eager to travel that spider's thread of attachment between himself and Clarissa" (128). (He is probably motivated by jealousy of Peter Walsh.) There follows a long paragraph of forty-four printed lines, giving an account of Dalloway's thoughts about Clarissa (and other things). The paragraph begins, "But he wanted to come in holding something. Flowers? Yes, flowers" (128). These flowers will express his love for her: "they never spoke of it; not for years had they spoken of it; which, he thought, grasping his red and white roses together (a vast bunch in tissue paper), is the greatest mistake in the world" (128). Now he intends "to say straight out in so many words (...), holding out his flowers, 'I love you'" (129). "Here he was walking across London to say to Clarissa in so many words that he loved her. Which one never does say, he thought" (129). In the same paragraph his mind wanders to other parts of his life and efforts. He had "championed the downtrodden":

> It did make his blood boil to see little creatures of five or six crossing Piccadilly alone. The police ought to have stopped the traffic at once.

He had no illusions about the London police. Indeed, he was collecting evidence of their malpractices; and these costermongers, not allowed to stand their barrows in the streets; and prostitutes, good Lord, the fault wasn't in them, not in young men either, but in our detestable social system and so forth; all of which he considered, could be seen considering, grey, dogged, dapper, clean, as he walked across the Park to tell his wife that he loved her. (129–30)

This little section gives a different and more attractive view of his character—and the end of the section, if not the goal, is his love for Clarissa. This paragraph is linked to the next long paragraph of thirty-one printed lines: "For he would say it in so many words, when he came into the room" (130). And later in the paragraph: "But he would tell Clarissa that he loved her, in so many words" (130). And at the end of the next paragraph: "Indeed, his own life was a miracle (...); here he was (...) walking to his house in Westminster to tell Clarissa that he loved her. Happiness is this, he thought" (131). And this paragraph is linked to the next: "It is this, he said, as he entered the Dean's Yard. Big Ben was beginning to strike..." (131). And the sound of Big Ben repeated in the next paragraph links us to Clarissa: "The sound of Big Ben flooded Clarissa's drawing room, where she sat..." (131). Dalloway comes in:

> He was holding out flowers—roses, red and white roses. (But he could not bring himself to say he loved her; not in so many words.)
> But how lovely, she said, taking his flowers. She understood; she understood without his speaking; his Clarissa. (132)

A few paragraphs later: "(But he could not tell her he loved her. He held her hand. Happiness is this, he thought)" (133). And then: "He had not said 'I love you'; but he held her hand. Happiness is this, he thought" (133). And then: "He must be off, he said, getting up. But he stood for a moment as if he were about to say something, and she wondered what? There were the roses" (134). Thus the episode is a ring: it begins and ends with flowers (128 and 134). Dalloway is unable to articulate his feelings, but the flowers speak for him. On the one hand, Dalloway is the dull and conservative person Clarissa chose to marry instead of the dashing and imaginative Peter Walsh; this episode, on the other hand, suggests that he has emotional depths that are not otherwise much in evidence. Flowers have a thematic resonance throughout the story, but it is not easy to say exactly what that resonance is; they can represent vitality, and also impermanence, but they seem, too, to represent a kind of social bond, as they are often used as gifts, though at times that bond seems perhaps somewhat superficial.

Some of Woolf's repetitions represent the way the mind mulls over an idea, as we find in our own minds that an idea tends to drift back into consciousness from time to time. Thus Peter Walsh speaks to himself: "Clarissa refused me, he thought. He stood there thinking, Clarissa refused me" (53–54). Just a page later he is musing on his youthful promise and his failure: "He had been a Socialist, in some sense a failure—true. Still the future of civilization lies, he thought, in the hands of young men like that," and then at the end of the same paragraph, "The future lies in the hands of young men like that, he thought" (55). At the end of Peter Walsh's visit to Clarissa, she tells him as he is leaving, "Remember my party tonight!" Peter picks this up at the beginning of the next paragraph (in a paragraph link): "Remember my party, remember my party, said Peter Walsh as he stepped down the street" (52), and then a few pages later, "Clarissa's voice saying, Remember my party, Remember my party, sang in his ears" (59). The party is on his mind. It is also on Clarissa's mind that Lady Bruton did not invite her to lunch: "Millicent Bruton, whose lunch parties were said to be extraordinarily amusing, had not asked her" (31); and a full page later, "Lady Bruton, whose lunch parties were said to be extraordinarily amusing, had not asked her" (32).

Some repetitions in *Mrs. Dalloway* mark the beginning and ending of a segment, to form a ring—as we saw above; these rings range from paragraphs to episodes to the whole book. A fully developed ring should create the sense that what is in the middle of the ring constitutes a real narrative unit: it is, in effect, the meat in the sandwich. The smaller the ring, in general, the less substantial the filling. Here is a very small ring as Mrs. Dalloway's servants prepare for the party—the filling is the congeries in the middle:

> The Prime Minister was coming, Agnes said: so she had heard them say in the dining-room, she said, coming in with a tray of glasses. Did it matter, did it matter in the least, one Prime Minister more or less? It made no difference at this hour of the night to Mrs. Walker among the

plates, saucepans, cullenders, frying-pans, chicken in aspic, ice-cream freezers, pared crusts of bread, lemons, soup tureens, and pudding basins which, however hard they washed up in the scullery, seemed to be on top of her, on the kitchen table, on chairs, while the fire blared and roared, the electric lights glared, and still supper had to be laid. All she felt was, one Prime Minister more or less made not a scrap of difference to Mrs. Walker. (186)

A more substantial ring encloses Peter Walsh's dream as he dozes on a park bench, sitting beside a nurse, after his visit to Clarissa:

The grey nurse resumed her knitting as Peter Walsh, on the hot seat beside her, began snoring. In her grey dress, moving her hands indefatigably, yet quietly, she seemed like the champion of the rights of sleepers, like one of those spectral presences which rise up in twilight in woods made of sky and branches. The solitary traveller, haunter of lanes, disturber of ferns, and devastator of great hemlock plants, looking up suddenly, sees the giant figure at the end of the ride. (62)

Peter sleeps for about a page and a half. There are a number of repetitions within the passage: "Such are the visions which proffer great cornucopias full of fruit to the solitary traveller," "Such are the visions," "overpowering the solitary traveller," "Such are the visions. The solitary traveller is soon beyond the wood," "So, as the solitary traveller advances," "But to whom does the solitary traveller make reply?" (63–64). And the ring ends: "So the elderly nurse knitted over the sleeping baby in Regent's Park. So Peter Walsh snored. / He woke with extreme suddenness, saying to himself, 'The Death of the soul.'" (64). His snoring marks the beginning and ending of the ring, and the middle is made up of the visions of the solitary traveler. (See also the repetition of "snored" on 124 and 125, as Lady Bruton takes a nap.)

Other rings are less strict. In the middle of the story, Septimus Warren Smith goes to a medical appointment with Sir William Bradshaw. Before the account of the appointment itself Woolf provides some background narrative, including a small portrait of Sir William's wife, Lady Bradshaw; as a hobby she took photographs, "which were scarcely to be distinguished from the work of professionals" (106). Then, a few pages later, after Septimus has left the appointment, we hear once again about Lady Bradshaw, who "took photographs scarcely to be distinguished from the work of professionals" (110). The repetitions seem to form a ring, with the appointment itself as the filling of the sandwich, but the ring itself is not of great significance.

Another ring in this episode seems more meaningful. During the appointment Sir William advises a rest cure for Septimus; "Trust everything to me," he says, and dismisses them. "Never, never had Rezia felt such agony in her life! She had asked for help and been deserted! He had failed them! Sir William Bradshaw was not a nice man" (110). Then we read a section of some four pages characterizing Sir William and his idea of proportion (discussed above); the section ends:

> Naked, defenceless, the exhausted, the friendless received the impress of Sir William's will. He swooped; he devoured. He shut people up. It was this combination of decision and humanity that endeared Sir William so greatly to the relations of his victims.
> But Rezia Warren Smith cried, walking down Harley Street, that she did not like that man. (114)

I am not sure if this varied repetition is supposed to represent one thought in two slightly different forms or two similar thoughts at different moments.

The narrative as a whole is organized as a ring. The day of the story in a sense is a ring, as it begins with preparations for the party and ends with the party itself. At the very beginning of the story Clarissa recalls her conversation some thirty years ago with Peter Walsh, when she was eighteen and he was twenty: he found her in the garden at Bourton and said, "Musing among the vegetables? (...) I prefer men to cauliflowers"; and she now says to herself, "it was his sayings one remembered (...)—a few sayings like this about cabbages" (1). Evidently cauliflower and cabbages are interchangeable in her memory of his sayings. Toward the middle of the story Peter himself recalls the cauliflowers and cabbages at Bourton (83). They return to complete the ring at the end. Peter has met Sally Seaton for the first time in many years at Clarissa's party: "Last time they met, Peter remembered, had been among the cauliflowers in the moonlight" (211); and a few pages later: "But no, he did not like cabbages; he preferred human beings, Peter said" (217).

Another possible ring is formed by reference to a passage from Shakespeare's *Cymbeline*. Early in the story Clarissa remembers the passage: "Fear no more the heat o' the sun / Nor the furious winter's rages," and she comments to herself, "This late age of the world's experience had bred in them all, all men and women, a well of tears. Tears and sorrows; courage and endurance; a perfectly upright and stoical bearing" (8). This passage suggests early on that the story will not flinch from looking at the darker sides of human life. When Clarissa discovers that Lady Bruton has invited Richard to lunch but without Clarissa, she repeats to herself, "Fear no more, said Clarissa. Fear no more the heat o' the sun" (31). And part of the passage is picked up while Clarissa is repairing the tear in her dress: "Fear no more, says the heart. Fear no more, says the heart . . ." (42). Later on, as Septimus lies on his sofa, the line comes to his mind: "Fear no more, says the heart in the body; fear no more. // He was not afraid" (157). This phrase is one of the most definite connections between Clarissa and Septimus. And the phrase comes back near the end, as Clarissa watches the old lady next door and ponders the death of Septimus: "The young man had killed himself; but she did not pity him, with the clock striking the hour, one, two, three, she did not pity him, with all this going on. There! the old lady had put out her light! the whole house was dark now with this going on, she repeated, and the words came to her, Fear no more the heat of the sun" (210). The repetition thus marks not just the outside elements of the ring, but some of the filling, as well.

At her party, Clarissa hears from Lady Bradshaw about the death of Septimus: "What business had the Bradshaws to talk of death at her party. A young man had killed himself" (207). Clarissa vividly imagines how he died, and then she recalls: "She had once thrown a shilling into the Serpentine, never anything more. But he had flung it away" (208). And this leads to a long meditation on life and death, a meditation which has been prepared throughout the novel. This moment is carefully anticipated at the very beginning, in Clarissa's first meditation: "She remembered throwing a shilling into the Serpentine" (7).

The very end of the narrative also reaches back into the story:

"I will come," said Peter, but he sat on for a moment. What is this terror? what is this ecstasy? he thought to himself. What is it that fills me with extraordinary excitement?

> It is Clarissa, he said.
> For there she was. (219)

This moment is anticipated around the middle of the story, as Peter muses after his visit to Clarissa: "But it was Clarissa one remembered. Not that she was striking; not beautiful at all; there was nothing picturesque about her; she never said anything specially clever; there she was, however; there she was" (84). And perhaps also at the beginning, as Clarissa recalls what Peter said about her when they were young: "She would marry a Prime Minister and stand at the top of a staircase; the perfect hostess he called her" (6).

Woolf's poetics, aesthetics, and thematics are all of a piece; if you pursue any one of them you will eventually touch them all. The segmentation and overlapping of focalized sections represent the spider threads of attachment which tie one person to another. The repetitions represent actions of the mind but also the passage and return of time. The beauty of the prose and of the portraits, her sense of how to construct and connect a story, this story, are all closely connected to her understanding of the ebb and flow of consciousness and the ebb and flow of life.

2
Ring Composition

Ring composition is an important element of narrative technique, and the analysis of rings provides a model for narrative analysis in general. Rings occur at every level of composition, from sentences to whole narratives; there are several different kinds of rings, though they all count as versions of the same figure; and it is often possible to understand the meaning or the function of a ring.

The term "ring composition" was used first by the Dutch classicist W. A. A. Van Otterlo in two articles and a book published in the 1940s, all concerning compositional technique in ancient Greek literature and particularly in Homer.[1] The sociologist Mary Douglas wrote an interesting book on rings, especially rings with complex internal structure. My impression, however, is that rings have not been of much interest to general literary critics, even though they are common in literature of all periods.[2]

Ring composition is a particular kind of repetition, where the beginning and the end of a text, small or large, are the same or similar. Rings can take various forms: (ABA), (ABBA), (ABAB), (ABABA), (ABCBA), (ABACADA), and so on; some of these variations show complex internal structure or the overlapping of two or more rings. A fully developed ring should create the sense that what is in the middle of the ring constitutes a real narrative unit: the middle, in effect, is the meat in the sandwich. Repetition does not in itself create a ring; rings are created by repetition which creates a middle. But the smaller the ring, in general, the less substantial the filling. Chiasmus (AB/BA) might seem to be a kind of ring, but it's not, because it lacks a middle.

Small Rings

At the level of the sentence, a ring is the same as the rhetorical figure epanalepsis. Sentence epanalepsis will ordinarily be of the simplest form, "A

[...] A." The middle of an epanalepsis, however, is usually not of great importance. Lanham's example of epanalepsis comes from Sir Philip Sidney's *Astrophel and Stella:* "I might, unhappy word, O me, I might." This sentence is almost a kind of diacope—the repetition of a word or phrase with something in between; so "I might, I might" becomes "I might, [unhappy word, O me,] I might," where the judgment "unhappy word, O me" is the middle. Epanalepsis is not common, but examples can be found. Here's one from Porter's *Ship of Fools*—"Fine, that would be just fine" (127). A sentence of this form can be thought of in two ways: either the repeated word is extracted from the main sentence and then put at the front, or an isolated word is stated and then placed in a sentence. It is easy enough to construct sentences on this model: "Delicious, that soup was just delicious!" Here is a better example, from Yuval Noah Harari's *Homo Deus: A Brief History of Tomorrow.* Harari is explaining why large animals, such as mammoths, were killed off by early humans, while smaller animals survived: mammoths live in small groups and breed slowly, so a troop will die off even if only a few are killed each year. "Rabbits, in contrast, breed like rabbits" (87).

Paragraph rings are common; I have noted several in chapter 1 and others in *How to Reread a Novel.* Here is another, the last paragraph of Henry Roth's *Call It Sleep.* The hero, the young boy David, has just received a great electrical shock from the third rail of the streetcar; now at home in bed he falls into a sort of sleep:

> He might as well call it sleep. It was only towards sleep that every wink of the eyelids could strike a spark into the cloudy tinder of the dark, kindle out of shadowy corners of the bedroom such myriad and such vivid jets of images—of the glint on tilted beards, of the uneven shine on roller skates, of the dry light on grey stone stoops, of the tapering glitter of rails, of the city sheen on the night-smooth rivers, of the glow on thin blonde hair, red faces, of the glow on the outstretched, open palms of legions upon legions of hands hurtling towards him. He might as well call it sleep. It was only towards sleep that ears had power to cull again and reassemble the shrill cry, the hoarse voice, the scream of fear, the bells, the thick-breathing, the roar of crowds and all sounds that lay fermenting in the vats of silence and the past. It was only towards sleep one knew himself still lying on the cobbles, felt the cobbles under him, and over him and scudding ever towards him like a black foam, the

perpetual blur of shod and running feet, the broken shoes, new shoes, stubby, pointed, caked, polished, bunion, pavement-bevelled, lumpish, under skirts, under trousers, shoes, over one and through one, and feel them all and feel, not pain, not terror, but strangest triumph, strangest acquiescence. One might as well call it sleep. He shut his eyes. (441)

Here is a paragraph ring from near the beginning of Henry James's *The Wings of the Dove*. Kate Croy has come to visit her father, who keeps her waiting:

> When her father at last appeared she became, as usual, instantly aware of the futility of any effort to hold him to anything. He had written her he was ill, too ill to leave his room, and that he must see her without delay; and if this had been, as was probably, the sketch of a design he was indifferent even to the moderate finish required for deception.

The paragraph ends:

> The inconvenience—as always happens in such cases—was not that you minded what was false but that you missed what was true. He might be ill and it might suit you to know it, but no contact with him, for this, could ever be straight enough. Just so he even might die, but Kate fairly wondered on what evidence of his own she would some day have to believe it. (23)

The repetition of "ill" makes a verbal ring, but there is also the semantic ring created by words having to do with deceit and falsehood. One effect of this ring, and of many other paragraph rings, is to make the whole of the paragraph into a single unit of meaning, as if it were possible to say all the words simultaneously. The same effect is achieved, or at least attempted, in many larger rings as well.

An example of another kind of relatively small ring is found in book 11 of the *Odyssey*, when Odysseus is in the Land of the Dead. There he meets the shade of his mother; he asks her four questions, in this order: (A) How did you die? (B) What about my father, Laertes? (C) What about my son, Telemachus? (D) What about Penelope? She answers in reverse order: (D) Penelope is waiting for you. (C) Telemachus is taking care of your land and property. (B) Laertes stays on his estate in the country. (A) I died of grief for you (*Od.* 11.171–203). This kind of ring could be called a Responsive Ring. This kind of mirroring response is a feature of oral technique; indeed, one often hears reverse responses in oral questioning still today: "I'll answer your questions in reverse order."

Many rings are larger than a paragraph but smaller than a chapter. The following comes from the beginning of book 3 of Arnold Bennett's *The Old Wives' Tale*. Book 3 is all about Sophia, from her elopement to her eventual commercial success as a hotel owner. The beginning of book 3 picks up from the very end of book 1, where Mrs. Baines is told that Sophia has run off with Gerald Scales. At the beginning of book 3 Sophia is in a hotel room in London waiting for Gerald:

> There was a knock at the door apparently gay and jaunty. But she thought, truly: "He's nearly as nervous as I am!" And in her sick nervousness she coughed, and then tried to take full possession of herself. The moment had at last come which would divide her life as a battle divides the history of a nation. Her mind in an instant swept backwards through an incredible three months.

There follows a long paragraph of thirty-some lines, then a short paragraph of four lines, both summarizing the events of the three months leading up to the elopement, and then the closing of the ring:

> The knock at the door was impatiently repeated.
> "Come in," she said timidly.
> Gerald Scales came in. (311–312)

The beginning of Dickens's *Little Dorrit* is a ring extending over two pages. The first sentence of the book is "Thirty years ago, Marseilles lay burning in the sun, one day" (39). This is followed by four paragraphs of vivid description of Marseilles in the heat, and at the end of this description: "Marseilles, a fact to be strongly smelt and tasted, lay broiling in the sun one day" (40). This sentence then becomes a link to the first sentence of the following paragraph, which also adds a new element: "In Marseilles that day there was a villainous prison."

Rings are often used to mark the beginning and the end of a digression. The *Odyssey* provides a famous example. In book 19 Odysseus, disguised as a beggar, is talking with Penelope, who does not know who he really is (though some critics believe that she has suspicions). At the end of the conversation, Penelope has the old nurse Eurykleia wash his feet. Odysseus realizes that Eurykleia will probably recognize him by the scar on his leg, a scar he received when he was a young boy; and indeed she does: "She came up close and washed her lord, and at once she recognized / that scar, which once the boar with his white tusks had inflicted / on him, when he went to Parnassos, to Autolycus and his children" (*Od.* 19.392–94).

The narrator now tells the story: when Odysseus is born, his maternal grandfather, Autolycus, takes him on his lap and names him; later on Odysseus goes to visit Autolycus, and on a hunting trip Odysseus is wounded by a boar; when he goes back home he tells the whole story to his parents. So the digression ends, and the main story picks up again: "The old woman, holding him in the palms of her hands, recognized / this scar as she handled it. She let his foot go, so that / his leg, which was in the basin, fell free, and the bronze echoed" (*Od.* 19.467–69).

The beginning and the end of the digression are marked by the repetition of the words "scar" (οὐλήν at 19.393 and 19.464) and "recognized" (ἔγνω at 19.392 and γνῶ at 19.468). Erich Auerbach, in the famous first chapter of *Mimesis*, argued that the past time in this digression completely takes over the present, and so the digression does not create any feeling of suspense: "What [Homer] narrates is for the time being the only present, and fills both the stage and the reader's mind completely. . . . When the young Euryclea sets the infant Odysseus on his grandfather Autolycus' lap after the banquet, the aged Euryclea, who a few lines earlier had touched the wanderer's foot, has entirely vanished from the stage and from the reader's mind" (3). I am not sure that I react to this episode as Auerbach does. I do feel suspense as Odysseus's foot is literally suspended for many lines. I propose another way to read this episode: the past has left its mark on the present—in this case literally, as a scar.

Another famous example of a digressive ring is found in Laurence Sterne's *Tristram Shandy*. At the beginning of chapter 21 of Volume I, Tristram's father and his uncle Toby are sitting downstairs as Tristram is being born upstairs:

> —I wonder what's all that noise, and running backwards and forwards for, upstairs, quoth my father, addressing himself, after an hour and a half's silence, to my uncle *Toby*,—who you must know, was sitting on the opposite side of the fire, smoking his social pipe all the time, in mute contemplation of a new pair of black-plush-breeches which he had got on;—What can they be doing, brother?—quoth my father,—we can scarce hear ourselves talk.
>
> I think, replied my uncle *Toby*, taking his pipe from his mouth, and striking the head of it two or three times upon the nail of his left thumb, as he began his sentence,—I think, says he:—But to enter rightly into my uncle *Toby's* sentiments on this matter, you must be made to enter first a little into his character, the outlines of which I shall just give you, and then the dialogue between him and my father will go on as well again. (55)

The digression interrupts Uncle Toby in midsentence. A page later Tristram remarks, "But I forget my uncle *Toby,* whom all this while we have left knocking the ashes out of his tobacco pipe" (56)—as if Uncle Toby were knocking out the ashes as we read. But rather than letting Uncle Toby knock out his pipe and finish his sentence, Tristam digresses again, and gives the history of Uncle Toby's wound and his consequent fascination with military fortifications. Then at the end of chapter 4 in Volume II he promises "to return back to the parlour fire-side, where we left my uncle *Toby* in the middle of his sentence" (79)—but the digression continues until the beginning of the next chapter, which begins:

> —What can they be doing, brother, said my father.—I think, replied my uncle Toby,—taking, as I told you, his pipe from his mouth, and striking the ashes out of it as he began his sentence—I think, replied he,—it would not be amiss, brother, if we rung the bell. (84–85)

Sterne overlays two different times; in the main narrative, Uncle Toby is frozen with his pipe in his hand and his sentence incomplete, while in the digression he is wounded, he spends years as an invalid, and he develops his fascination with fortifications. Then he is allowed to finish his sentence. This ring seems to be saying something about both the management of narrative and the nature of time; the narrator has frozen the characters in midsentence while the narrative wanders.

Digressions in dialogue, such as this passage from *Tristam Shandy,* are very common. Here is an example from Gertrude Stein's story "The Good Anna," in *Three Lives:*

> "Well, Julia, is your mamma out?" Anna asked, one Sunday afternoon, as she came into the Lehntman house.
>
> [Four paragraphs]
>
> She came to the Lehntman house, where she had not been for several days, and opening the door that is always left unlatched in the houses of the lower middle class in the pleasant cities of the South, she found Julia in the family sitting room alone.
>
> "Well, Julia, where is your mamma?" Anna asked. (25)

This ring, like many others, has two elements at each end: AB [. . .] BA. Just why Stein varies Anna's question in this ring sentence I don't know. The variation, I think, highlights the fictionality of the story: there is no reality here, nothing which is outside the control of the author, even to the extent that the author (unlike God) can change a reality which has already been established. We will see similar variation in some other examples.

Anthony Trollope is very fond of digressions in dialogue, which he uses as a way to add commentary on the action while the characters are put on hold. The following passage, from Trollope's *Framley Parsonage,* comes from a conversation involving Lady Lufton, her son, Lord Lufton, and Griselda Grantly, who has some hopes of marrying Lord Lufton. Lady Lufton asks her son if he intends to join in the dancing; he suggests that dancing might interrupt the conversation, but then he asks Griselda her opinion.

> "I have not thought about it," said Griselda, turning her face away from Lord Lufton.
>
> It must not, however, be supposed that Miss Grantly had not thought about Lord Lufton, or that she had not considered how great might be the advantage of having Lady Lufton on her side if she made up her mind that she did wish to become Lord Lufton's wife.

The digression continues for a long paragraph exploring her thoughts about Lord Lufton and another possible suitor, Lord Dumbello, and then the main action begins again, with a repetition of the line that began the digression: "'I have not thought about it,' said Griselda, very coldly" (355). Griselda's words at the beginning of the ring are exactly those at the end; we are not supposed to think that she said them twice; rather, the tape has been rewound just enough so that we hear the same words over again. The narrator's commentary, however, has changed. At first he just notes that Griselda turns away; when he repeats he adds that she spoke "coldly." The ring is an opportunity to add a comment. Trollope uses digressive rings several times in *Framley Parsonage*.[3] Clearly this technique has become a regular tool in his kit. It is interesting to note that the repetitions are not always exact.

Many digressive rings are easy to see, because the words marking the ring are fairly close together, but the ring words of a larger digression may be separated by several pages, or more. Thus *Framley Parsonage* begins, "When young Mark Robarts was leaving college, his father might well declare that all men began to say all good things to him, and to extol his fortune in that he had a son blessed with so excellent a disposition" (33). There follow five pages of background, from Mark's childhood through his career in college: "and after that came the period at which we will begin our story. But before doing so, may I not assert that all men were right in saying all manner of good things to the Devonshire physician, and in praising his luck in having such a son" (38). We can note the repetition of key words and ideas: "say"/"saying," "all men," "all good things"/"all manner of good things," "fortune/luck."

A ring can also enclose a complete chapter. Here is the first sentence of the first chapter of Thomas Hardy's *The Return of the Native:* "A Saturday afternoon in November was approaching the time of twilight, and the vast tract of unenclosed wild known as Egdon Heath embrowned itself moment by moment" (33). The rest of this first chapter is a long account of Egdon Heath itself, with no characters and no action. The chapter ends by bringing the reader back to the moment of the opening sentence and to move towards actual narration: "On the evening under consideration it would have been noticed that, though the gloom had increased sufficiently to confuse the minor features of the heath, the white surface of the road remained almost as clear as ever" (36). The first sentence of the second chapter then follows with a link: "Along the road walked an old man" (37).

Medium Rings

A section larger than a chapter can also be a ring. A famous early instance occurs in books 2 to 4 of Virgil's *Aeneid*. In book 1, Aeneas has landed on the coast of Africa and he has been welcomed by Dido. At the end of the book, at a great feast, Dido asks Aeneas to tell about the fall of Troy and about his wanderings. The first line of book 2 is "All faces now were fixed on him in silence" ("conticuere omnes, intentique ora tenebant"), and the last line of book 3 is "At last he reached the end and sat in silence" ("conticuit tandem, factoque hic fine quievit"). The translator (Sarah Ruden) places the ring word "silence" at the end of the two lines, whereas Virgil placed it (as a verb) at the beginning of the lines. The ring marks the boundaries of this extensive retrospect, which is an element in the architecture of the epic.

Virgil here is imitating and attempting to improve a passage from the *Odyssey*. In book 6 Odysseus lands in the country of the Phaiakians, where he is welcomed and entertained, although he does not reveal his identity. Finally at a great feast, the king of the Phaiakians, Alkinoös, asks him to tell who he is; this is at the very end of book 8, and at the beginning of book 9 he starts to tell his story. In the middle of book 11, as he is telling about his trip to the Land of the Dead, he stops and says that he doesn't want to keep everyone from sleep: "So he spoke, and all of them stayed stricken in silence / held in thrall by the story all through the shadowy chambers" (11.333–34). At the urging of the Phaiakians he continues, ending finally at the end of book 12. Book 13 then begins, "So he spoke, and all of them stayed stricken to silence, held in thrall by the story all through the shadowy chambers" (13.1–2). The Greek wording of these two passages is identical. Homer has created a kind of ring, but he has joined the middle of the story to the end. Clearly Virgil noticed this ring in the *Odyssey* and decided that he could improve it.

In *Little Dorrit*, Dickens created a ring that covers two full chapters and parts of two more. Chapter 5 of book 1 ends as Arthur decides that he has to find out more about Little Dorrit, as he fears that an action by his parents may have caused her family's poverty: "His original curiosity augmented every day, as he watched for her, saw or did not see her, and speculated about her. Influenced by his predominant idea, he fell into a habit of discussing with himself the possibility of being in some way associated with it. At last he resolved to watch Little Dorrit to know more of her story." Then the next chapter begins, not with Arthur's investigation, but with the narrator explaining the situation and the history of the Dorrit family: "Thirty years ago there stood, a few doors short of the church of Saint George, in the borough of Southwark, on the left-hand-side of the way going southward, the Marshalsea Prison." The narrator spends two chapters explaining how it was that Mr. Dorrit fell into debt and was imprisoned; how his family lived in the prison with him; how his youngest daughter, Amy—Little Dorrit—was born in the prison; how his wife died there; and so on. And this digression ends, at the very end of chapter 7: "This was the life, and this the history, of Little Dorrit; now going home upon a dull September evening, observed at a distance by Arthur Clennam. This was the life, and this the history, of Little Dorrit; turning at the end of London Bridge, recrossing it, going back again, passing on to Saint George's Church, turning back suddenly once more, and flitting in at the open outer gate and little court-yard of the Marshalsea" (118). Chapter 8 begins: "Arthur Clenham stood in the street, waiting to ask some passerby what place that was." So the end of chapter 5 forms a ring with the beginning of chapter 8, and the beginning of chapter 6 forms a ring with the end of chapter 7. Thus there are two rings, one outside the digression—Arthur's watching for Little Dorrit—and one inside—the prison and its environs.

A Complex Ring in Trollope's *Doctor Thorne*

One of the most complicated rings I have come across occurs in Trollope's *Doctor Thorne*. This ring structure, as I see it, covers about one hundred pages of text, from the beginning of chapter 1 to the end of chapter 8. This whole section of the novel is centered on a single day, July 1, 1854, which is the twenty-first birthday of young Frank Gresham, but the section also includes extensive flashbacks. The rings are a way of controlling the complex organization of time in the section. At a deeper level of analysis, I would suggest that ring structures can represent the complexity of the human experience of time, in which the present is interwoven with the past and the future. The boundaries of the various elements of this complex ring structure are not definite, because the boundaries of human time are not definite, and there is considerable overlapping of the narrative strands. With this warning I will attempt a rough analysis of the section; as complex as the analysis may seem, the narrative is in fact more complex, but a map can show only so much of the territory.

The first sentence of the novel sets up a ring by announcing a digression before the story even gets going: "Before the reader is introduced to the modest country medical practitioner who is to be the chief personage of the following tale, it will be well that he should be made acquainted with some particulars as to the locality in which, and the neighbours among whom, our doctor followed his profession" (5). We can call the story of Dr. Thorne the A strand of the complex ring structure.

The narrator then introduces several characters, in particular Frank Gresham and his son, also named Frank Gresham. The present time of the story begins at young Frank Gresham's coming-of-age party, in the middle of chapter 1: "It was in July, and tables were spread under the oaks for the tenants" (12). The party counts as the B strand of the section, but there are strands within the party as well; the tenants, first mentioned in this sentence, count as the C strand, but the introduction of this C strand is immediately followed by a long digression about the place where the party is being held, Greshamsbury Park. This ends after about five pages: "But we have kept the Greshamsbury tenantry waiting under the oak-trees by far too long" (17). The words "oaks" and "tenants" clearly mark the boundaries of this ring. In the next sentence we are brought back to the party itself, the B strand: "Yes, when young Frank came of age . . ." (17). We note the repetition of "came of age" (12 and 17) and "gala doings" (12 and 19).

Almost at the end of chapter 1 we are introduced to a new set of characters, Lady de Courcy and her children, who also attend the party: "Indeed, the party at Greshamsbury was not a large one, and consisted chiefly of Lady de Courcy and her suite." This section also introduces what one might call the middle-class guests: "Then there were the Bakers and the Batesons, and the Jacksons . . . ; there was the Reverend Caleb Oriel, the high church rector, with his beautiful sister, Patience Oriel; there was Mr. Yates Umbleby, the attorney and agent; and there was Dr. Thorne, and the doctor's modest, quiet-looking little niece Miss Mary" (19). For convenience I place both groups of guests together in the D strand.

This final sentence of chapter 1 also brings back the A strand, Dr. Thorne, and it introduces an important new character, Mary Thorne. Chapter 1 is linked then to the beginning of chapter 2: "As Dr. Thorne is our hero—or I should rather say my hero, a privilege of selecting for themselves in this respect being left to all my readers—and as Miss Mary Thorne is to be our heroine, a point on which no choice whatsoever is left to anyone, it is necessary that they shall be introduced and described in a proper, formal manner" (20). This digression from the party is a reprise of the A strand, but it also leads to the development of new material, the story of Dr. Thorne's niece Mary, which we can call the E strand. She is named in the first sentence of chapter 2, but her story doesn't really begin until the middle of chapter 3.

Most of chapter 2 is taken up with the story of Dr. Thorne, his brother Henry, Henry's seduction of Mary Scratcherd, Henry's death at the hands of Mary Scratcherd's brother Roger, and eventually the birth of Dr. Thorne's niece, Mary. The story of the Scratcherds, which we can call the F strand, may count as the middle of the whole complex ring structure (22–30); we will see that this strand will link to chapter 9, which follows the long account of Frank's birthday party (111).

The story of Dr. Thorne's career (the A strand) continues with a link from the end of chapter 2 to the beginning of chapter 3. Well into chapter 3 we hear that Mary came to live with Dr. Thorne (37); this picks up the E strand from the beginning of chapter 2 (20) and is continued later in chapter 3: "So much for Dr. Thorne. A few words must still be said about Miss Mary before we rush into our story; the crust will then have been broken, and the pie will be open to the guests" (41). This E strand continues to the very end of chapter 3: "And so Mary Thorne grew up under the doctor's eye, and at the beginning of our tale she was one of the guests assembled at Greshamsbury on the coming of age of the heir, she herself having arrived at the same period of her life" (44). This final sentence of chapter 2 then links to the reprise of the B strand at the beginning of chapter 4: "It was the first of July, young Frank Gresham's birthday, and the London season was not yet over: nevertheless, Lady de Courcy had managed to get down into the country to grace the coming of age of the heir" (45).

And now the party finally begins. At this point rings are partly replaced by other structural devices. Chapter 4 is composed of several blocks of narration: first, a conversation between Lady Arabella and her sister Lady de Courcy (45–48); second, a conversation between Frank and his cousin John (48–52); third, a conversation between Mr. Gresham and Dr. Thorne (52–56); and fourth, a conversation between Mary Thorne and Beatrice Gresham and some others (56–64). We can also note a small ring within the last of these sections, as Mary's arrival is told three times: "Mary came in" (56); "When Mary came in" (57), "At this moment the door opened gently, and Mary Thorne entered the room" (59).

The beginning of chapter 5 continues the party and picks up the list of guests from chapter 1 (19 and 65); this reference belongs to the C strand of the narrative. Most of the chapter is taken up with the banquet, Frank's speech at the banquet, and conversation afterwards, in the present time of the narrative.

Chapter 6 begins, "It was, we have said, the first of July" (76); this in effect picks up the B strand, Frank's birthday and coming of age. The chapter begins with Frank's flirtation with Patience Oriel; it then moves to consider the upcoming marriage of Augusta, Frank's sister, to Mr. Moffat, the son of a wealthy tailor; and then moves back to Frank, in a flashback: "Some days before the commencement of our story, young Frank had sworn in sober earnest [...] that he loved Mary Thorne with a love for which words could find not sufficient expression": "Oh, oh! Mary; do you love me? Don't you love me? Won't you love me? Say you will. Oh, Mary, dearest Mary, will you? won't you? do you? don't you? Come now, you have a right to give a fellow an answer." (83) This little speech begins a small digressive ring in which the narrator gives some account of Frank's relationship to Mary; this takes a couple of pages, and then this little ring is closed: "When Frank declared that Mary had a right to give him an answer, he meant that he had a right to expect one. Mary acknowledged this right, and gave it him" (85). She says no. Frank leaves in despair and contemplates suicide, but "he managed to live though the subsequent period; doubtless with the view of preventing any disappointments to his father's guests" (86); this, the end of chapter 6, bring us back to the C strand, the guests at the party.

Chapter 7 shifts from Frank to Mary, her feelings about Frank, and her questions about her own mysterious background. This chapter begins with another small ring: "Mary had contrived to quiet her lover with considerable propriety of demeanour. Then came on her the somewhat harder task of quieting herself" (87); "When Mary had, as she thought, properly subdued young Frank [...] then she found it necessary to subdue herself" (88). She questions her uncle about her status—the time of this conversation is calculated in relation to the B strand, the present time of the narrative; it happens "a day or two afterwards, on the evening before Frank's birthday" (89). The chapter ends with another small ring; after his conversation with Mary, in which he does not reveal the truth about her birth and family, Dr. Thorne ponders the situation:

> And then he walked slowly by himself, backward and forwards through the garden, thinking of what he had done with reference to this girl, and doubting whether he had done wisely and well. (93)

> And so he walked slowly backwards and forwards though the garden, meditating these things painfully enough. (96)

Chapter 8 returns to the party, the B strand, but now from Mary's point of view, with a backward glance at events from chapter 4 (62) and chapter 5 (72):

> Such had been her feelings when she protested that she would not be Augusta Gresham's bridesmaid, and offered to put her neck beneath Beatrice's neck; when she drove the Lady Margaretta out of the room, and gave her own opinion on the construction of the word humble; and also had been her feelings when she kept her hand so rigidly to herself while Frank held the dining-room door open for her to pass through. (98)

As chapter 8 continues, Lady de Courcy (who belongs to strand D) urges Frank to visit her so that he can meet a rich heiress, Miss Dunstable, and it ends with a final reference to his birthday, strand B:

> "Beatrice," said he, "I am to go to Courcy Castle tomorrow."
> "So I heard mamma say."
> "Well I only came of age today, and I will not begin by running counter to them. But I tell you what, I won't stay above a week at Courcy Castle for all the de Courcy's in Barsetshire. Tell me, Beatrice, did you ever hear of a Miss Dunstable?" (110)

This closes the complex ring structure of these eight chapters; by my reckoning, the rings form this pattern: ABCCDAEFABEBDBDB. Of these rings, the B ring, Frank's coming of age, is probably the most important, followed by the A ring, Dr. Thorne, and the E ring, Mary Thorne. Some of the others, such as the C ring, the tenants at the party, are less important, but still part of the structure. In addition, there are several small rings that I have mentioned but not included in the count, as well as one or two that I have left without comment. Altogether the analysis shows that this set of eight chapters is astonishingly complex, but still a unity—and the unity is created by the rings. Nor does the careful construction of the story end with the end of chapter 8, but further discussion would take us beyond the specific topic of this chapter.

Plot Rings: Ending with the Beginning

An entire plot can be formed as a ring if the beginning of a narrative is in some way mirrored by the ending—with some wiggle room for exactly what counts as the beginning and the end. A plot may be constructed so that an event or situation from the beginning is recapitulated in some way at the end; often language used at the beginning is used also at the end. A ring of this kind can be called Ending with the Beginning. (In chapter 5 I will discuss Beginning with the Ending, where an event or situation from the end is anticipated at the beginning.)

The whole plot of the *Iliad* is a ring: the events of book 1 are closely mirrored by the events of book 24:[4]

1. Agamemnon refuses to return Chryseis to her father Chryses; Apollo sends a plague; funeral pyres in the Greek camp;
2. a council of the chiefs where Achilles and Agamemnon quarrel;
3. Thetis consoles Achilles and agrees to take a message to Zeus;
4. Thetis appeals to Zeus, who adopts the hero's cause;
5. the gods assemble, and Hera opposes Zeus.

These are then mirrored in book 24:

5. the gods assemble, and Hera opposes Zeus;
4. Thetis receives notice from Zeus that the gods no longer support Achilles;
3. Thetis consoles Achilles and brings him a message from Zeus;

2. Achilles restores Hector's body to Priam;
1. the funeral of Hector, with the construction of a funeral pyre for him.

The symmetry is not exact, but the general correspondence is striking. A more detailed analysis would note subtle and not-so-subtle variations. Here I will mention just one variation: in book 1 Agamemnon rudely dismisses Chryses, but at the end Achilles gives Hector's body back to Priam; moreover, the child of Chryses is alive, while Priam's son Hector is dead; so in both situations there is a kind of reversal, as well as a change in characters. The combination of repetition and difference creates the meaning of the ring. The structure of the poem asks us to compare these two situations, and specifically to compare Agamemnon to Achilles. The middle of this ring—that is, the whole of the poem in between—creates and explains the comparison. This ring of the whole creates the sense that the whole of the *Iliad* is a unified structure of meaning.

These, then, are two important functions of ring composition: the creation of unified narrative structures, and the invitation to compare. In addition, we see in this ring some general principles in the composition of plot rings: a ring can be a repetition of action rather than words; the second element of the ring can be the reverse or the negation of the first element; and there can be a transference of characters from the beginning of the ring to the end.

The causal connection between the beginning and the ending of the *Iliad* is very strong: the abduction of Chryseis is the beginning of a causal chain which ends with the return of Hector's body, so the end of the ring is a direct consequence of the beginning. If, however, Homer had decided to begin his version of the story with the Judgment of Paris or to end it with the death of Patroclus, then there would be no ring.

The plot ring in Henry James's *Roderick Hudson* is less clearly motived than the plot ring of the *Iliad*. At the beginning of the story Rowland Mallet goes to visit his cousin Cecilia in Northampton, Massachusetts. There he meets a promising young sculptor, Roderick Hudson, and Hudson's fiancée, Mary Garland. Mallet enables Hudson to go to Europe to study, and Mary eventually follows. Mallet falls in love with Mary, and Hudson wastes his talent in dissipation. Almost at the end of the story, Hudson dies, in an accident or perhaps by suicide. In the penultimate paragraph Mary flings herself on Hudson's body "with a loud tremendous cry." And here is the final paragraph of the novel:

> That cry still lives in Rowland's ears. It interposes persistently against the reflection that when he sometimes—very rarely—sees her, she is unreservedly kind to him; against the memory that during the dreary journey back to America, made of course with his assistance, there was a great frankness in her gratitude, a great gratitude in her frankness. Mary Garland lives with Mrs. Hudson, at Northampton, where Rowland visits his cousin Cecilia more frequently than of old. When he calls upon Mary he never sees Mrs. Hudson. Cecilia, who having her shrewd impression that he comes to see the young lady at the other house as much as to see herself, does not feel obliged to seem unduly flattered, calls him whenever he reappears the most restless of mortals. But he always says to her in answer, "No, I assure you I am the most patient." (249–50)

The final paragraph has a lot of work to do. It takes the major characters all the way from Europe to America, it establishes a new pattern of Rowland's visits to Northampton, and it delicately suggests something about Mary's reception of these visits and Mallet's hopes. This ending is certainly satisfying, and the satisfaction I think is increased by the ring structure, but the ending lacks the inevitability that we find in the ending of the *Iliad*. There is nothing in the causal sequence of events that requires a return to Northampton; but the ending is nonetheless essential to the investigation of Mallet's character and psychology.

A ring may be created by the repetition at the end of language from the beginning, even if there is no direct causal chain. Here is the beginning of William Faulkner's *Light in August*, as Lena arrives in Jefferson: "Sitting beside the road, watching the wagon mount the hill toward her, Lena thinks, 'I have come from Alabama: a fur piece. All the way from Alabama a-walking. A fur piece.' Thinking *although I have not been quite a month on the road I am already in Mississippi, further from home than I have ever been before. I am now further from Doane's Mill than I have been since I was twelve years old*" (3).

Lena is pregnant, and she is looking for the father of her child, Lucas Burch. The narrator describes her journey: "a long monotonous succession of peaceful and undeviating changes from day to dark and dark to day again, through which she advanced in identical and anonymous and deliberate wagons as though through a succession of creakwheeled and limpeared avatars, like something moving forever and without progress across an urn" (6). The end of the first chapter creates a small ring: "My, my," she says; "here I aint been on the road but four weeks, and now I am in Jefferson already. My, my. A body does get around" (27).

Lena arrives in Jefferson and meets Byron Bunch; at the end of the story they leave Jefferson together. Most of the novel, however, is taken up with other characters, particularly Joe Christmas, Joanna Burden, and Gail Hightower, whose intertwined stories are only tangentially connected to the story of Lena and Byron. The plot is quite complicated, and I will not attempt a full summary here. It is enough to say that Christmas, who is (probably?) of mixed race, runs a bootlegging business with Lucas Burch, who has taken the name Joe Brown. Brown works at a planing mill with Byron Bunch. Christmas has been having an affair with Joanna Burden, who lives in Jefferson, but who is an outcast in the town because she comes from the North and opposes racism. She tries to kill Christmas, and he kills her instead. Lucas Burch sets fire to her house in order to cover up the crime, but Joe Christmas is arrested for murder. Lena delivers her baby, assisted by Gail Hightower, who had been a pastor in the town until his wife left him in scandalous circumstances; Lucas Burch once again leaves Lena in the lurch. Joe Christmas escapes from custody; he takes refuge at Hightower's house, but he is caught and killed. At the end of the story, Byron Bunch proposes to Lena. She declines to marry him, but they leave Jefferson together.

At the very end, after Lena and Byron Bunch have left Jefferson, she speaks the last words: "My, my. A body does get around. Here we aint been coming from Alabama but two months, and now its already Tennessee" (511). These words create a clear ring with the beginning and end of the first chapter.

Lena's story is connected to the story of Joe Christmas and Joanna Burden through Lucas Burch, but, as Michael Millgate argues, her story and the story of Joe Christmas are strands, each of which retains its own identity even as they are woven together (1987, 37).

Lena's departure from Jefferson is not caused by the events of the main story, but it makes a good closure nonetheless. The ring creates an invitation to compare—the reader is invited to compare Lena's situation at the beginning of the story and her situation at the end. The ring suggests the repetition and variation of a pattern, as once again Lena sets off down the road, but this time with her baby and Byron Bunch. As the narrator says at the beginning, Lena is forever moving but never making any progress. As Millgate notes, Lena's story is "essentially plotless" (1987, 37).

Most stories move more or less steadily forward in time—though of course in any story there may be minor deviations from the steady forward movement—*anachronies,* as Gérard Genette (1980) calls them. The forward movement of time is a fundamental feature of our perception of reality. The story of Joe Christmas, for instance, moves forward in time, from his birth to his death. The stories of Joanna Burden and Gail Hightower also move forward. This forward motion is not, however, the whole story of time and how we perceive it. Sometimes we perceive time as cyclical rather than progressive, and a plot ring may suggest this cyclical mode of time and experience. Lena's story is cyclical rather than progressive: she is always moving, but never really getting anywhere. The ring encloses and provides a commentary on the inner stories of Joe Christmas, Joanna Burden, and Gail Hightower. The ring has the "effect of requiring the action as a whole to be viewed from a distanced perspective, seen within the context of the long history of humanity itself—a history as steady and repetitious in terms of individual lives as the yearly progress of the seasons" (Millgate 38).

Another kind of Ending with the Beginning is found in Lewis Carroll's *Alice's Adventures in Wonderland* and *Alice Through the Looking Glass;* in both of these fantasies, the events of the story turn out to be dreams: the story begins as Alice falls asleep and it ends as she wakes up. James Branch Cabell's *The High Place* is another story with a dream ring, and there are many others, including the great dream allegories, such as *Piers the Ploughman,* by William Langland, *Le Roman de la Rose,* by Guillaume de Lorris and Jean de Meun, and *The Pilgrim's Progress,* by John Bunyan.

The ending of Robert Heinlein's science fiction novel *Starman Jones* initially looks like part of a dream ring. The story begins:

> Max liked this time of day, this time of year. With the crops in, he would finish his evening chores early and be lazy. When he had slopped the hogs and fed the chickens, instead of getting supper he followed a path to a rise west of the barn and lay down in the grass, unmindful of

chiggers. He had a book with him that he had drawn from the county library last Saturday, Bonforte's *Sky Beasts: A Guide to Exotic Zoology*, but he tucked it under his head as a pillow....

Max kept his eyes to the northwest. He favoured this spot because from it he could see the steel stilts and guide rings of the Chicago, Springfield, & Earthport Ring Road emerge from a slash in the ridge to his right. There was a guide ring at the mouth of the cut, a great steel hoop twenty feet high....

Max kept his eyes fixed on the cut; the *Tomahawk* was due any instant. Suddenly there was a silver gleam, a shining cylinder with needle nose burst out of the cut, flashed through the last ring and for a breathless moment was in free trajectory between the ridges. Almost before he could swing his eyes the projectile entered the ring across the gap and disappeared into the hillside—just as the sound hit him.

It was a thunderclap that bounced around the hills. Max gasped for air. "Boy," he said softly, "Boy, oh boy!" (5–6)

Max runs away from home, away from his stepmother and her new husband. He fakes his way onto the crew of a space ship; various exciting adventures happen; and in a skillfully contrived wish-fulfillment plot Max ends up the captain of the ship and he saves everyone from disaster. Then the last chapter begins:

Max liked this time of day, this time of year. He was lying in the grass on the little rise west of the barn, with his head propped up so he could see to the northwest. If he kept his eyes there, on the exit ring of the C.S.&E. Ring Road, he would be able, any instant now, to see the *Tomahawk* plunge out and shoot across the gap in free trajectory. At the moment he was not reading, no work was pushing him, he was just being lazy and enjoying the summer evening....

There was a breathless hush, then suddenly a silver projectile burst out of the exit ring on the far side—just as the sound hit him.

"Boy, oh boy!" he said softly. "It never looks like they'd make it." (313)

The reader at this point might well suspect that this story will turn out to be a dream story, like the Alice stories or *The High Place*. But no; all the exciting adventures really did happen, and Max really did end up as the captain of a spaceship. He has just returned home now, before his next assignment in space. The house he ran away from is in ruins, the farm is abandoned, his stepmother and step-stepfather have disappeared. The dream is reality.

William Golding's *Pincher Martin* has a ring something like a dream ring, but more sinister. The eponymous hero of the story is one of the crew of a ship that is attacked and sunk in the North Atlantic. He is thrown into the water, but he manages (so it seems) to inflate his lifebelt and to kick off his sea boots, which threaten to drag him down into the water (10). He swims until he finds a barren island, where he survives for some time. Most of the story consists of his memories and hallucinations. But in the last chapter of the book, Martin's body is found washed up on shore, and, in the last sentence of the book, one of the officers who deals with the body remarks, "He didn't even have time to kick off his seaboots" (208). This ring is contrived, but it is crucial to the interpretation of the novel—the story of Martin's survival is false, perhaps the creation of his dying mind or some kind of postmortem fantasy. It is easy to find other examples of Ending with the Beginning; I will leave this task to the reader. In this chapter I have identified a few types of ring composition and I have made some general comments about how rings work and what they mean, but each ring creates its own meaning in the context of the narrative in which it occurs.

3
The Composition of *The Good Soldier* and *Catch-22*

The Good Soldier

Critical discussion of Ford Madox Ford's *The Good Soldier* has understandably concentrated on questions of character and morality, as well as on the narrator's fragmented and unreliable discourse, but critics have also noted the remarkable formal features of the novel. According to Mark Schorer, "the novel renews a major lesson of all classic art: from the very delimitation of form arises the exfoliation of theme," and he goes on to say that this novel "has perfect clarity of surface and nearly mathematical poise" (128). I must admit that I don't know what Schorer means. I would say that *The Good Soldier* is a mess—a deliberate mess, but still a mess. It is easy enough to talk about the exfoliation of theme and about mathematical poise, but literary critics, like scholars in other fields, should be able to show their work. Michael Levenson I think comes closer to the reality of the novel when he notes the narrative's "insistent formal dislocations" and "its inversions, postponements, repetitions, reversals" (Levenson 1984, 374).

Robert Ray argues that "the strength of Ford Madox Ford's *The Good Soldier* may be found in Ford's style"; he notes that Ford's metaphors have received critical attention, and then he adds a list of "four other stylistic techniques": repetition of thematic elements, parallelism, hypothesis, and negation. Each of these is responsible for a particular effect: thematic repetition "creates a consistent world-view"; parallelism "suggests a helpless movement toward a purposeless end and [. . .] also embodies the order that underlies apparent chaos"; hypothesis "reveals the reflective and anxious uncertainty of the narrator"; and negation "indicates the narrator's passive response to some of the problems that face man in contemporary society" (Ray 1963, 61). Each item in Ray's list could benefit from clarification, but the analysis in his brief article provides a suggestive starting point. Style and compositional technique are indeed an inescapable part of the reader's experience of this novel, and they somehow help create the meaning, though exactly how is not easy to say. The composition of the narration therefore deserves examination in some detail, which this section attempts to provide. The discussion can be understood in four general and sometimes overlapping aspects: repetition, both verbal and thematic; negation and rhetorical questions; correction; and fragmentation of the narrative stream.

The basic story of *The Good Soldier* is (ostensibly) a relatively simple tale of adultery, but things quickly become more complicated. The story involves two couples—an American couple, John and Florence Dowell, and a British couple, Edward and Leonora Ashburnham. The two couples meet in Nauheim in 1904, where Edward and Florence begin an affair; Leonora knows about the affair—indeed, Edward has had a series of affairs—but Dowell (who is the rather naïve and unreliable narrator of the whole novel) seems not to know for a very long time. (He also did not know about Florence's affair with a young artist named Jimmy.) After some years of this situation, Florence sees Edward in a tête-à-tête with a young friend, Nancy, who is Leonora's ward; on the same night Dowell finds out about Florence's affair with Jimmy. Florence kills herself. Edward and Nancy then begin a tormented and unconsummated relationship. Nancy goes to India; Edward kills himself, and Nancy goes insane. Leonora remarries. Dowell buys the Ashburnhams' manor, where he takes care of Nancy. These seem to be the facts of the story, but there is some reason to doubt important elements of Dowell's account.

Along the way there are several secondary stories; the most important of these concerns Maisie Maidan, the young wife of one of Ashburnham's subordinate officers in India; Ashburnham has developed an interest in her, but it is not clear if she has become his mistress. Maisie suffers from a heart condition, and Leonora has decided to pay for her to accompany them to Nauheim. Leonora's motives are not entirely clear. Maisie overhears Edward and Florence talking about her; evidently she realizes that she has been used and she fears that Ashburnham's affections are turning to Florence; she writes a bitter letter to Leonora and then she dies of a sudden heart attack, at the very end of part 1 of the novel.

Ashburnham seems to have been a serial adulterer. The first of Ashburnham's various sexual escapades, what Dowell calls the Kilsyte case, occurred when Ashburnham "kissed a servant girl in a railway train, and it was only by the grace of God, the prompt functioning of the communication cord and the ready sympathy of what I believe you call the Hampshire Bench, that kept the poor devil out of Winchester Gaol for years and years" (45). In Dowell's judgment it seems to be Ashburnham who is to be pitied, and not the girl he assaulted. "He left servants alone after that" (46). Instead he turned his attentions to the mistress of a Russian grand duke, then the wife of a fellow officer, then Maisie Maidan, then Florence, and finally Nancy.

The events of the novel are tawdry. Other readers may judge otherwise, but I find the characters shallow, trivial, cruel, and thoughtless, and hardly worth our consideration, if it were not for the fascination of the narration. In this section I will be mostly interested in how the story is composed, but I begin with a few words on the narrative situation.

This is foregrounded very early. On the second page of the text Dowell notes that Florence's family came from Fordingbridge in England: "From there, at this moment, I am actually writing" (14). (As it turns out, this moment of writing is not the last moment of the story, and Dowell tells later events from a later perspective.) "You may well ask why I write," Dowell says to the reader, who thus becomes the narratee; addresses to the narratee are frequent throughout. He writes, he explains, because "the death of a mouse from cancer is the whole sack of Rome by the Goths, and I swear to you that the breaking up of our little four-square coterie was such another unthinkable event" (14).

A few pages later, at the beginning of the second section, Dowell has more to say about his method of writing: "I don't know how it is best to put this thing down—whether it would be better to try and tell the story from the beginning, as if it were a story; or whether to tell it from this distance of time, as it reached me from the lips of Leonora or from those of Edward himself" (19). Then he imagines himself as sitting in a cottage, telling his story to "a sympathetic soul," the narratee: "You, the listener, sit opposite me. But you are so silent. You don't tell me anything" (21). The narrative has the characteristics of a conversational confession—unplanned, rambling, disorganized, inconsistent, and remarkably repetitive—even though Dowell is writing, not speaking—but evidently not rewriting: "And it occurs to me that some way back I began a sentence that I have never finished..." (27)—the ellipsis is his, as he fails to finish a sentence about not finishing a sentence (see also 81). At the beginning of the fourth and final part he returns to his initial image of the narrative situation:

> I have, I am aware, told this story in a very rambling way so that it may be difficult for anyone to find their path through what may be a sort of maze. I have stuck to my idea of being in a country cottage with a silent listener, hearing between the gusts of the wind and amidst the noises of the distant sea, the story as it comes. And, when one discusses an affair—a long, sad affair—one goes back, one goes forward. One remembers points that one has forgotten and one explains them all the more minutely since one recognizes that one has forgotten to mention them in their proper places and that one may have given, by omitting them, a false impression. I console myself with thinking that this is a real story, and that, after all, real stories are probably told best in the way a person telling a story would tell them. They will then seem most real. (147)

Dowell's description of his imagined narrative situation comes in a ring at the beginning and at the beginning of the ending. Dowell may be rambling, but Ford is carefully shaping the presentation of the story.

Dowell's narration itself is remarkably repetitive. There are far too many repetitions to enumerate. I begin with a few examples of repetitions at roughly the level of the sentence, and then I will move on to repetitions that occur over larger stretches of text. These examples could be vastly multiplied, but what matters is experience rather than enumeration.

> *Epizeuxis:* "And he swore and swore and swore, that there was nothing else in the world against him" (56; see also 176, 181, 183, etc.).
> *Extended epizeuxis:* "I know nothing—nothing in the world—of the hearts of men" (16; see also 25, 56, 119–20, 143, 166, 182, etc.).
> *Anadiplosis:* "... the consolations of her spiritual advisors. Her spiritual advisors..." (121; see also 20, 77, 121, 176, etc.).
> *Anaphora:* "I like catching the two-forty; I like the slow, smooth roll of the great big trains [...]. I like being drawn through the green country..." (39–40; see also 138–39, 160, 186–87, etc.).

Epistrophe: "At any rate, he would have had fewer chances of ruining and or remorse. For Edward was great at remorse" (53; see also 71, 95, 152, etc.).
Chiasmus: "the burning logs were just logs that were burning" (173; see also 178, 195, 197, etc.).
Polyptoton: "And I burst out crying and I cried and cried for the whole eleven miles" (17; see also 60–61, 95, 103, 141, 148, 162, etc.).
Polysyndeton: "And my function in life was to keep that bright thing in existence. And it was almost as difficult as trying to catch with your hand that dancing reflection. And the task lasted for years" (21; see also 41).
Epanalepis: "But her passion for Jimmy was not even a passion" (77).

In addition, many passages use kinds of repetition that don't quite fit the traditional terminology: "Yet Leonora adored him with a passion that was like an agony, and hated him with an agony that was as bitter as the sea" (29); "I stood on the carefully swept steps of the Englischer Höf, looking at the carefully arranged trees in tubs upon the carefully arranged gravel whilst carefully arranged people walked past in carefully calculated gaiety, at the carefully arranged hour . . ." (26).

These accumulating repetitions suggest that Dowell is obsessed, continually chewing and chewing and chewing over each word and phrase. This obsessive quality is increased by the repetitions at larger levels of composition. The repetitions begin to swamp the progression of the story.

Repetition and figuration often occur at moments of high emotion; the following passage comes from part 4, when Nancy and Edward are working out their mutual infatuation:

> What had happened was just Hell. Leonora had spoken to Nancy; Nancy had spoken to Edward; Edward had spoken to Leonora—and they had talked and talked. And talked. You have to imagine horrible pictures of gloom and half lights, and emotions running through silent nights—through whole nights. You have to imagine my beautiful Nancy appearing suddenly to Edward, rising up at the foot of his bed with her long hair falling, like a split cone of shadow, in the glimmer of a night-light that burned beside him. You have to imagine her, a silent, a no doubt agonized figure, like a spectre, suddenly offering herself to

him—to save his reason! And you have to imagine his frantic refusal—and talk. And talk! My God! (160)

The gradatio in the second sentence turns around on itself and bites its tail; then there is epizeuxis of "talked"; the quadruple anaphora of "You have to imagine"; and the end recapitulates the epizeuxis of "talked" from the beginning of the passage. These are stylistic figures, but they are used in the composition of the paragraph as a whole.

Ford often uses figures to express emotion, but figures can also organize thought. In the following passage, from part 3, Dowell is musing on love and a man's interest in making a new conquest:

> With each new woman that a man is attracted to there appears to come a broadening of the outlook, or, if you like, an acquiring of new territory. A turn of the eyebrow, a tone of the voice, a queer characteristic gesture—all these things, and it is these things that cause to arise the passion of love—all these things are like so many objects on the horizon of the landscape that tempt a man to walk beyond the horizon, to explore. He wants to get, as it were, behind those eyebrows with the peculiar turn, as if he desired to see the world with the eyes that they overshadow. He wants to hear that voice applying itself to every possible proposition, to every possible topic; he wants to see those characteristic gestures against every possible background. (96–97)

The thought is almost analytical. Some of the difference between these two passages has to do with what they are about; the first represents the agonies of these particular people and asks the reader to imagine those agonies, with words such as *Hell, horrible, gloom, agonized,* and *frantic;* while the second is abstract and general, with less-charged words, such as *territory, horizon, explore,* and *landscape.* Both passages use anaphora, but with very different effect: the repetition in the first passage of "you have to imagine," "you have to imagine," "you have to imagine" pulls the reader into the text, but the repetition in the second passage of "he wants," "he wants," "he wants" focalizes the generalized figure of a man attracted to a woman. And the second passage uses an analytical figure, dinumeratio, where items are first listed and then elaborated: "A turn of the eyebrow, a tone of the voice, a queer characteristic gesture" becomes

He wants to get, as it were, behind those eyebrows with the peculiar turn, as if he desired to see the world with the eyes that they overshadow. He wants to hear that voice applying itself to every possible proposition, to every possible topic; he wants to see those characteristic gestures against every possible background.

These repetitions occur in short passages—a sentence up to a paragraph. But repetitions can function over larger stretches as well, as repeated epithets, clusters, key words, links, refrains, or rings.

Epitheton: An epithet can be just a single adjective used to add meaning to the passage in which it occurs, but a repeated epithet can have a general influence on the meaning of the whole narrative, as a sort of key word. One frequent epithet in *The Good Soldier* is "poor." It occurs twice on the first page, in the phrase "poor Florence"; on the next page it occurs once without a name, but referring to Florence, and then again in the phrase "poor Florence"; then on pages 16 and 20 "poor dear Florence"; "poor dear thing" on page 21; "poor dear Florence" on page 22; "poor dear wife" on page 23. The reader's initial impression of Florence is surely guided by the frequent application of this epithet—but then on pages 23 and 24 we find it applied to Florence's uncle John. On page 26 the epithet is once again applied to Florence, but on page 30 the phrase "poor girl" applies to one of Ashburnham's tenants, and on page 31 to Ashburnham himself. On page 38 it is applied to Florence; on page 40 it is applied to a cow; it is applied to Edward on page 45 and three times on page 46; then on page 47 to "poor little Mrs. Maidan." At various times it is applied to Florence, her uncle John, Mrs. Maidan, Edward, Leonora, Nancy, a tenant—and a cow. Such a wide and indiscriminate application bleaches the specific meaning out of the word, but a kind of tone remains to color the whole story.

When we first see the narrator apply it to Florence, we might take it as an indication of a kind of sympathetic pity, and that impression might be strengthened a few pages later when Dowell details the attention he paid to "poor dear Florence" (22), but soon enough this impression is dispelled: "For I hate Florence. I hate Florence with such a hatred that I would not spare her an eternity of loneliness" (61). Dowell's judgment is thoroughly inconsistent and unreliable.

Key words: The key words in the novel include *heart, sentimental, intimacy, good people, nice people, passion, remorse, sad,* and *hate; The Good*

Soldier is lavish in its repetitions. The effect is a kind of spider web of associations in which the reader gets tangled.

Of these key words *heart* is the most frequent and probably the most important. I have found the word fifty-nine times in 187 pages of the Penguin edition of the novel, about once every three pages. Some of these refer to the heart as an organ of the body, because some of the principal characters may (or may not) suffer from heart disease, but some refer to the heart as the center of emotion, and the two usages are surely connected. Here are a few instances:

> ... one of us had, as the saying is, a "heart" (13)
>
> You will gather Captain Ashburnham also had a heart (13)
>
> I know nothing—nothing in the world—of the hearts of men (16)
>
> ... the storm that seemed irretrievably to have weakened her heart (16)
>
> ... or with heart whispering to heart (17)
>
> ... with his weak and fluttering heart (23)
>
> And so, guarded against his heart.... (24)
>
> He wasn't obtrusive about his heart (24)
>
> ... quite an extraordinary kind of heart (24)
>
> ... in which she locked up her heart and her feelings (33)[1]

Florence's supposed heart disease is essential to the plot of the novel, and essential to her plot against Dowell, since it excuses her from sexual relations with him and facilitates her affairs with Jimmy and then with Ashburnham; and for some period after she dies, Dowell thinks she has died from heart disease rather than from self-administered poison. There is a hint early on, however, that symptoms can be deceiving. Florence's Uncle John was supposed to suffer from his heart, but at the age of eighty-four he died of bronchitis and his heart was discovered to be healthy (24).

Florence's heart condition supposedly begins during their sea crossing to Europe and it determines the shape of her life and her relationship with her husband, who becomes her assiduous nurse: "For I was solemnly informed that if she became excited over anything or if her emotions were really stirred her little heart might cease to beat. For twelve years I had to watch every word that any person uttered in any conversation and had to head it off what the English call 'things'—off love, poverty, crime, religion, and the rest of it. Yes, the first doctor that we had when she was carried off the ship at Havre assured me that this must be done" (22). This passage seems consistent with the image of Florence as poor Florence and of Dowell as her devoted caregiver. And yet this image is destroyed by the very next sentence: "Good God, are all these fellows monstrous idiots, or is there a freemasonry between all of them from end to end of the earth? . . ." (22). (The ellipses are Dowell's.) Either Dowell had suspicions from the beginning, or else this sentence violently juxtaposes his past ignorance and his current knowledge.

The death of Florence is narrated at the end of part 2 and the beginning of part 3. Dowell is sitting in the lounge at the spa where the two couples spend the summer together; he is talking with a stranger named Bagshawe when Florence rushes in from outside: "And then, quite suddenly, in the bright light of the street, I saw Florence running. It was like that—Florence running with a face whiter than paper and her hand on the black stuff over her heart. I tell you my own heart stood still. I tell you I could not move" (84). Florence has seen Ashburnham talking intimately with Nancy; now Florence sees her husband talking with Bagshawe: "She struck her hands over her face as if she wished to put her eyes out. And she was not there any more" (84). Bagshawe has recognized her, and he says to Dowell, "The last time I saw that girl she was coming out of the bedroom of a young man called Jimmy at five o'clock in the morning" (85). When Dowell goes to their room he finds her stretched out on her bed holding the vial that he supposed contained her heart medicine.

Dowell, however, seems not to have realized at the time that Florence has killed herself. Later in the story, though only a few pages later in the telling of the story, after Ashburnham has also killed himself, Leonora says to Dowell, "I think it was stupid of Florence to commit suicide" (90), and he replies, "Did Florence commit suicide? I didn't know" (91). And he tells the reader, "So that was the first knowledge I had that Florence had committed suicide. It had never entered my head. You may think that I had been singularly lacking in suspiciousness, you may consider me even to have been an imbecile. But consider exactly the position" (91). And he goes on to deliver an extended explanation of his obtuse ignorance; in this explanation the word *heart* occurs four times in quick succession (91, 92).

There is more to be said about this key word, and about other key words: *sentimental, intimacy, good people, nice people, passion, remorse, sad,* and *hate*.[2] My goal here, however, is not a complete analysis of these words in the composition of the narrative, but only a sort of notice to the re-reader of the novel to pay attention to these repetitions and their complex interplay.

Epimone: the rhetorical figure *epimone* designates a refrain, a phrase or sentence repeated throughout a narrative. Often a refrain is typical of a particular character, as for example, Alex in Burgess's *A Clockwork Orange* says, "What's it going to be then, eh?" (3, 5, 6, 85, 86, 87, 88, etc.). The repetitions don't have to be exact, of course.

Dowell's refrain is some variation of "I don't know" or "I know nothing"; this refrain is related to repetitions of the word "nothing"; and it is often associated with unanswered rhetorical questions. It is also related to the frequent use of the figure correctio, which I discuss below. The word "nothing" is thematic; as Michael Levenson notes, "in important respects, let us recognize, Dowell is nothing. No 'paradigm of traits' can describe him, because there is nothing substantial to describe: no determining past, no consistency of opinion, no deep belief, no stable memory" (383).

This theme of ignorance and vacuity is suggested at the very beginning of the story, in the first paragraph: "My wife and I knew Captain and Mrs. Ashburnham as well as it was possible to know anybody, and yet, in another sense, we knew nothing at all about them" (13). Dowell's professions of ignorance are profuse, and I will note only enough to give some of the flavor:

> I don't know . . . (16; Dowell's ellipses)
>
> I know nothing—nothing in the world—of the hearts of men. (16)
>
> I don't know; I don't know; (17)
>
> Who knows? (17)
>
> I don't know how it is best to put this thing down (19)
>
> Is this a digression or isn't it a digression? Again I don't know. (21)
>
> I don't know why I had gone to New York. I don't know why I had gone to the tea. (21)

> I don't know. (33)
>
> I don't know what Leonora knew or what she didn't know. (39)

Some of these are just simple statements, dropped in as isolated comments, but some are more extensive:

> But upon my word, I don't know how we put in our time. How does one put in one's time? How it is possible to have achieved nine years and to have nothing whatever to show of it? Nothing whatever, you understand. (36)
>
> I don't know. And there is nothing to guide us. And if everything is so nebulous about a matter so elementary as the morals of sex, what is there to guide us in the more subtle morality of all other personal contacts, associations, and activities? Or are we meant to act on impulse alone? It is all a darkness. (19)
>
> Here were two noble people—for I am convinced that both Edward and Leonora had noble natures, drifting down life, like fire-ships afloat on a lagoon and causing miseries, heartaches, agony of the mind and death. And they themselves steadily deteriorated. And why? For what purpose? To point what lesson? It is all a darkness. (132)

A good many of these come at the beginning of the story, but they continue here and there throughout and at the very end: "Anyhow, I don't know whether, at this point, Nancy Rufford loved Edward Ashburnham. I don't know whether she even loved him when, on getting, at Aden, the news of his suicide she went mad. Because that may just as well have been for the sake of Leonora as for the sake of Edward. Or it may have been for the sake of both of them. I don't know. I know nothing. I am very tired" (191).

Clusters: Ford often repeats a word several times within a paragraph or so. Here, for instance, is a paragraph from very early in the novel, as Dowell compares the relationship of the two couples to a stately minuet and then bemoans the breakup of this dance:

> Permanence? Stability? I can't believe it's gone. I can't believe that that long, tranquil life, which was just stepping a minuet, vanished in four crashing days at the end of nine years and six weeks. Upon my

word, yes, our intimacy was like a minuet, simply because on every possible occasion and in every possible circumstance we knew where to go, where to sit, which table we unanimously should choose; and we could rise and go, all four together, without a signal from any one of us, always to the music of the *Kur* orchestra, always in the temperate sunshine, or, if it rained, in discreet shelters. No indeed, it can't be gone. You can't kill a *minuet de la cour*.[3] You may shut up the music-book, close the harpsichord; in the cupboard and presses the rats may destroy the white satin favours. The mob may sack Versailles; the Trianon may fall, but surely the minuet—the minuet itself is dancing itself away into the furthest stars, even as our minuet of the Hessian bathing places must be stepping itself still. Isn't there any Nirvana pervaded by the faint thrilling of instruments that have fallen into the dust of wormwood but that yet had frail, tremulous, and everlasting souls?

No, by God, it is false! It wasn't a minuet that we stepped; it was a prison—a prison full of screaming hysterics. (15)

The obsessive repetitions of "minuet" here occur in a kind of cluster.

Clusters can be found throughout the text. Here, for instance, is a passage which immediately follows the cluster of "minuet":

And yet I swear by the sacred name of my creator that it was true. It was true sunshine, the true music, the true splash of the fountains from the mouth of stone dolphins. For, if for me we were four people with the same tastes, the same desires, acting—or, no, not acting—sitting here and there unanimously, isn't that the truth? If for nine years I have possessed a goodly apple that is rotten at the core and discover its rottenness only in nine years and six months less four days, isn't it true to say that for nine years I possessed a goodly apple? (15–16)

Here we note the repetitions of "true" and also the repetition of "nine years and six months," which links the two passages. It is easy and appropriate to interpret the repetitions in these passages as an expression of Dowell's emotions, his frenzy, the conflict between his desire to have a goodly apple and his discovery that the apple was always rotten.

Quotation of passages with clusters would quickly become excessive, but I will list some for the reader to examine at leisure. On page 30, there is a cluster with four repetitions of *perfectly,* three repetitions of *pink,* including two of *brick pink,* and two of *blue.* On page 95 the word *glad* or *gladness* is used three times, and then on the next page it is used three times more. On pages 96–97 the word *passion* is used five times in one long paragraph and three times more on the next two pages (and many times more throughout the novel). On page 103, there is a passage of three paragraphs with five repetitions of *complicated* or *complication* and two of *innocence.* On page 161 we find the phrases *intense, maternal love, intense jealousy, intense disgust, intense pity,* and *a feeling equally intense [. . .] a feeling of respect.* On page 175 there are five repetitions of the phrase *she remembered.* On pages 183–84 there are four repetitions of the word *pathetic.* On pages 186–87 there are nine repetitions of the word *normal, normally,* and *abnormal.* A long passage on pages 29 and 30 is a dense network of key words and clusters: *adored, passion, agony, hated, agony, sentiment; sentimentalists, constancy, intimacy, sentimental, constancy; constancy, poor dear Edward, sentimental, sad, sentimental; sentimental, constant, poor girl, sentimental,* and *poor girl.*

Fragmented Narration: Several of the important events in the story are told in fragments. This manner is excused by the conversational narrative situation Dowell imagines. The Kilsyte affair, for instance, when Ashburnham assaulted a servant girl on a train, is first told, in bits and pieces, on pages 45–46, then referred to again on pages 51 and 54; then on page 81; then again on pages 122 and 126–27. Ashburnham's affair with Mrs. Basil, the wife of his fellow officer, is mentioned on pages 49 and 52 and then again on pages 98 and pages 135–38. His affair with the mistress of the grand duke is mentioned on pages 50–52, again on page 98, and again on pages 128–32. Florence's lover Jimmy is mentioned on pages 23, 67, 69 and 73–77, 82, 85, 98, and 100. Various parts of the story of Maisie Maidan are given on pages 46–48, 56–57, 62–64, 139, and 150–51. Dowell is simply incapable of telling a story once through in some reasonable order. Ford, of course, is managing all this to give a psychological portrait of Dowell.

Shortly after the Dowells and the Ashburnhams first meet, they decide to go on an outing to a famous castle at M—(I don't know why Ford has Dowell suppress the name of the town, which is Marburg) where Luther either did or did not spend the night. Florence takes the opportunity to flaunt her learning. In the course of her little lecture on the Protestant Reformation, she puts a finger on Ashburnham's wrist. Dowell senses "something treacherous, something frightful, something evil in the day." He was horribly frightened and feels that his heart has skipped a beat. Leonora clutches him by the wrist. "'I can't stand this,' she said, with a most extraordinary passion. 'I must get out of this.'" She takes him out to a terrace. "'Don't you see,' she said, 'don't you see what's going on?'" Dowell claims ignorance. Leonora manages to compose herself. "'Don't you know,' she said, in her clear hard voice, 'don't you know that I'm an Irish Catholic?'" (42–43).

There is then a section break; the next section begins: "Those words gave me the greatest relief that I have ever had in my life" (43). Dowell then goes off on digressions about his taste for caviar; his impatience about missing trains; Florence's heart condition and what he calls his profession as Florence's nurse (44); Ashburnham's heart condition, or lack thereof (45); the Kilsyte case (46); and so on. Not until page 58 do we return to Dowell and Leonora on the terrace: "At any rate the measure of my relief when Leonora said that she was an Irish Catholic gives you the measure of my affection for the couple" (58). The word "relief" is the specific verbal link between the two passages.

Dowell maintains throughout his narrative that he had no suspicions that Florence was having an affair with Ashburnham. This passage suggests otherwise. Why is he so relieved to believe that Leonora is just offended by Florence's attitude towards Catholics? It must be because he felt something else in the air. Indeed, his initial fear and subsequent relief make sense only if he knew in some way that something else was going on. The reader may conclude that Dowell knew about the affair all along and simply suppressed that knowledge.

At any rate, he responds to Leonora by apologizing for Florence's "silly jibes at the Irish and at the Catholics," and he ends with an appeal: "Do accept the situation." She replies, "'Oh, I accept the situation,' she said at last, 'if you can.'" They probably mean different things. There is then another section break. So this whole section, pages 43 to 58, is contained within these two parts of a single fragmented conversation, which then continues in the next section: "I remember laughing at the phrase, 'accept the situation,' which she seemed to repeat with a gravity too intense"; "from that moment," Dowell tells us, "until after Edward and the girl and Florence were all dead together, I had never the remotest glimpse, not the shadow of a suspicion, that there was anything wrong" (59). It is difficult to believe him.

There is then another gap, in which Dowell fills in, either from later discoveries or from speculation, something about how Florence and Leonora managed their relation during the period of the affair. Then on page 62 the narrative loops back to make a brief return to the excursion and then moves forward to the death of Maisie Maidan, which occurred significantly on the same day.

The narration is both fragmented and linked. We have already seen the word "relief" as a link from page 43 to page 58; there is also a link from page 43 ("And she laid one finger on Captain Ashburnham's wrist") to page 151 ("It went to pieces at the moment when Florence laid her hand upon Edward's wrist"); the key caught in Maisie's hair links several of the fragments (33, 48, 64), as does the screen in the hotel corridor (27, 31, 48).

The very ending of the story takes advantage of the fragmentary manner of narration. We have known for some time that after Nancy left for India, Edward killed himself and that when Nancy heard the news she went insane (see 182–83). On the penultimate page, Dowell says, "It suddenly occurs to me that I have forgotten to say how Edward met his death" (198), and he proceeds to do so. A linear chronological narration would have been forced to place the death of Edward earlier; the fragmentary manner allows Ford to choose what he wants for an ending. This choice places Edward's death, rather than Nancy's insanity, as the culmination of the events; it also allows for a certain symmetry: the ending of part 1 is the death of Maisie Maidan, the ending of part 2 is the death of Florence, and the end of the whole story is the death of Edward.

Links: A list of the links in *The Good Soldier* would quickly become tiresome. These links occur at every level, from sentence links, to links within and across paragraphs, to section links, to links from one part to another. All of these are in addition to the general and pervasive linkage provided by the network of key words and by verbal clusters.

I begin with a few examples of links within a paragraph. On page 36, the first paragraph begins "But upon my word, I don't know how we put in our time" and the fifth sentence begins "Upon my word, I couldn't tell you offhand." On page 40, past the middle of a very long paragraph, Dowell says "I was pleased to be off duty" and a little later he says "I was so relieved to be off duty." At the beginning of the last paragraph on page 41, Dowell says that Florence spoke with "an accent of gaiety, of triumph, and of audacity" and two sentences later he says "I was extremely happy at her gaiety, in her triumph, in her audacity."

Links from one paragraph to the next are very common. In the following examples I indicate a paragraph break by a double vertical line: "From there, at this moment, I am actually writing. || You may well ask why I write" (14). "Well, that was a sort of frenzy with me. || It was a frenzy that now I can hardly realise" (44). "And she went off to England. || Yes, she went off to England" (50). "And it was then that they really quarrelled. || Yes, they quarrelled bitterly" (51). "You see, she was childless herself. || She was childless herself . . ." (52). "She was hitting a naughty child who had been stealing chocolates at an inopportune moment. || It was certainly an inopportune moment" (56).[4] These links are immediate, in a form of strict paragraph anadiplosis, but links can also be separated by a few words or sentences. Or a word can occur several times in a few paragraphs, in what amounts to a small cluster.[5]

Sometimes the link covers a little more distance, as the phrase "an extraordinarily steady boat" on page 72 is picked up by "a steady ship" on page 73. The phrase "at that moment" begins a paragraph on page 165 and then begins the third paragraph on page 166. A link can cross an even greater distance, as "She just boxed Mrs. Maidan's ears" on page 47 is picked up by "her boxing Maisie's ears" and "she had boxed Maisie's ears" on page 151.

A link can join one section to the next. The last sentence of section 5, part 1, is "'Oh, I accept the situation,' she said at last, 'if you can'" and the first sentence of the next section is "I remember laughing at the phrase 'accept the situation'" (58–59). The last sentence of section 6, part 4, is "And then I came on the scene" and the next section begins "My coming on the scene certainly calmed things down" (189).

A link can occur from one part to the next: part 1 ends with the death of Maisie Maidan: "He never could bear the sight of a corpse. And, since she never gave him an idea that Maisie had written to her, he imagined that the death had been the most natural thing in the world. He soon got over it. Indeed, it was the one affair of his about which he never felt much remorse" (64). Part 2 begins "The death of Mrs. Maidan occurred on the 4th of August, 1904" (67). Part 2 ends (in a sort of ring) with the death of Florence; the last sentence is "That was on the 4th of August, 1913" (85), and the first sentence of part 3 begins "The odd thing is that what sticks out in my recollection of the rest of that evening . . ."; the two parts are continuous but not linked. At the end of part 3, Dowell tells us (in retrospect) about Leonora's plotting to get her husband's affections back from Maisie Maidan; the last sentence is "Florence knocked all that on the head" (144). Part 4 begins with a look back at the description of the narrative situation explained at the beginning: "I have, I am aware, told this story in a very rambling way" (147); the two parts are neither continuous nor linked, but there is a ring from here back to the beginning.

Correctio: Dowell has a habit of making a statement and then correcting it. As Paul Armstrong notes, "In recounting his original 'impression' and then correcting it, Dowell gives the past as he understood it and the present in which he reconsiders this unreflected understanding" (Armstrong 1987, 199). I think we can say more: in this narrative the reader can never really know what to believe. As Michael Levenson says, "No matter how generous our standards of behavior, as long as they are standards, they will not contain Dowell, who defies familiar notions of consistency and purpose, who credits the most implausible lies, whose moral valuations shift from sentence to sentence, whose memory leaks like an old man's, and whose attention wanders like a child's" (Levenson 1984, 379).

The first instance of *correctio* occurs in the very first paragraph: "My wife and I knew Captain and Mrs. Ashburnham as well as it was possible to know anybody, and yet, in another sense, we knew nothing at all about them" (13). A little later Dowell says that Ashburnham only ever talked about certain subjects, such as horses, boots, brandy, shooting: "I hardly ever heard him talk of anything else. Not in all the years that I knew him did I hear him talk of anything but these subjects. Oh, yes," Dowell says, Ashburnham told him where to buy a particular shade of tie and also advised him to buy a stock (28–29). "And that was absolutely all that I knew of him until a month ago—that and the profusion of his cases, all of pigskin and stamped with his initials, E. F. A." The reader wonders what other afterthoughts there may be. And then two paragraphs later, Dowell tells us, "And I have given a wrong impression of Edward Ashburnham if I have made you think that literally never in the course of our nine years of intimacy did he discuss what he would have called 'the graver things'"; no, Dowell admits, at times, late at night, "he would say that constancy was the finest of the virtues" (29).

One important *correctio* has to do with the amount of time Florence had to carry on her affairs. "I don't believe that for one minute she was out of my sight," Dowell claims, but then adds a qualification, "except when she was safely tucked up in bed and I should be downstairs, talking to some good fellow or other." And a few sentences later, "It must have been when I was taking my baths, and my Swedish exercises, being manicured. Leading the life I did, of the sedulous, strained nurse, I had to do something to keep myself fit. It must have been then!" (16). And somewhat later: "But, looking over what I have written, I see that I have unintentionally misled you when I said that Florence was never out of my sight. Yet that was the impression that I really had until just now. When I come to think of it she was out of my sight most of the time" (75).

Nor is *correctio* limited to facts; Dowell's moral evaluation of the story is also corrected. At first (in passages we have already examined) Dowell seems to regret the loss of the minuet which the two couples danced: "Permanence? Stability? I can't believe it's gone.... Upon my word, yes, our intimacy was like a minuet." Then he rejects that image: "No, by God, it is false! It wasn't a minuet that we stepped; it was a prison—a prison full of screaming hysterics." But this correction is corrected: "And yet I swear by the sacred name of my creator that it was true" (15). The reader is left spinning.

All these corrections create Dowell as thoroughly unreliable, both in matters of fact and more fundamentally in matters of moral judgment, in particular his judgment of Ashburnham—and also his judgment of himself. Very early in the story, before we know much at all about Ashburnham's affairs, Dowell says, "I don't want you to think that I am writing Teddy Ashburnham down a brute. I don't believe he was. God knows, perhaps all men are like that" (18). Here Dowell has his judgment and eats it, too; his assurance that Ashburnham is not a brute is also a suggestion that of course he was. Later on he praises Ashburnham: "Have I conveyed to you the splendid fellow that he was—the fine soldier, the excellent landlord, the extraordinarily kind, careful and industrious magistrate, the upright, honest, fair-dealing, fair-thinking, public character? I suppose I have not conveyed it to you" (78). After such praise the reader can only become suspicious.

Dowell admits that Ashburnham's behavior to Nancy was "monstrously wicked," but within a sentence he adds, "It is impossible of me to think of Edward Ashburnham as anything but straight, upright, and honourable.

That, I mean, is, in spite of everything, my permanent view of him. . . . He was such a fine fellow" (96). Towards the end of the story, he reports that Leonora "considered it her duty to warn the girl of the sort of monster that Edward was"; she told Nancy about all his affairs, and she told her that he was "violent, overbearing, vain, drunken, arrogant, and monstrously a prey to his sexual necessities" (188). This is Leonora's judgment, not Dowell's, but it is Dowell's report, so we know at least that he knew Leonora's judgment of her husband and he passes it on to the reader.

Dowell's evaluation of the Kilsyte case is also unreliable, or perhaps just confused. When he first mentions the case he doesn't give much detail, but his comment that Ashburnham might have received seven years in Winchester Gaol suggests a serious offense (46). But when Dowell tells the story later, Ashburnham was innocent; he was simply trying to comfort a poor girl who was crying in the train: "he assured me that he felt at least quite half-fatherly when he put his arm around her waist and kissed her" (122). Ashburnham "saw himself as the victim of the law," but he was merely fined five shillings for "an ill-placed desire to comfort a member of the opposite sex" (127).

Ashburnham "was very well built, carried himself well, was moderate at the table and led a regular life" and "he had, in fact, all the virtues that are usually accounted English." (123). "I hope I have not given you the idea that Edward Ashburnham was a pathological case. He wasn't. He was just a normal man and very much of a sentimentalist" (143).

Dowell's judgment of Ashburnham turns out to be his judgment of himself, or of his illusion of himself: "In my fainter sort of way I seem to perceive myself following the lines of Edward Ashburnham. I suppose that I should really like to be a polygamist." But he hastens to assure us that he is "a strictly respectable person. . . . I have only followed, faintly, and in my unconscious desires, Edward Ashburnham" (185).

> I guess that I myself, in my fainter way, come into the category of the passionate, of the headstrong, and the too-truthful. For I can't conceal from myself the fact that I loved Edward Ashburnham—and that I loved him because he was just myself. If I had had the courage and virility and possibly also the physique of Edward Ashburnham I should, I fancy, have done much what he did. He seems to me like a large elder brother

who took me out on several excursions and did many dashing things while I just watched him robbing the orchards, from a distance. (197)

Thus Dowell sees himself as Ashburnham's double. But a double is often a rival. Did Dowell offer Florence as a gift for his hero? I don't mean to suggest that Dowell's love for Ashburnham was in a direct sense homosexual—though it is notable that Dowell lived a life without any sexual relationship with a woman.

Just after Dowell tells us that he loved Ashburnham he recounts, out of its place in the chronology, Ashburnham's death: "It suddenly occurs to me that I have forgotten to say how Edward met his death" (198). Dowell and Ashburnham were in the stables when Ashburnham received a telegram from Nancy saying that she was having a good time in Brindisi, on her way to India. Ashburnham takes from his pocket "a little neat penknife—quite a small penknife." He glares at Dowell. "I guess he could see in my eyes that I didn't intend to hinder him. Why should I hinder him?" Dowell has said earlier in the story that he thought Ashburnham would be better off dead (137), and he says so again at the end: "I didn't think he was wanted in the world" (198). "When he saw that I did not intend to interfere with him his eyes became soft and almost affectionate" (199). Ford is hardly hiding anything here. Dowell says that he loved Ashburnham as a boy might love his stronger and more daring older brother; Dowell admits that he might have stopped Ashburnham if he had wanted to; and Dowell claims that at the end Ashburnham regarded him with affection, even as he went to kill himself. Ashburnham's death is the climax of the story—and Ford has made it the climax by placing it artificially at the end.

Grammatical structures, rhetorical figures, and narrative figures generally accommodate a range of meanings. None of the figures and devices I have noted in *The Good Soldier* determines in any simple or direct way the meaning or the effect of the novel as a whole, and all of these devices can create quite differing effects in different contexts.

The Composition of *Catch-22*

Joseph Heller's *Catch-22* is stuffed full of rhetorical tricks. Here is a passage from early in the novel, when Yossarian is a patient in the hospital; this passage concerns another patient, a colonel, who does not play any further part in the story. The passage does nothing to further the plot, but it does help establish the style and the tone of the whole story:

> The colonel dwelt in a vortex of specialists who were still specializing in trying to determine what was troubling him. They hurled lights in his eyes to see if he could see, rammed needles into his nerves to hear if he could feel. There was a urologist for his urine, a lymphologist for his lymph, an endocrinologist for his endocrines, a psychologist for his psyche, a dermatologist for his derma; there was a pathologist for his pathos, a cystologist for his cysts, and a bald and pedantic cetologist from the zoology department at Harvard who had been shanghaied ruthlessly into the Medical Corps by a faulty anode in an I.B.M. machine and spent his sessions with the dying colonel trying to discuss *Moby Dick* with him.
> The colonel had really been investigated. There was not an organ of his body that had not been drugged and derogated, dusted and dredged, fingered and photographed, removed, plundered and replaced. (15)

The phrase "to see if he could see" counts as the figure *ploce,* which Lanham defines as "repetition of a word or a name with a new signification after the intervention of another word or words"—the first "see" means something like "find out," while the second means "perceive with the eyes." I don't know of any specific name in traditional rhetoric for "to hear if he could feel"; one effect of the figure, I think, is to encourage the reader to hear the colonel scream. The series urologist/urine, lymphologist/lymph, endocrinologist/endocrines, and so on, is a congeries and also polyptoton, since the words occur in different forms, but Heller extends the series to include forms that are not usual English words. The second part of the passage is another congeries, this time with alliteration. The whole passage would count as *paronomasia,* a rather vague rhetorical term for general word play. The trickiness of this passage is typical of the whole book.

It is easy enough to find instances of traditional rhetorical figures in *Catch-22*—we can find epistrophe (18); gradatio (18, 43, 118, 225); tricolon (52, 72); anadiplosis (57); antithesis (187, 244); anaphora (412); and so on—but this listing of the traditional figures does not, I think, give a real sense of what Heller is up to. Heller has developed a particular set of figures—not a very large set—which he uses over and over to great effect. I don't suppose any of Heller's figures is entirely his own invention, though they don't all appear in the traditional lists of figures, but the way he uses them is distinctive. In this section I will be particularly interested in the way he uses inversions and paradoxes, links, repetitions and refrains, and fragmentary narration. Many of these figures overlap, but it makes sense to try to separate them out initially for identification and analysis.

Inversions and Paradoxes: Much of *Catch-22* consists of jokes, and many of the jokes are based on comic or not so comic inversions. At the very beginning of the novel, when Yossarian is in the hospital, we meet a minor character known to us only as The Texan: "The Texan turned out to be good-natured, generous, and likable. In three days no one could stand him" (9). This statement cheats our expectations; we expect that someone who is likable will be liked. The technical term for this figure is *para prosdokian*, which means "against expectation"; our word "paradox" is closely related. There are many jokes like this throughout the novel. Early on Yossarian tells the chaplain, "Nately had a bad start. He came from a good family" (12). Later on, the "sordid, vulturous, diabolical old man" who lived in the brothel in Rome "reminded Nately of his father because the two were nothing at all alike" (244). And we learn that Nately "did not hate his mother and father, even though they had both been very good to him" (248). These three passages all involve Nately, but the device is applied broadly. "Doc Daneeka was Yossarian's friend and would do just about nothing in his power to help him" (28). Yossarian "had decided to live forever or die in the attempt" (29). "Even among men lacking all distinction [Major Major] inevitably stood out as a man lacking more distinction than all the rest, and people who met him were always impressed by how unimpressive he was" (83). An extensive character description can be constructed para prosdokian:

> Colonel Cargill, General Peckem's troubleshooter, was a forceful, ruddy man. Before the war he had been an alert, hard-hitting, aggressive marketing executive. He was a very bad marketing executive. Colonel Cargill was so awful a marketing executive that his services were much sought after by firms eager to establish losses for tax purposes. Throughout the civilized world, from Battery Park to Fulton Street, he was known as a dependable man for a fast tax write-off. His prices were high, for failure often did not come easily. He had to start at the top and work his way down, and with sympathetic friends in Washington, losing

money was no easy matter. It took months of hard work and careful misplanning. A person misplaced, disorganized, miscalculated, overlooked everything and opened every loophole, and just when he thought he had it made, the government gave him a lake or a forest or an oilfield and spoiled everything. Even with such handicaps, Colonel Cargill could be relied on to run the most prosperous enterprise into the ground. He was a self-made man who owed his lack of success to nobody. (27)

In a related kind of joke, the text sets up an expectation which is then immediately violated. Yossarian asks Major Major to relieve him of flying any further missions, and Major Major wonders how to answer him:

> One thing he could not say was that there was nothing he could do. To say there was nothing he could do would suggest he *would* do something if he could and imply the existence of an error or injustice in Colonel Korn's policy. Colonel Korn had been most explicit about that. He must never say there was nothing he could do.
> "I'm sorry," he said. "But there's nothing I can do." (103)

The men in the squadron panic when they are given the assignment to bomb Bologna. The mission is postponed by bad weather, but their fears only increase. They come to hate and fear the bomb line on the map, the line that shows how far the allied troops have advanced; if the bomb line passes Bologna before the weather clears, they won't have to go on the mission:

> "I really can't believe it," Clevinger exclaimed to Yossarian in a voice rising and falling in protest and wonder. "It's a complete reversion to primitive superstition. They're confusing cause and effect. It makes as much sense as knocking on wood or crossing your fingers. They really believe that we wouldn't have to fly that mission tomorrow if someone would only tiptoe up to the map in the middle of the night and move the bomb line over Bologna. Can you imagine? You and I must be the only rational ones left."
> In the middle of the night Yossarian knocked on wood, crossed his fingers, and tiptoed out of his tent to move the bomb line up over Bologna. (119)

And the mission is canceled—for a while, anyway.

Another related kind of joke is based on the misuse of grammatical or logical forms. The most important of these is Catch-22 itself:

> There was only one catch and that was Catch-22, which specified that a concern for one's own safety in the face of dangers that were real and immediate was the process of a rational mind. Orr was crazy and could be grounded. All he had to do was ask; and as soon as he did, he would no longer be crazy and would have to fly more missions. Orr would be crazy to fly more missions and sane if he didn't but if he was sane he had to fly them. If he flew them he was crazy and didn't have to, but if he didn't want to he was sane and had to. Yossarian was moved very deeply by the absolute simplicity of this clause of Catch-22 and let out a respectful whistle.
> "That's some catch, that Catch-22," he observed.
> "The best there is," Doc Daneeka agreed. (42)

Violations of logic and grammar run through the whole story. In an important passage early in the novel, Yossarian says to Clevinger "They're trying to kill me"; Clevinger replies that they are trying to kill everyone, and Yossarian asks, "What difference does that make?" Yossarian drives Clevinger into wordless sputtering. "Clevinger really thought he was right, but Yossarian had proof, because strangers he didn't know shot at him with cannons every time he flew up into the air to drop bombs on them, and it wasn't funny at all. And if that wasn't funny, there were lots of things that weren't even funnier" (17). The normal construction here would be "there were lots of things that were even less funny"; the impropriety of the construction somehow adds to the absurdity of the situation.

> Sharing a tent with a man who was crazy wasn't easy, but Nately didn't care. He was crazy too, and had gone every day to work on the officers' club that Yossarian had not helped build.
> Actually, there were many officers' clubs that Yossarian had not helped build, but he was proudest of the one on Pianosa. (18)

Some of the jokes depend on what could be considered a kind of *zeugma,* a figure that uses one construction to join two items that do not match.

"Yossarian could run into the hospital whenever he wanted to because of his liver and because of his eyes; the doctors couldn't fix his liver condition and couldn't meet his eyes each time he told them he had a liver condition" (165). At the beginning of the sentence we expect that Yossarian is having trouble (or claiming to have trouble) with his liver and also with his eyes, but the end of the sentence destroys that parallelism. (We can also note the interweaving of liver/eyes/liver/eyes/liver.) "He could enjoy himself in the hospital, just as long as there was no one really very sick in the same ward. His system was sturdy enough to survive a case of someone else's malaria or influenza with scarcely any discomfort at all. He could come through other people's tonsillectomies without suffering any postoperative distress, and even endure their hernias and haemorrhoids with only mild nausea and revulsion. But that was just about as much as he could go through without getting sick" (165). The joke here is that Yossarian is suffering from the illnesses of other people. A few pages later another patient, a warrant officer, who has malaria and a mosquito bite on his ass, complains that there is no sense in who has which illness. "If I had gotten syphilis or a dose of clap for my five minutes of passion on the beach instead of this damned mosquito bite, I could see some justice. But malaria? Malaria? Who can explain malaria as a consequence of fornication?" Yossarian replies, "I stepped out of my tent in Marrakech one night to get a bar of candy and caught your dose of clap when that Wac I never even saw before hissed me into the bushes." The warrant officer says, "That sounds like my dose of clap, all right." Another patient says, "I've got somebody else's three hundred thousand dollars." He explains that the money was left to him and he has done nothing to deserve it. "I wonder who it really belongs to?" he asks. Dunbar says, "Maybe it belongs to my father.... He spent a lifetime at hard work and never could make enough money to even send my sister and me through college. He's dead now, so you might as well keep it." And the warrant officer says, "Now if we can just find out who my malaria belongs to, we'd be all set" (170–71).

 Heller here is playing with some ordinary turns of phrase. If I say, "I have your cold," I mean "You have a cold and I caught it from you." Two people can have what we call the same cold at the same time. A cold doesn't belong to anyone. But if I say, "I have your wallet," then presumably you don't have it, even though it belongs to you. A wallet is not the kind of thing that two people can have at the same time. If you were in a competition and your opponent was unfairly awarded the prize, I can say "He has your prize," meaning "He has the prize that should have been yours," but barring some re-adjudication the prize will stay in the possession of your opponent. If I say to you, "George gave me your ten dollars to give back to you," I probably don't mean a specific bill, and you probably will accept two fives; money is usually an abstract amount rather than a particular object. Heller is mixing up all these various ways of speaking.

Underlying all these jokes is a fundamental inversion of the realist project—a project often proclaimed by writers and critics, but manifest more in ideology than in actual practice. The realist project assumes that there is a real world, independent of our perception of it; it is the task of language to correspond to and thus to represent that external real world; and this is also the task of specialized forms of language, such as novels. If that were all that realism amounts to, I would say that it's kind of boring. Reading a novel would be something like looking at someone's vacation slides. The great realists, however, are not content with showing us the world, they show us something about the world. And many great writers are not realists at all.

Heller often inverts the realist project. Instead of showing that language can copy reality, he shows that reality can copy language, at least in the world of the novel:

> Yossarian sidled up drunkenly to Colonel Korn at the officers' club one night to kid with him about the new Lepage gun that the Germans had moved in.
> "What Lepage gun?" Colonel Korn inquired with curiosity.
> "The new three-hundred-and-forty-millimeter Lepage glue gun," Yossarian answered. "It glues a whole formation of planes together in mid-air." (124)

A little later Captain Black comes into the club:

> "Boy, are you bastards in for it!" he announced exuberantly.... "I just got a call from Colonel Korn. Do you know what they've got waiting for you at Bologna? Ha! Ha! They've got the new Lepage glue gun. It glues a whole formation of planes together right in mid-air."
> "My God, it's true!" Yossarian shrieked, and collapsed against Nately in terror. (125)

The most consequential example of the inversion of reality and language comes in the episode when McWatt flies over the beach and accidentally slices Kid Sampson in two. When he realizes what he has done, he flies his plane into the side of a mountain. On the ground the soldiers watching all this unfold have been asking who else was in the plane. Sergeant Knight tells them that Doc Daneeka was, because he was listed on the pilot's manifest—Heller prepares this element of the incident back in chapter 4—even though Doc Daneeka is there on the ground trying to talk to them. "The first person in the squadron to find out that Doc Daneeka was dead was Sergeant Towser, who had been informed earlier by the man in the control tower that Doc Daneeka's name was down as a passenger on the pilot's manifest McWatt had filed before taking off. Sergeant Towser brushed away a tear and struck Doc Daneeka's name from the roster of squadron personnel. With lips still quivering, he rose and trudged outside reluctantly to break the bad news to Gus and Wes, discreetly avoiding any conversation with Doc Daneeka himself . . ." (340). The episode continues with further absurdities caused by the persistent presence of Doc Daneeka despite his official death. Back in Staten Island Mrs. Daneeka is officially informed that her husband has died. At first she is distraught, but then she finds out that she is the beneficiary of her husband's GI insurance policy, a life-time pension, and social security payments until her children reach the age of eighteen; in addition, Doc Daneeka had four of his own insurance policies worth $50,000 each. "The husbands of her closest friends began to flirt with her. Mrs. Daneeka was simply delighted with the way things were turning out and had her hair dyed" (343). Meanwhile in Pianosa Doc Daneeka himself no longer is drawing any pay, nor is he entitled to rations or a place to live. "Colonel Cathcart refused to see him, and Colonel Korn sent word through Major Danby that he would have Doc Daneeka cremated on the spot if he ever showed up at Group Headquarters" (343). In despair he writes to his wife, but on the day she receives his letter she also receives a letter from Colonel Cathcart:

> *Dear Mrs., Mr., Miss, or Mr. and Mrs. Daneeka:*
> *Words cannot express the deep personal grief I experienced when your husband, son, father, or brother was killed, wounded or reported missing in action.*

Mrs. Daneeka moved with her children to Lansing, Michigan, and left no forwarding address. (344)

Links: We have seen paragraph links in other authors, and Heller certainly has his share:

> ... young Huple, who lived on the wrong side of the railroad tracks in the tent in the administration area in which Hungry Joe lay screaming in his sleep every night.
> The administration area in which Hungry Joe had pitched his tent by mistake lay in the center of the squadron.... (25)

* * *

Doc Daneeka did mind. He was beginning to lose confidence in Gus and Wes and was thinking of having them both transferred back to the motor pool and replaced by someone who *could* find something wrong.

Doc Daneeka was personally familiar with a number of things that were drastically wrong. (33)

* * *

These were two disappointments to which [Yossarian] had resigned himself: he would never be a skeet shooter, and he would never make money.

"It takes brains not to make money," Colonel Cargill wrote in one of the homiletic memoranda he regularly prepared for circulation over General Peckem's signature. (36)

Paragraph links ordinarily create smooth transitions. Many of Heller's links, however, don't really link; instead they highlight a discontinuity through an artificial juxtaposition. In the last example in the group above, there is no connection between Yossarian's disappointment that he will never make money and Colonel Cargill's comment that it takes brains not to make money. The comment is made in a memorandum which is in no way about Yossarian and which has no temporal or causal connection to Yossarian and his disappointment. The connection is simply the similarity of the phrases "never make money" and "not to make money." A link that does not link foregrounds an abrupt transition. In the following passage, Colonel Korn and Colonel Cathcart are discussing Captain Black's loyalty oath campaign, which is designed against Major Major. Colonel Korn says:

> "Don't worry, this will probably run its course soon. The best thing to do now is send Captain Black a letter of total support and hope he drops dead before he does too much damage." Colonel Korn was struck with a whimsical thought. "I wonder! You don't suppose that imbecile will try to turn Major Major out of his trailer, do you?"
>
> "The next thing we've got to do is turn that bastard Major Major out of his trailer," Captain Black decided. "I'd like to turn his wife and kids out into the woods, too. But we can't. He has no wife and kids." (115)

Captain Black's words repeat what Colonel Korn has just said, but there is no real connection between their words; the link lies in the words—but it does represent a kind of connection beyond causality which often operates in *Catch-22*. These nonlinking links create a narrative world in which connections don't connect.

Abrupt transitions, where the topic shift and the grammatical divisions don't match, can occur within a paragraph or even within a sentence. The second sentence of the following passage makes an abrupt transition from Colonel Cathcart's phony courage to Appleby's skill at Ping-Pong: "Colonel Cathcart had courage and never hesitated to volunteer his men for any target available. No target was too dangerous for his group to attack, just as no shot was too difficult for Appleby to handle on the Ping-Pong table. Appleby was a good pilot and a superhuman Ping-Pong player with flies in his eyes who never lost a point. Twenty-one serves were all it ever took for Appleby to disgrace another opponent" (55). And the paragraph continues with the description of a particular Ping-Pong game. There is no connection between Colonel Cathcart's courage in risking the lives of others and Appleby's skill in Ping-Pong except the verbal connection Heller constructs through a grammatical parallelism.

Near the beginning of the book, Yossarian has a nonsensical conversation with Orr: "When I was a kid," Orr says, "I used to walk around all day with crab apples in my cheeks" (22). When Yossarian asks him why, Orr manages to keep the conversation off track with a long series of unresponsive answers. This conversation takes a couple of pages. Finally, "Yossarian decided not to utter another word. It would be futile. He knew Orr, and he knew there was not a chance in hell of finding out from him why he had wanted big cheeks. It would do no more good to ask than it had done to ask him why that whore had kept beating him over the head with her shoe that morning in Rome in the cramped vestibule outside the open door of Nately's whore's kid sister's room" (24). The passage now continues with two long paragraphs about this incident, but then it returns to the initial situation and then quickly back to the whore in Rome:

> Whatever he had done or tried to do or failed to do behind the closed door of Nately's whore's kid sister's room was still a secret. The girl wouldn't tell Nately's whore or any of the other whores or Nately or Yossarian. Orr might tell, but Yossarian had decided not to utter another word.
> "Do you want to know why I wanted big cheeks" Orr asked.
> Yossarian kept his mouth shut.
> "Do you remember that time in Rome when that girl who can't stand you kept hitting me over the head with the heel of her shoe? Do you want to know why she was hitting me?" (25)

But no answer is forthcoming to either question—and that lack of an answer is the only connection between the two incidents. The lack of satisfactory answers is one of the great problems of the book.

Heller also uses many chapter links. The book is divided into forty-two chapters and about twenty-five of these are linked.[6] Here is the end of chapter 1: "In less than ten days, the Texan drove everybody in the ward back to duty—everybody but the C.I.D. man, who had caught cold from the fighter captain and come down with pneumonia" (15). And the beginning of chapter 2: "In a way the C.I.D. man was pretty lucky, because outside the hospital the war was still going on" (16). The link to the C.I.D. man is really just a way of moving to the discussion of the general conditions of the war: "Men went mad and were rewarded with medals. All over the world, boys on every side of the bomb line were laying down their lives for what they had been told was their country, and no one seemed to mind, least of all the boys who were laying down their lives" (16).

The two parts of a link don't have to be in immediate proximity. The first part of the link between chapter 2 and chapter 3 comes a few paragraphs before the end of chapter 2: "Yossarian eyed everyone he saw warily when he returned to the squadron from the hospital" (20). This is followed by about thirty lines describing the situation in the squadron, and then chapter 3 begins: "Actually, no one was around when Yossarian returned from the hospital but Orr and the dead man in Yossarian's tent" (22). Chapter 3 links immediately to chapter 4; here is the end of chapter 3:

> Hungry Joe was babbling incoherently when they fished him out from the dank bottom of the slit trench, babbling of snakes, rats and spiders. The others flashed their searchlights down just to make sure. There was nothing inside but a few inches of stagnant rain water.
> "You see?" cried Havermeyer. "I told you. I told you he was crazy, didn't I?" (31)

And the beginning of chapter 4: "Hungry Joe *was* crazy and no one knew it better than Yossarian, who did everything he could to help him" (32). "Crazy" is probably the key word of the whole novel.

I don't see a link from chapter 4 to chapter 5, from chapter 5 to chapter 6, or from chapter 6 to chapter 7. But the end of chapter 7 is closely linked to the beginning of chapter 8. Here is the end of chapter 7: "But Yossarian still didn't understand either how Milo could buy eggs in Malta for seven cents apiece and sell them at a profit in Pianosa for five cents" (67). And the beginning of chapter 8: "Not even Clevinger understood how Milo could do that, and Clevinger knew everything. Clevinger knew everything about the war except why Yossarian had to die while Corporal Snark was allowed to live" (68). Here we see at the level of chapter transitions the same kind of arbitrary juxtaposition we saw in paragraph and sentence links. There is no real connection between Milo's business practices and the threat that Yossarian might die in the war, except that Clevinger doesn't understand either of them. It is interesting to see what happens if we slightly revise the passage, to place the first sentence of chapter 8 at the end of chapter 7:

> But Yossarian still didn't understand either how Milo could buy eggs in Malta for seven cents apiece and sell them at a profit in Pianosa for five cents. Not even Clevinger understood how Milo could do that, and Clevinger knew everything.

Chapter 8

> Clevinger knew everything about the war except why Yossarian had to die while Corporal Snark was allowed to live. (68)

The transition is somewhat smoother, because the chapter division seems to make a better match with the shift of topics. Of course Heller's version is better.

Chapter links can also jump over an intercalated chapter. The beginning of chapter 10—"Clevinger was dead. This was the basic flaw in his philosophy" (104)—is in no way connected to the end of chapter 9, but there is a connection to the end of chapter 8. This chapter takes place earlier in the narrative stream, when Yossarian and Clevinger are at cadet school in California; Clevinger is brought before a disciplinary board on unspecified charges, and his interrogation is one of Heller's brilliant surrealistic set pieces. Clevinger in his naivety is bewildered by the hatred his three inquisitors display (there is an anticipation here of the interrogation of Yossarian at the end of the novel). The end of chapter 8 thus links to the beginning of chapter 10; chapter 9, which tells the story of Major Major Major Major, is intercalated.

It is interesting to see how and why Heller links, but also how and why he doesn't; when there are so many links, the absence of a link becomes meaningful. There is, for instance, a significant lack of a link from chapter 5 to chapter 6. The end of chapter 5 is the first narration of the death of Snowden:

> "The bombardier, the bombardier," Dobbs answered in a cry when Yossarian spoke. "He doesn't answer, he doesn't answer. Help the bombardier, help the bombardier."
> "I'm the bombardier," Yossarian cried back at him. "I'm the bombardier. I'm all right. I'm all right."
> "Then help him, help him," Dobbs begged. "Help him, help him."
> And Snowden lay dying in back. (50)

Everything here is emphatically doubled, except for the final line. There is nothing more to be said—for the moment.

Repetition and Fragmentary Narration: Repetitions are a fundamental tool of Heller's humor. Words spoken by one person may be repeated, sometimes spoken by another person, either by accident or by design. General Peckem explains to Colonel Cargill that he doesn't plan to fly combat missions: "You see, my most precious abilities are mainly administrative ones. I have a happy facility for getting different people to agree." And Colonel Cargill tells ex-P.F.C. Wintergreen, "He has a happy facility for getting different people to agree what a prick he is." Then ex-P.F.C. Wintergreen suggests that Colonel Cargill might fly combat missions, and Colonel Cargill replies, "Of course I wouldn't really mind going into combat, but my best abilities are mainly administrative ones. I too have a happy facility for getting different people to agree." And ex-P.F.C. Wintergreen tells Yossarian, "He too has a happy facility for getting different people to agree what a prick he is" (121).

In chapter 25 General Dreedle sees the chaplain in the officers' club house and exclaims to Colonel Cathcart, "That's really a fine thing when a man of God begins hanging around a place like this with a bunch of dirty drunks and gamblers." Colonel Cathcart assumes that General Dreedle is blaming the chaplain and says, "I don't know what's happening to the clergy these days," to which the general replies, "They're getting better, that's what's happening to them," and Colonel Cathcart quickly agrees (283). Then some days later in the club the general roars with laughter because his son-in-law, Colonel Moodus, has been punched in the nose and knocked down on the seat of his pants—"until he saw the chaplain standing close by gawking at him grotesquely in tortured wonder. The General stomps off to the bar and says, 'That's really a fine thing. When a man of god begins hanging around a place like this with a bunch of dirty drunks and gamblers.'" This time Colonel Cathcart assumes that General Dreedle means what he meant the last time he used these words and hastens to take credit for the chaplain's presence; then he realizes that the general this time is angry to see the chaplain in the club, and he quickly blames Colonel Korn (284).

Other repetitions work over longer stretches of the story. Doc Daneeka, for instance, has a refrain: "You think you've got troubles? [...] What about me?" (28); "He thinks he's got troubles? What about me?" (32); "You think you've got troubles? [...] What about me?" (40); "They think they've got troubles? What about me?" (42); "*He's* sick? How does he think I feel?" (51); "You think you've got something to be afraid about? [...] What about me?" (173). Another refrain is Milo's frequent reminder that everyone has a share in M&M Enterprises.[7]

Some repetitions are caused by the convoluted storyline of the novel, as the fragmented narrative doubles back on itself and incidents are repeated, sometimes from different points of view. Clevinger, for instance, is dead at the beginning of chapter 10 (104), but he is alive in chapter 12 (122). The chronological time of the story can be reconstructed to some extent by tracking the number of combat missions required at any point in the story. In chapter 2 (21), when Yossarian gets out of the hospital, we discover that Colonel Cathcart has raised the number of missions to fifty. At the beginning of chapter 6, the number is still fifty, but a couple of pages into the chapter we find that the story has doubled back to the time when the number was twenty-five, then raised to thirty (53); at the end of the chapter the number has been raised to fifty-five (58). In chapter 7 the number is still fifty-five (65), and still fifty-five in chapter 10 (107), but on the same page the story doubles back to the time when the number was only thirty-five. At the end of chapter 16, forty missions are required (164) and Yossarian checks himself into the hospital; he stays there ten days, and when he comes out he discovers that the number is now forty-five (165), and he goes back into the hospital. This hospital stay is the one that begins the book. At the end of the chapter he is out of the hospital and the number has been raised to fifty (174). In chapter 19 (189) and again in chapter 22 (226), the number is raised to sixty; in chapter 30 (339) the number is sixty-five, and in chapter 31 (340) it is seventy. But the story time can move around in between these markers. In chapter 7, for instance, the number of missions is fifty-five, but then chapter 8 moves back to the time when Yossarian and Clevinger were in cadet school in California. Chapter 9 is mostly concerned with the history of Major Major, and so it covers a lot of time. We can track the time of one moment in the chapter, however: "Major Major began forging Washington Irving's name the day after the first C.I.D. man showed" (90), so this moment in chapter 9 is around the time of the beginning of the novel.

During Yossarian's hospitalization in chapter 1 he was assigned the task of censoring letters written by enlisted men. He finds the task monotonous and starts to play games with his censoring. "Catch-22 required that each censored letter bear the censoring officer's name." Instead of his own name, Yossarian starts to write "Washington Irving" or "Irving Washington" and a C.I.D. man is sent to investigate. There are many references thereafter to Washington Irving and to the C.I.D. man—eventually two or more C.I.D. men. In chapter 9 a C.I.D. man interrogates Major Major about someone forging Washington Irving's name, and the next day Major Major starts doing it himself (90–97). In chapter 20 Corporal Whitcomb tells the chaplain that the C.I.D. man is investigating the chaplain for signing letters with the name Washington Irving; the chaplain protests that he hasn't been doing that, and the corporal says that he himself has been forging the name for the chaplain (205–7). And so on. All of this at first seems like simple buffoonery, but later the chaplain is arrested and interrogated partly on the charge that he has been forging the name Washington Irving (386).

Because the narrative time is fragmented and discontinuous, several incidents and episodes happen more than once. In chapter 1 we encounter the soldier in white for the first time (9–11), again in chapter 17, which is named after him (166–69), and again briefly in chapter 25 (267–68). The dead man in Yossarian's tent is mentioned first in chapter 10 (107), again in chapter 17 (169), and twice in chapter 24 (255 and 263).

After the mission over Avignon, when Snowden dies in the back of the plane, Yossarian decides not to wear his uniform or any clothes at all, as we learn in chapter 24 (260). But we have already read in chapter 21 that Yossarian has been awarded a Distinguished Flying Cross after the mission over Avignon, and he receives the medal from General Dreedle stark naked.

In chapter 24, Yossarian watches Snowden's funeral from a distance, sitting in a tree, with no clothes on (261–66). The chaplain, who is officiating at the funeral, sees him from a distance and thinks that he is seeing a vision. We hear about the chaplain's vision briefly in chapter 20—"Had the naked man in the tree at Snowden's funeral been merely a hallucination? Or had it been a true revelation? The chaplain trembled at the mere idea. He desperately wanted to confide in Yossarian" (204)—and then again in chapter 25 (268–69; 271–72), which seems to pick up directly from chapter 20: "[The vision was] the most extraordinary event that had ever befallen him, an event perhaps marvellous, perhaps pathological—the vision of the naked man in the tree. [. . .] Was it a ghost, then? The dead man's soul? An angel from heaven or a minion from hell? [. . .] The possibility that there really had been a naked man in the tree [. . .] never crossed the chaplain's mind" (272).

By far the most important instance of fragmentary narration, however, is the story of Snowden dying in the back of the plane. Snowden's death is mentioned briefly several times (35, 163, 165, 166, 172, 204, 260, 263, 345) and more extensively in chapter 5 (50), chapter 22 (225–26), chapter 30 (331), and chapter 41 (436–40); this penultimate chapter in the book is titled "Snowden." Each time the story is told, we are given more vivid detail. Snowden's death is a kind of recurring nightmare. Even though it occurs fairly early in the chronology of the story—before Yossarian meets the chaplain in chapter 1, for instance—it is the thematic and emotional climax of the book.

Heller's style foregrounds rhetorical and compositional devices, and they provide much of the pleasure of reading. The sheer number of the jokes and the complexity of their interaction are beyond any reasonable account, but somehow the reader assimilates all these paradoxes and links and repetitions and inversions and fragments and puts them together into a unified reading experience. The tricks are not just tricks, nor do they detract from the emotional impact of the story—to the contrary, they heighten the emotion. What begins as humor ends as horror.

Rings: In writing *Catch-22* Heller had to solve (at least) two aesthetic problems: first, how to make all the tricks and devices hang together in some kind of unified structure, so that it would be one book rather than a collection of random jokes, and second, how to make the story move towards some kind of intelligible ending, some kind of goal. I think he solved the first problem; I'm not sure he solved the second, though he made a good try.

Unification comes partly through repetition, and in particular through rings. Here is a small ring from the very beginning of the novel. As noted above, in chapter 1, Yossarian is given the task of censoring letters: "All the officer patients in the ward were forced to censor letters written by all the enlisted men patients, who were kept in wards of their own. It was a monotonous job"—and so Yossarian starts to sign his censored letters Washington Irving or Irving Washington. A C.I.D. man is sent to investigate: "They all knew he was a C.I.D. man because he kept inquiring about an officer named Irving or Washington and because after his first day there he would not censor letters. He found them too monotonous" (8). This little incident, which introduces a recurring element of the novel, is contained within the ring of "monotonous/ monotonous." The reader is reminded of this ring later on, when Major Major starts to forge the name Washington

Irving on official documents: "Signing Washington Irving's name to official documents was not much of a career, perhaps, but it was less monotonous than signing 'Major Major Major.' When Washington Irving did grow monotonous, he could reverse the order and sign Irving Washington until that grew monotonous" (93).

There are a number of middle-sized rings. In chapter 23 an old man in the brothel reminds Nately of his father "because the two were nothing at all alike" (244); at the end of the chapter Nately wishes the old man would clean up, shave, get a haircut, and wear a good shirt and a good suit, "so that Nately would not have to suffer such confusing shame each time he looked at him and was reminded of his father" (250).[8]

But the most important rings connect the early part of the narrative to the later parts. Heller in effect tells the reader to look out for this kind of connection; in chapter 41 the chaplain is telling Yossarian about the deal that has been cooked up which would allow Yossarian to go home:

> Yossarian listened to the chaplain's news with enormous relief. "That's good."
>
> "Yes," said the chaplain, a pink flush of impish pleasure creeping into his cheeks. "Yes, that is good."
>
> Yossarian laughed, recalling his first conversation with the chaplain. (433)

Yossarian is recalling these phrases from that first conversation: "pretty good," "That's good," "Yes, that is good," "That's too bad," "That's too bad," "Yes, that is too bad," "That's too bad," "Yes, that is too bad," and "That's good," "That's good," and "Yes, that is good" (11–14). But this recollection encourages the reader to recollect other rings.

Heller makes the point again a little later, in the last chapter of the book, in a conversation between Yossarian and Major Danby. Yossarian is thinking about deserting in order to avoid flying more missions, and Danby tries to justify the war on patriotic and moral grounds. Yossarian objects:

> The Germans will be beaten in a few months. And Japan will be beaten a few months after that. If I were to give up my life now, it wouldn't be for my country. It would be for Cathcart and Korn. So I'm turning my bombsight in for the duration. From now on I'm thinking only of me.

Major Danby replied indulgently with a superior smile. "But Yossarian, suppose everyone felt that way."

"Then I'd certainly be a damned fool to feel any other way, wouldn't I?" Yossarian sat up straighter with a quizzical expression. "You know, I have a queer feeling that I've been through this exact conversation before with someone else." (446)

Indeed, he has been, back in chapter 9, when Yossarian is trying to convince Major Major to let him stop flying combat missions:

"Would you like to see our country lose?" Major Major asked.

"We won't lose. We've got more men, more money, and more material. There are ten million men in uniform who could replace me. Some people are getting killed and a lot more are making money and having fun. Let somebody else get killed."

"But suppose everyone on our side felt that way."

"Then I'd certainly be a damned fool to feel any other way. Wouldn't I?" (103)

Another important ring begins in chapter 1, just before Yossarian starts to sign the name Washington Irving to the letters he is censoring: "One time he blacked out all but the salutation, 'Dear Mary' from a letter, and at the bottom he wrote, 'I yearn for you tragically. A. T. Tappman, Chaplain, U.S. Army'" (8). This comes back late in the story, when the chaplain is being interrogated; he is shown a letter "in which everything but the salutation "Dear Mary" had been blacked out and on which the censoring officer had written 'I yearn for you tragically. A. T. Tappman, Chaplain, U.S. Army'" (382). The chaplain tells the interrogators that this is not written in his handwriting, and so they accuse him of forging the handwriting of someone else to write his own name. Then they accuse him of several crimes, including forging the name Washington Irving on the letters, and also crimes that they don't even know about yet (386). Eventually they let him go, but this incident is an important moment in the gradual darkening atmosphere of the end of the book.

In chapter 12 Hungry Joe has a dream "that Huple's cat was sleeping on his face, suffocating him, and when he woke up, Huple's cat *was* sleeping on his face" (129–30). Then in chapter 41 the chaplain brings Yossarian the bad news that Hungry Joe has died. "God, no!" Yossarian cries. "On a mission?" And the chaplain answers, "He died in his sleep while having a dream. They found a cat on his face" (435).

The climax of the story comes with another ring. In chapter 3, Orr and Yossarian have an inconclusive conversation about why Orr used to walk around all day with crab apples or chestnuts in his cheeks and then about why the whore in Rome kept beating him over the head with her shoe (25). At the very end of the book, Yossarian learns that Orr has probably ditched his plane deliberately in order to desert to Sweden. "He knew what he was doing every step of the way," Yossarian says. "Bring me apples, Danby, and chestnuts, too." He explains to Danby that Orr practiced getting shot down. "Now I understand what he was trying to tell me. I even understand why that girl was hitting him on the head with her shoe. . . . Because he was paying her to, that's why. But she wouldn't hit him hard enough, so he had to row to Sweden" (449–50). Yossarian realized that Orr was always trying to get out of the fighting; finally he ditched his plane and managed to row to Sweden. Yossarian decides to follow him, and the book ends as he runs away.

These five rings from early to late in the novel tie the book together. In addition, some of these rings contribute towards the goal of the book, which also is the moral problem Heller presents and tries to resolve. Yossarian's desertion is at best morally ambiguous, and to many readers it will seem simply wrong. Desertion may be justifiable under particular circumstances, but few readers will agree that the Allied position in World War II meets those circumstances.

Heller clearly understood and anticipated this likely response, for instance in Yossarian's conversation with Major Major in chapter 9, recapitulated in his conversation with Major Danby in chapter 42. The war is won already, Yossarian argues, so there's no need for him to risk his life anymore. He is certainly wrong. The war is not yet won, and many more soldiers will have to die before it is won.

Yossarian also argues that the management of the war is corrupt. He asks Major Danby, "How can you work along with people like Cathcart and Korn? Doesn't it turn your stomach" (444). "I do it to help my country. . . . Colonel Cathcart and Colonel Korn are my superiors, and obeying their orders is the only contribution I can make to the war effort. I work along with them because it's my duty"—but then he undercuts his own argument:

"And also [. . .] because I am not a very aggressive person" (445). And Yossarian answers, "Between me and every ideal I always find Scheisskopfs, Peckems, Korns, and Cathcarts. And that sort of changes the ideal" (445). There is a real moral problem here, and Heller presents the evidence of corruption very vividly throughout the whole story.

The machinations of Milo Minderbinder contribute to this side of the argument. Indeed, in the last telling of the story of Snowden's death, in chapter 41, Yossarian opens the first-aid kit: "The twelve syrettes of morphine had been stolen from their case and replaced by a cleanly lettered note that said: 'What's good for M & M Enterprises is good for the country. Milo Minderbinder'" (436). Milo is perhaps the most corrupt person in the novel, and his Enterprise exemplifies the corruption that is an essential feature of capitalism. But Yossarian's explicit justifications for his desertion do not mention Milo—who is, oddly, one of Yossarian's friends.

Part of the problem with the ending—for those readers who find it problematic—is inherent in the fantastic elaboration that is the essence of the narration. So long as the story stays in the realm of fantasy, the story is consistent with itself, and the reader can be content. The problem arises with application. As soon as the story is applied to the actualities of World War II, the reader may feel some discomfort. The book begins, before the beginning, with an explicit remark on the abstraction from reality which allows for the fantasy: "The island of Pianosa lies in the Mediterranean Sea eight miles south of Elba. It is very small and obviously could not accommodate all of the actions described. Like the setting of this novel, the characters, too, are fictitious" (3). The war, too, is fictitious, at least until the reader makes the application to reality.

4
Simple Plot Forms

Plots and Stories

It is always worth asking why a narrative begins where it begins, why it ends where it ends, and what kinds of events in the middle either hinder or facilitate the progression from the beginning to the end. But before we can talk about beginnings, middles, and ends, these terms need to be clarified, along with the idea of plot time and the distinction between story and plot.

Something like the distinction between story and plot goes back at least to the Russian Formalists of the early part of the twentieth century. As Robert Scholes explains,

> In their writings on fiction the formalists employ a distinction between two aspects of narrative: story (*fable*) and plot (*sujet*). The *story* is the raw material of the narrative, that is, the events in their chronological sequence. The *plot* is the narrative as actually shaped. We can think of the story as being analogous to the facts of history itself, always running on at the same speed, in the same direction. In a *plot*, the speed may be changed, the direction reversed at will. . . . The art of fiction is, then, most apparent in the artificial rearrangement of chronology which makes a story into a plot. Time is indeed crucial to fiction, and the formalists are aware not only of how crucial it is but of the ways in which it becomes crucial. (Scholes 1974, 80; see also Erlich 1965, 240)

Something like this distinction is made by many theorists, but in terminology which is complicated and inconsistent. I have seen the terms *story, fable, plot, sujet, histoire, récit, narration, narrative,* and *text* used variously by various theorists. This terminological mess can only lead the student of narrative to despair.[1]

All these theorists, whatever terms they use, seem to distinguish an underlying chronological order from the rearrangement of that order. According to Scholes, story runs on "at the same speed, in the same direction," while it is "the artificial rearrangement of chronology which makes a story into a plot." According to Rimmon-Kenan, story "designates the narrated events, abstracted from their disposition in the text and reconstructed in their chronological order" (1983, 3).

There is some value in making at least a provisional distinction between the underlying order of the events in a story and the arrangements of these events in the story as narrated, and to express this distinction I will adopt Scholes's distinction between *story* and *plot*. The expression side of narrative must, however, include much more than the arrangement of events, and for this aspect of narrative I will use Chatman's term *discourse*. It is a matter of discourse, for instance, that *Paradise Lost* is verse rather than prose, or that *Mrs. Dalloway* includes extensive use of free indirect speech; it is a matter of plot that *Paradise Lost* begins *in medias res,* or that *Mrs. Dalloway* is a One-Day Novel.

The relationship between story time and plot time can be conceptualized in three ways. One could imagine that the chronological ordering of the story comes first, I suppose in the mind of the author, and then this time is rearranged to make the plot (though the priority of story to plot may be theoretical). This is the relation implied by Scholes. Or one could imagine that the plot comes first, as presented in the text, and the story time is created by abstraction from the plot. This is the relation implied by Rimmon-Kenan. I would suggest, however, that the distinction between the story and the plot is artificial. As an analytical tool this artificial distinction between story and plot has its use, but in reading, the story time and the plot time are experienced simultaneously: the story has no existence independent of the plot and the plot has no existence independent of the story. The reality of the narrative is the story as arranged in a plot.

Scholes exaggerates when he says that "the art of fiction is, then, most apparent in the artificial rearrangement of chronology which makes a story into a plot." The art of fiction is manifold and goes far beyond chronological rearrangements. He is right, however, when he notes that "time is indeed crucial to fiction." Story telling is always at least partly about time, and most particularly the human experience of time. Human time is not

Simple Plot Forms 91

measured by the regular ticking of the clock. Human time is a complex compound of the past, the present, and the future. Human time is the time of living and dying, the time of feeling young and growing old, the time of waiting and hoping and finding satisfaction and losing hope. It is the time of an individual life and the time of generations. It is the time of remembering and anticipating. It is the time of watching other people pass through time as we pass through time ourselves. All of these times, and many others, find expression in the various temporal structures of narrative.

Beginning, Middle, and End

The beginning of a novel could be anything at all on the first page. Even material before the first page, such as the title, or an epigraph, if there is one, or a dedication, or whatever, could be counted as part of the beginning, since all these are part of the beginning of the reading experience. In this section, however, I am interested in what one might loosely call the beginning of the plot. Many famous first sentences, such as the first sentence of *Pride and Prejudice* or the first sentence of *Anna Karenina* would not count as the beginning of the plot, though they are worth discussing in other terms. For convenience I will call such a non-beginning beginning the Opening, and a corresponding non-ending ending the Close, and reserve the terms Beginning, Middle, and Ending, capitalized, for the beginning, middle, and ending of the plot, as I describe below.

Plot time can be understood, approximately, as the moment when the clock of the story begins to tick. This moment is sometimes specifically noted at the start of a novel, as in Henry James's *The American:* "On a brilliant day in May, in the year 1868, a gentleman was reclining at his ease on the great circular divan which at that period occupied the centre of the Salon Carré, in the Museum of the Louvre" (1981, 5). This is the first moment of the plot, the zero point on the timeline. There is also a negative side to the timeline—the lives of the characters before the plot time starts. These earlier lives are accessible through flashbacks and retrospects, some of which I will discuss in chapter 5.

It is a commonplace of criticism that most narratives begin with some kind of disruption of an equilibrium and end when a new equilibrium is established; the middle consists (partly) of obstacles to be overcome. As James Phelan says, "Plot dynamics typically develop through patterns of instability–complication–resolution. That is, an author generates a plot through introducing one or more characters in unstable situations, he advances the plot by complicating those instabilities, and he ends the plot by resolving those instabilities to one degree or another—or thematizing the impossibility of resolution" (Phelan 2017, 10–11).

The ancestor of this critical commonplace can be found in Aristotle's *Poetics:* "A beginning is something that does not come necessarily after something else, although something exists naturally or comes to be after it. An end, on the contrary, is what naturally comes after something else, either by necessity or for the most part, but has nothing following it. A middle is what both comes after something else and is itself followed by something" (1450b). I propose a revision of Aristotle's account:

> Beginning: In many novels, some social, psychological, or material equilibrium is upset by some specific event, which normally occurs at or near the beginning of both the text and the chronology of the events. This upsetting event enables the story to unfold. Only six Beginnings are in common use: Arrival, Departure, Meeting, Need, Birth, and Death.
>
> Ending: At or near the end of both the text and the chronology of events, a new equilibrium may be established by some specific event. Some typical Endings are Departure, Return, Marriage, Death, Discovery, and Satisfaction.
>
> Middle: The material between the Beginning and the Ending will consist of events that either hinder or facilitate the movement towards the Ending, along with character analysis, descriptions, digressions, and commentary.[2]

Novels (though not, I think, short stories) have a short list of common Beginnings and a short list of common Endings—as well as a long list of uncommon Beginnings and Endings. In addition, a Beginning often matches up with the Ending: a narrative that begins with a Meeting often ends with a Marriage (though there are many exceptions); an Arrival Beginning often ends with a Departure; a Departure Beginning often ends with a Return; a Lack Beginning often ends with the Satisfaction of that Lack; but Birth and Death beginnings have no particularly common counterpart. Of these common patterns, the Arrival/Departure pair and the Departure/

Return pair are rings; a Meeting and a Marriage do not in themselves form a ring, though a particular Meeting/Marriage story may be constructed as a ring, as may any kind of Beginning and Ending.

These Beginnings establish general categories—Birth Beginning Plots, Arrival Plots, and so on—but within each category there can be innumerable variations. The Meeting of Elizabeth and Mr. Darcy at the beginning of Austen's *Pride and Prejudice* leads to their Marriage, while the Meeting at the beginning of James's *The American* leads to a parallel plot structure. The beginning of the first chapter of Gabriel García Márquez's *Love in the Time of Cholera* is the death of Jeremiah de Saint-Amour, but the beginning of the plot is the death of Dr. Juvenal Urbino at the end of the first chapter. The many variations are to be elucidated in the interpretations of specific novels.

Temporal transformations, such as Beginning with the Ending or Second Chapter Retrospects, which I discuss in chapter 5, can complicate the narrative architecture; in such cases it may be possible to deduce an underlying form which follows the conventions—if, for example, the Beginning occurs within a Retrospect, as in James's *The Wings of the Dove* the Meeting of Kate Croy and Merton Densher is told in a Retrospect in Volume I, book 2, section 1: "The beginning—to which she often went back—had been a scene, for our young woman, of supreme brilliancy . . ." (1964, 48). This Meeting comes before but is narrated after the scene when Kate visits her father, which opens the novel.

These Beginnings do not necessarily occur right at the beginning, nor do the Endings necessarily occur right at the end. A Departure Beginning, for instance, may be preceded by an account of the society the hero is leaving behind, as in Twain's *Adventures of Huckleberry Finn;* a Marriage Ending may be followed by a brief account which disposes of the other characters in the story, as the last chapter of *Pride and Prejudice* tells us not only that Elizabeth and Mr. Darcy are married, as are Jane and Mr. Bingley, but also tells us what happens to Kitty, to Mary, to Wickham and Lydia, to Mr. Darcy's sister, Georgina, and to Lady Catherine. Some stories begin with a particular moment that creates the instability, but some begin in a more leisurely fashion, setting the scene and introducing the characters before things really get going. We can call this the Set-up.

Sometimes it is hard to say exactly why a story begins where it does or why it ends where it does. Zero beginnings and zero endings—beginnings and endings that are not strongly marked—usually make some kind of point, but each one has to be examined and interpreted on its own. Some narratives have a composite Beginning: Quest, for instance, usually combines Lack and Departure at the beginning with Satisfaction and Return at the end, and Arrival often combines with Meeting. Subsections of a narrative often are marked by a subordinate internal Beginning and Ending, and many of these also draw on the list of common Beginnings. All these patterns are only tendencies, not laws—ideal forms in a sense. The term "ideal" is descriptive rather than evaluative; deviations from the ideal may be particularly interesting.

The list of six common Beginnings is derived from an overview of a large selection of novels; it is a matter of fact, not theory. It is not hard to see, however, why these Beginnings would be common: all of them naturally enough lead to the kinds of instabilities which generate a story. But instabilities are not simply fixed by nature. In societies where marriages are arranged, for instance, the Meeting/Marriage plot might not be common. On the other hand, Marriage in some societies might be a source of instabilities rather than a resolution. Epic narratives, such as the *Iliad* and the *Song of Roland*, may begin with an Insult, which I believe is no longer a productive Beginning.[3] Later in this chapter I discuss some less common Beginnings, and in chapter 5 I discuss temporal transformations of plots, such as the Second Chapter Retrospect and Beginning with the Ending.

Lack or Need

In most plots which Begin with a Lack, what is lacking is some material and inanimate object of value, but occasionally what is lacking is a person or an abstraction. The Ending of such a plot is often called Lack Liquidated. At the beginning of James Branch Cabell's *Jurgen*, the title character's wife is stolen by the devil, and Jurgen goes off, somewhat reluctantly, to find her. The Lack could also be something intangible; at the beginning of Rudyard Kipling's *Kim*, the Tibetan lama Teshoo Lama is searching for a river which will bring him enlightenment. But most Lack stories are about money.

Lack combined with Departure becomes Quest. A classic Quest is found in the *Argonautica* (also known as *Jason and the Golden Fleece*) written by Apollonius of Rhodes sometime in the third century BC, but based on traditional materials. Jason is the rightful heir to the throne of Iolkos, which has been usurped by Jason's uncle, Pelias. Pelias fears that Jason will dethrone him, so he sends Jason on what he hopes will be a fruitless and fatal quest for the Golden Fleece, which is in the possession of King Aietes of Colchis, situated at the far end of the Black Sea. Jason gathers a crew—the Argonauts—and sets sail. After a series of adventures the Argonauts come to Colchis, where Medea, the daughter of King Aietes, falls in love with Jason. She helps him get the Golden Fleece and then she flees with the Argonauts. On their way, Jason and Medea get married, and after more adventures they reach Iolkos. (The later lives of Jason and Medea are told in other stories, such as Euripides' play *Medea*.) It is clear that this narrative begins with a Lack or a Need, which is satisfied either when Jason gets the Fleece in Colchis or when he returns with it to Iolkos. It also begins with a Departure, which is closed by the Return at the end. And within the larger story there is also a Meeting and a Marriage, and an Arrival and a Departure.

The plot of Robert Louis Stevenson's *Kidnapped* is somewhat like the outside plot of the *Argonautica:* an uncle, Ebenezer Balfour, has purloined the property of his nephew, David Balfour. Ebenezer arranges for David to be kidnapped. After a series of adventures, David returns and recovers his property. There are, of course many differences between the two stories. In any case, *Kidnapped* is also a story that Begins with Lack and Departure and Ends with Return and Lack Liquidated. Stevenson's *Treasure Island* is another of this type, as is J. R. R. Tolkien's *The Hobbit*. *The Lord of the Rings* introduces a variant form in inversion, since the task is to destroy the Ring rather than to find it. *The Lord of the Rings* is also a Gift plot, since Bilbo gives Frodo the Ring at the Beginning. Gifts, especially including inheritances, serve to articulate the Middles of some narratives, such as Gaskell's *North and South,* Trollope's *Doctor Thorne,* and James's *The Portrait of a Lady*.

H. Rider Haggard's *King Solomon's Mines* is a Quest, as Allan Quartermain, Sir Henry Curtis, his friend Captain Good, and their crew, including the mysterious porter Umbopa, set out to find Sir Henry's lost brother and the treasure of King Solomon. In the middle of the story, the travelers reach the "Lost World" of Kukuanaland, which is ruled by the cruel king Twala. It turns out that Twala is the uncle of Umbopa, who is the rightful king of Kukuanaland. After a battle, Twala is killed and Umbopa resumes the throne. Thus the Quest story has a Revenge of the Nephew plot in the middle. The Englishmen manage to find at least some of King Solomon's treasure. On their way back, they find Sir Henry's brother. They eventually return to England and live happily ever after (until the sequel, *Allan Quartermain*). *King Solomon's Mines* shares a number of the formal features of the Quest stories we have described, and it is also one of the foundation stories of the Lost World genre, which includes Kipling's *The Man Who Would Be King*, Edgar Rice Burroughs' *The Land That Time Forgot*, James Hilton's *Lost Horizon*, and many others.

Most Lack/Lack Liquidated plots concern some material object of value, and therefore they tend to foreground the material aspects of life, even in novels which otherwise foreground psychological analysis. Many nineteenth-century English novels, for instance, are concerned with money; even if the ostensible goal of the plot is a marriage, that marriage may be blocked by a lack of money or it may be favored because it will bring money or it may occur despite the absence or apparent absence of money. Examples are obvious: Austen's *Pride and Prejudice*, Charlotte Brontë's *Jane Eyre*, Gaskell's *North and South*, Trollope's *Doctor Thorne*, and so on.

George Eliot's *Silas Marner* is organized around theft, which creates a form of Lack. At (or near) the beginning of the story Marner is falsely accused of stealing money from the small Christian sect he belongs to. One might expect that a false accusation would lead to vindication, especially since Marner says repeatedly "God will clear me," but Eliot takes the story another direction. Marner leaves the sect and settles in a town in central England called Raveloe. Thus the story has a threefold beginning: Lack (in the form of Theft); Departure; and Arrival.

In Raveloe Marner works as a weaver and lives a solitary life. Gradually he accumulates a hoard of gold, but this is stolen by the younger son of the local squire, who then disappears. This theft mirrors the theft that begins the story.

One night a little orphan girl, a toddler whose mother has died of drink and cold, finds her way to Silas's cottage. With his bad eyesight he takes her golden hair for his lost treasure:

> Turning towards the hearth, where the two logs had fallen apart, and set forth only a red uncertain glimmer, he seated himself on his fireside chair, and was stooping to push his legs together, when, to his blurred vision, it seemed as if there were gold on the floor in front of the hearth. Gold!—his own gold—brought back to him as mysteriously as it had been taken away! He felt his heart begin to beat violently; and for a few

moments he was unable to stretch out his hand and grasp the restored treasure. The heap of gold seemed to flow and get larger beneath his agitated gaze. He leaned forward at last, and stretched forward his hand; but instead of hard coin with the familiar resisting outline, his finger encountered soft warm curls. (167)

Marner adopts the girl, whom he names Eppie, and she becomes a substitute for his lost gold. Towards the end of the story the thief's body and Marner's gold are found in the bottom of a pond. It turns out that Eppie is the unacknowledged daughter of the older son of the squire, the brother of the thief who stole Marner's gold. Eppie humanizes Marner and brings him into the society of the town, and so the Lack is Liquidated at a higher moral level.

Departure

We have seen that Lack is often paired with Departure to form a Quest, but Departure can also be a Beginning on its own. An obvious example is Twain's *Huckleberry Finn*. Huck's (delayed) Departure occurs in chapter 6, when Huck's father kidnaps him. The story then continues with Huck's travels until he reaches the Phelps's farm; each of the subordinate episodes is a little Arrival/Departure story. Twain uses this form to give a varied picture of Southern society at the time. This kind of examination of society through a journey can also be found in Voltaire's *Candide* and Samuel Johnson's *Rasselas*.

A Departure may come with or because of a change in the circumstances in the life of one or more of the characters. William Thackeray's *Vanity Fair* begins when Amelia Sedley and Becky Sharp leave school. Guy de Maupassant's *A Woman's Life* begins the day after Jeanne has left the convent.

Many science-fiction stories Begin with a Departure. Robert Heinlein's *Starman Jones* begins when the young hero, Max, leaves his home in the Ozark Mountains and manages to lie his way onto a spaceship. The ship gets lost in space; after various adventures, Max becomes the astrogator and captain of the ship, which he successfully brings back to Earth. The Departure of *Have Spacesuit, Will Travel* occurs when its young hero, Kip Russell, is kidnapped and taken into space, and it ends when he Returns to Earth (along with his new friend, Peewee Reisfeld, who also had been kidnapped). The Departure of *Time for the Stars* occurs when Tom Bartlett is chosen to be in the crew on a journey of space exploration—leaving behind his identical twin brother, Pat, with whom he can communicate telepathically.

Many Departure plots lead to travel and thus to a kind of diffusion of action through space and in various social groups, but a Departure novel can be intense and dramatic if the characters are passengers in a ship or a train or some other vehicle, as in Katherine Anne Porter's *Ship of Fools,* or Herman Melville's *Moby-Dick.*[4] Variations of the passenger story form may be found in Agatha Christie's *Murder on the Orient Express* or Graham Greene's *Stamboul Train.*

Arrival

An Arrival can be a Return, as in Hardy's *The Return of the Native* or Austen's *Persuasion.* An Arrival plot can focus the action on a small group of characters within a confined area; this kind of story is likely to be intense and dramatic. At the beginning of Ken Kesey's *One Flew Over the Cuckoo's Nest,* McMurphy arrives at the ward, and the action plays out there, until the Departure of Chief Broom at the end of the book. At the beginning of Émile Zola's *Germinal,* the hero, Étienne Lantier, arrives at the coal mining town of Montsou, and the action takes place there until his departure. At the beginning of William Faulkner's *Light in August,* Lena arrives in Jefferson, Mississippi, and the action takes place there until her departure. At the beginning of Thomas Mann's *The Magic Mountain,* Hans Castorp arrives at the sanatorium, and the action takes place there until his departure. In Charles G. Finney's remarkable satire *The Circus of Dr. Lao,* a strange circus arrives, out of nowhere, in the small Arizona town of Abalone. The story recounts the various experiences the people of the town have with this circus: they see unnatural creatures, including a satyr, a roc, a sea serpent, and Medusa; one woman looks at Medusa and is turned into a statue; and so on. At the end of the story the circus simply leaves town.

Some stories begin with a preliminary Departure, which then leads to an Arrival at a specific location, where the story then plays out; the story may then end with a Departure and Return to the place where the journey started; the form then is Departure+Arrival/Departure+Return. Many fantasy and science-fiction stories as well as utopian stories take this form: L. Frank Baum's *The Wonderful Wizard of Oz,* Edgar Rice Burroughs's *A Princess of Mars,* Sir Thomas More's *Utopia.* In these stories the characters travel in space, sometimes to a fantasy land, but characters can also travel in time; in Octavia E. Butler's *Kindred,* the heroine, Dana, a young African American woman, jumps in time from 1976 to the antebellum South and back again.

In Robert Heinlein's *Tunnel in the Sky,* a group of high-school students is sent to an unexplored planet as their final examination in a survival course. They are supposed to be left there for only a few days, but technical problems with the matter-transportation system leaves them stranded for several years. The story tells how they meet the various challenges of their situation, both physical and social, as they gradually form a functioning government. Eventually they are rescued and return to Earth, but at the very end of the story the hero is shown as he is about to lead a group of settlers to a new planet; the plot form is thus Departure+Arrival/Departure+Return/Departure. This story can be compared to William Golding's *The Lord of the Flies,* which begins with the arrival of the boys onto the island where the story plays out and ends as they are rescued, but before they actually leave the island; the form is simply Arrival/(Departure). *Tunnel in the Sky* and *Lord of the Flies* differ in theme as well as in form: Heinlein imagines that the stranded children will be able to form a functional government, whereas Golding presents their descent into savagery.

Death

Death is the least common of the common Beginnings, except in murder mysteries, but it is common enough to deserve a spot on the list. Death also occurs frequently as the beginning of episodes within a larger narrative. Death often creates instability in real life, so it is not surprising that it creates instability in stories.

Ordinarily the person who dies is not available to be a character later in the story, but there are exceptions. The narrator of Flann O'Brien's *The Third Policeman* is murdered at the beginning of the second chapter, while he is looking for money which his companion Divney has hidden under the floorboards of a house:

> Without stopping to light another match I thrust my hand bodily into the opening and just when it should be closing about the box, something happened.

> I cannot hope to describe what it was but it had frightened me very much long before I had understood it even slightly. It was some change which came upon me or upon the room, indescribably subtle, yet momentous, ineffable. It was as if the daylight had changed with unnatural suddenness, as if the temperature of the evening had altered greatly in an instant or as if the air had become twice as rare or twice as dense as it had been in the twinkling of an eye. (20–21)

Divney has murdered him, but he doesn't understand what has happened and narrates the rest of the story without realizing that he is dead.

In book 1 of Robert Montgomery Bird's *Sheppard Lee: Written by Himself* the narrator injures himself as he is digging for what he believes is buried treasure; he falls into a sort of trance:

> When I awoke from this trance, it was almost daybreak.
>
> I recovered in some confusion of mind, and did not for a moment notice that I was moving away from the place of my disaster; but I noticed there was something strange in my feelings and sensations. I felt exceedingly light and buoyant, as if a load had been taken, not merely from my mind, but from my body; it seemed to me as if I had the power of moving whither I would without exertion, and I fancied that I swept along without putting my feet to the ground. (47)

He then finds that he is looking at his own dead body: "The sight was as bewildering as it was shocking; and the whole state of things was not more terrifying than inexplicable. *There* I lay on the ground, stiff and lifeless; and *here* I stood on my feet, alive and surveying my own corpse, stretched before me" (48). Eventually he realizes that he is dead and it is only his spirit that is able to see and hear and move around. He then discovers that his spirit can move into other dead bodies and revitalize them, and the rest of the narrative is taken up with a satirical account of his various changes of bodily abode.

The Third Policeman and *Sheppard Lee* are exceptions. By and large the person who dies in a Death Beginning stays dead. What matters to the story is not so much the dead person but the effect—social or psychological—of the dead person's death on the people who are still alive.

The heroine of Edith Wharton's *The Mother's Recompense,* Kate Clephane, is a woman in her forties who left her wealthy husband and her young daughter, Anne, years ago and has lived for years in Europe in a society made up of people with dubious backgrounds. Her husband has been dead now for some time, but her exclusion from decent society in New York has been maintained by her mother-in-law. At the beginning of the novel Kate receives a telegram informing her that her mother-in-law has died; almost immediately afterwards she receives another telegram, this one from her daughter, now an adult, inviting her to return to New York. Kate's mother-in-law is never an active character in the story, but so long as she is alive, the situation is static; it is her death that creates the instability that moves the plot along.

Kate does return to New York, and her return sets off the rather complicated series of events that make up the plot. Once back in New York, Kate discovers that her daughter, Anne, is in love with Chris Fenno, with whom Kate herself had had an affair a few years before. The middle of the story is thus a quasi-Oedipal conflict among three characters. The end of the story creates a ring, as Kate moves back to Europe in a second Return. The overall shape of the plot can be diagrammed—with the understanding that diagrams never do justice to the richness of the work itself; the events in parentheses occur before the story proper begins: (Preliminary Marriage) (Preliminary Departure) Death > Return/Three Person Plot/Return. But the point of the plot, or one point at least, is to create a situation in which we may examine Kate's character.

Death often creates some kind of social instability which is eventually resolved at the End, as in Austen's *Sense and Sensibility,* Dickens's *Nicholas Nickleby,* and Trollope's *Barchester Towers.* Dickens's *Oliver Twist* begins with a Birth, the birth of Oliver, and a Death, the death of his mother. Oliver is left an orphan, and the rest of the story is spent re-establishing his position within his family. The book ends with a ring, as Oliver dedicates a tombstone for his mother. Dickens's *Dombey and Son* begins with the Birth of Paul Dombey and the Death of his mother. There are many Deaths throughout Dickens's novels; they vary in their importance to the plot.

The Death of Bishop Grantly in *Barchester Towers,* the Death of the elder Nicholas Nickleby in *Nicholas Nickleby,* and the Death of old Mrs. Clephane in *The Mother's Recompense* are simply devices to set up the instability that drives the plot forward, and no one in the story displays very strong emotions about the person who has died, nor is much attention paid to the dead person once the story gets going. Some Deaths, however, hover over the whole of a story, as in James Agee's *A Death in the Family,* William Faulkner's *As I Lay Dying,* and Eudora Welty's *The Optimist's Daughter;* in all of these, the point of the story is to explore the various emotional reactions of the surviving characters.

Most murder mysteries almost by definition are about a Death, but different stories manage the Death in different ways.[5] Examination of a series of murder mysteries can demonstrate how the author deliberately varies the conventions of the genre. Rex Stout wrote many novels about the sedentary detective Nero Wolfe and his peripatetic assistant Archie Goodwin. At the very beginning of *Death of a Doxy,* Archie finds a body:

> I stood and sent my eyes around. It's just routine, when leaving a place where you aren't supposed to be, to consider it and where you have touched things, but that time it went beyond mere routine. I made certain. There were plenty of things in the room. [...] Deciding I had touched nothing, I turned and stepped back into the bedroom. Nearly everything there was too soft to take a fingerprint. [...] I crossed for another look at the body of a woman on the floor a couple of feet from the bed, on its back with its legs spread out and one arm bent. (1967, 1)

Thus the corpse is before the reader's eye in the very first paragraph. In *The Final Deduction,* Nero Wolfe is hired on a (purported) kidnapping case; the first murder doesn't occur until chapter 3, and the second in chapter 5. At the beginning of *The Silent Speaker,* Wolfe manages to get himself hired to investigate the murder of Cheney Boone, the director of the Bureau of Price Regulation, which has already occurred before the narrative begins. In *Before Midnight,* Louis Dahlman has been murdered before the story begins, but this time clients come to hire Wolfe. This story begins with what Archie calls an overture: "Not that our small talk that Tuesday evening in April had any important bearing on the matter, but it will do for an overture, and it will help to explain a couple of reactions Nero Wolfe had later" (1957, 1). Stout often opens with some kind of preliminary conversation between Wolfe and Archie, before the murder is announced or before the client arrives. In *Might As Well Be Dead,* Wolfe is hired to find the missing son of a businessman from Nebraska, only to discover that the son, under a different name, has just been convicted of first-degree murder; Wolfe's job then is to clear the son by finding the real murderer. In *If Death Ever Slept,* Wolfe is hired by Otis Jarrell, a wealthy financier, who believes that his daughter-in-law is cheating him out of business deals. Archie moves into Jarrell's opulent apartment, under the pretense that Jarrell has hired him to be his secretary. The first murder doesn't happen until several days and sixty-one pages later, in chapter 5. These examples show the care Stout takes to vary the circumstances within the conventions of the genre; additional examples from other mystery authors would confirm the point.

Birth

A biography may quite naturally begin with the Birth of the subject, or perhaps with an account of the subject's ancestors, and end with the subject's Death. An autobiography may begin with a Birth, though under normal circumstances autobiographers can give only a second-hand account of their own births and no account at all of their deaths. Fictional biographies and autobiographies mimic these nonfictional forms, but a fictional autobiography may end, for instance, with a Marriage. We will see examples in a moment.

Birth Beginnings, however, are not restricted to pseudo-biographies. At the Beginning of *Daphnis and Chloe,* written by an otherwise unknown author named Longus sometime in the second century BC, the foundling boy Daphnis is adopted by a goatherd and shortly thereafter the foundling girl Chloe is adopted by a neighboring shepherd. The two grow up together. After they suffer a series of adventures it is discovered that they come from wealthy families, and at the end they marry. *Daphnis and Chloe* belongs to a group of stories that begin with a mysterious birth. One of the most famous is the story of Oedipus—though the best-known version, the play by Sophocles, compresses the story so that the birth is told only in retrospect. Fielding's *Tom Jones* and Dickens's *Oliver Twist* are other examples of the Mysterious Birth, but these, unlike the story of Oedipus, have happy endings.

The first chapter of *David Copperfield* is titled "I am Born." It begins: "Whether I shall turn out to be the hero of my own life, or whether that station will be held by anybody else, these pages must show. To begin my life with the beginning of my life, I record that I was born (as I have been informed and believe) on a Friday, at twelve o'clock at night. It was remarked that the clock began to strike, and I began to cry, simultaneously" (1990, 9). Most of the first chapter is a detailed account of the day of David's birth. (There are also a few digressions, or as David calls them, meanderings.) But before this Birth, there was a Death, the death of David's father: "I was a posthumous child. My father's eyes had closed upon the light of this world six months when mine opened on it. There is something strange to me, even now, in the reflection that he never saw me; and something stranger yet in the shadowy remembrance that I have of my first childish associations with his white gravestone in the churchyard" (10). So the first paragraphs of the novel focus on Birth and Death.

David has been careful to explain to the reader how he comes by the details of the story of his birth ("as I have been informed"); the reader can also note the impersonal construction here: "It was remarked"—remarked by whom? Later he tells us that he makes no claim "to have any remembrance founded on the evidence of my own senses" (11). What he reports has been reported to him, even in its detail and quality: "My mother, I say, was sitting by the fire, that bright, windy March afternoon, very timid and sad, and very doubtful of ever coming alive out of the trail that was before her, when, lifting her eyes as she dried them, to the window opposite, she saw a strange lady coming up the garden path" (11). The lady—David's aunt, Betsey Trotwood—proceeds to take charge and to order everyone around. David as narrator recounts the actions and the words of his mother, his aunt, and the other characters, as if he had seen them and heard them. We can imagine that David's mother must have told him some of what happened, and he suggests that he received reports also from the servant Peggotty, her nephew, Ham Peggotty, and Mr. Chillip, the doctor. The reader is asked to believe that David is able to reconstruct a highly detailed episode, with extensive direct quotation of dialogue and inside views of the feelings of some of the participants, simply on the basis of reports. But David seems to limit his interior views. He feels able to say what his mother or Peggotty or Mr. Chillip felt, but in general he does not say what his aunt felt. Instead, he shows her feelings through her actions and her words, especially through her patterns of speech and the tone they imply:

> "I tell you I have a presentiment that it must be a girl," returned Miss Betsey. "Don't contradict. From the moment of this girl's birth, child, I intend to be her friend. I intend to be her godmother, and I beg you'll

call her Betsey Trotwood Copperfield. There must be no mistakes in life with *this* Betsey Trotwood. There must be no trifling with *her* affections, poor dear. She must be well brought up, and well guarded from reposing any foolish confidences where they are not deserved. I must make that *my* care."

There was a twitch of Miss Betsey's head, after each of these sentences, as if her own old wrongs were working within her, and she repressed any plainer reference to them by strong constraint. So my mother suspected, at least, as she observed her by the low glimmer of the fire: too much scared by Miss Betsey, too uneasy in herself, and too subdued and bewildered altogether, to observe anything very clearly, or to know what to say. (14)

Oskar, the hero and narrator of Günter Grass's *The Tin Drum*, narrates his own birth as an eye- and ear-witness: "I may as well come right out with it: I was one of those clairaudient infants whose mental development is completed at birth and after that merely needs a certain amount of filling in. The moment I was born I took a very critical attitude toward the first utterances to slip from my parents beneath the light bulbs. My ears were keenly alert. . . . And what my ear took in my tiny brain evaluated" (2010, 47). He hears his (putative) father say that Oskar would take over the grocery store; he hears his mother say that she knew all along the baby would be a boy, even when she said it would be a girl; and he hears his mother promise him a drum when he turns three. But what really impressed him was the sound of a moth beating against the light bulbs. "Today Oskar says simply: the moth drummed . . . that moth was Oskar's master" (48).

Outwardly wailing and impersonating a meat-colored baby, I made up my mind to reject my father's projects, in short everything connected with the grocery store, out of hand, but to give my mother's plan favorable consideration when the time came, to wit, on my third birthday.

From all this speculation about my future, I quickly realized that Mama and this Mr. Matzerath were not equipped to understand my decision whether positive or negative. Lonely and misunderstood, Oskar lay beneath the light bulbs, and figuring that things would go on like this for some sixty or seventy years, until a final short circuit should cut off all sources of light, he lost his enthusiasm even before this life beneath the light bulbs had begun. It was only the prospect of the drum that prevented me then from expressing more forcefully my desire to return to the womb.

Meanwhile, the midwife had already cut my umbilical cord. There was nothing more to be done. (48–49)

In Oskar's world, all this is possible; the reader will have to accept many odd and unnatural events before the story is over.

Meeting

In one very common plot type, two people Meet at the Beginning of a story and Marry at the End. The Middle is made up of obstacles to the Marriage—obstacles which are all overcome just before the End. It is easy to multiply examples. In chapter 1 of E. M. Forster's *A Room with a View,* Lucy Honeychurch Meets George Emerson and they Marry somewhere between chapter 19 and chapter 20. There are many variations on this basic form—the Meeting can be contrived in various ways, it can be delayed, it can occur in a retrospect. A Meeting may lead to a Marriage—or to a Marriage which does not happen, as in Balzac's *Eugénie Grandet* or James's *Washington Square*—but it may also lead to hostility and conflict, or to any other kind of human relationship.

The Beginning of *Pride and Prejudice* is a doubled Meeting—Elizabeth meets Mr. Darcy and Jane meets Mr. Bingley—and the End is a doubled Marriage. The Meetings are preceded by an Arrival, but it's clear that the interest of the story is the Meeting/Marriage plot rather than the Arrival. Austen's *Sense and Sensibility* begins with a Death, which sets up a Departure and a subsequent Arrival, but there are also two Meetings, which are really the point of the plot. Elinor Dashwood Meets Edward Ferrars, the brother of Mr. John Dashwood's wife, at the beginning of chapter 3, though this Meeting is not dramatized; we hear only of "a growing attachment between her eldest daughter and the brother of Mrs. John Dashwood, a gentlemanlike and pleasing young man, who was introduced to their acquaintance soon after his sister's establishment at Norland, and who had since spent the greatest part of his time there" (2001, 11). The Departure occurs in chapters 5 and 6. Marianne Meets Colonel Brandon in chapter 7. In chapter 50, Elinor Marries Edward and Marianne Marries Colonel Brandon. Austen's other novels present variations of the Meeting/Marriage pattern.

Of course not every Meeting is the beginning of a Marriage plot. The Beginning of Rudyard Kipling's *Kim* is the Meeting between Kim and Teshoo Lama; Kim undertakes to lead the lama on his quest for the river which will bring him enlightenment. Their relationship continues on and off throughout the story, which ends with the lama's discovery of the river.

The Beginning of Dickens's *Great Expectations* is the Meeting between Pip and the escaped convict Magwich, in chapter 1. Magwich then disappears from the story, or so it seems, until chapter 39, when the reader discovers that Magwich has been Pip's benefactor and thus a crucial character in Pip's life all along. In addition to Pip's Meeting with Magwich, there is also his Meeting with Miss Havisham and Estella in chapter 8, as well as his Meeting with Herbert Pocket in chapter 11; these relationships continue to the end of the story. (Dickens famously wrote two endings. In the original ending, which was not published, Estella has married, been widowed, and remarried; she and Pip meet accidentally and have a final brief and sad conversation. In the revised ending, which was published, they meet in the ruins of Miss Havisham's house; their final conversation is longer and ends, perhaps, with a suggestion that they will continue to be friends.)

A Meeting can involve more than two people. At the beginning of Vladimir Nabokov's *King, Queen, Knave,* a poor provincial young man, Franz Bubendorf, is on a train to Berlin hoping to get a job in the clothing store owned by his second cousin, Kurt Dreyer, whom he has never met. On the train Franz accidentally shares a compartment with Dreyer and his wife, Martha. They do not speak, but he is immediately attracted to Martha. The next day he goes to Dreyer's house and they all realize that they had met on the train. As the story continues, Martha and Franz have a love affair and plot to kill Dreyer, though Franz has lost interest in Martha, but then Martha dies of pneumonia.

At the beginning of Flaubert's *Sentimental Education,* a young man, Frédéric Moreau, while traveling on a steamboat, meets Jacques Arnoux and his wife, Marie. He is immediately attracted to Marie. This beginning is clearly somewhat like the beginning of *King, Queen, Knave.* In his preface to the English translation of the novel, Nabokov mentions the influence of Flaubert's *Madame Bovary,* but one wonders if the beginning of *Sentimental Education* was also in his mind. *King, Queen, Knave* and *Sentimental Education,* however, develop rather differently. Frédéric does fall in love with Marie Arnoux, but the subsequent story covers more time, includes more characters, and in general is more complex than Nabokov's story.

Uncommon Beginnings

There are many other, less common ways to begin a novel. Albert Camus's *The Plague* begins when Dr. Bernard Rieux discovers dying rats in the stairway of his apartment building. José Saramago's *Blindness* begins when people unaccountably start going blind.[6] In Mark Twain's *The Prince and the Pauper* two young boys in sixteenth-century England—a pauper named Tom Canty and Edward Tudor, the Prince of Wales—switch identities. Many science-fiction stories have uncommon Beginnings. The hero of Richard Matheson's *I Am Legend* seems to be the only normal human survivor of a pandemic, which has killed many and turned others into vampires. Matheson's novel *The Shrinking Man* is one of a number of stories in which the hero is transformed in some way; these include Apuleius's novel *The Golden Ass,* Nikolai Gogol's story "The Nose," Philip Roth's novella *The Breast,* and Robert Louis Stevenson's novella *The Strange Case of Dr. Jekyll and Mr. Hyde.*

Some stories begin without any clear initiating instability, without any clear moment of Beginning. Sometimes the Beginning is so far delayed that its initiating force becomes attenuated. Gaskell's *North and South* clearly has a Marriage plot; Margaret is introduced in the very first sentence of the novel, but Mr. Thornton is first mentioned in a prepositional phrase in chapter 4 and he does not appear in person until chapter 7; meanwhile there has been a Marriage in the first chapter, a Departure in chapter 2, another Departure in chapter 6, and an Arrival in chapter 7, and all these lead to instabilities, but they also all lead to the Meeting in chapter 7, which is the real beginning of the plot.

One-Day Novels, such as Woolf's *Mrs. Dalloway,* and also stories of long duration, such as Woolf's *The Years,* can call into question the whole idea of a single progressive timeline with a Beginning, Middle, and End. Some narratives, such as Robbe-Grillet's *La Jalousie,* deliberately confuse the idea of progressive time.

In a sense every novel has its own form. The point of analysis is not to fit living works of art into dead schemes, but to understand how the conventions, insofar as they exist, convey meaning, and also to understand how the departures from those conventions also carry meaning. When James, in *The Wings of the Dove,* puts Kate Croy's visits to her father and to her sister before her Meeting with Merton Densher, he emphasizes her need for money and her disreputable family; her Meeting with Densher and their subsequent relationship then occurs within that context.

The beginning of James's *The American* temporarily gives the reader a false impression of how the book will proceed. The first scene is the Meeting of the hero, Christopher Newman, with a young woman, Noémi Nioche, who is painting a copy of a Madonna in the Louvre. This initial Meeting may seem to set up a traditional Marriage plot. Indeed, Mlle. Nioche's father is concerned about Newman's intentions towards his daughter. Later in the novel James almost seems to apologize to the reader. Newman's friend Valentin de Bellegarde, who has taken an interest in Mlle. Nioche, discovers that she has left her father's house, presumably to facilitate her amorous career. "She has had other chances," Valentin tells Newman, "but she was resolved to take none but the best. She did you the honour to think for awhile that you might be such a chance. You were not; so she gathered up her patience and waited awhile longer. At last the occasion came along, and she made her move with her eyes wide open" (1981, 255–56). In chapter 15 Mlle. Nioche herself tells Newman that he has not been gallant to her, presumably because he wanted to purchase her paintings rather than her favors. Mlle. Nioche evidently expected something to come from her Meeting with Newman, and perhaps the reader did as well. This Beginning, however, is by no means a misstep.

The novel has two parallel plots; Newman is the center of one of these plots and Mlle. Nioche is the center of the other, and both are introduced at the Beginning. In chapter 3 Newman meets Claire de Cintré. He sees her again in chapter 6. He visits her frequently thereafter and he soon declares his desire to marry her. Her mother and older brother feel that Newman, this brash American businessman, is beneath them. They need money, however, and so, at first, they agree not to oppose Newman's suit. In chapter 18 they force her to break the engagement; they want her to marry their distant English relative, Lord Deepmere, but instead she decides to become a Carmelite nun. Newman and Mme. de Cintré have their last meeting in chapter 20, nearly a hundred pages before the end of the novel. Newman learns that the family is hiding a scandal; he now has a weapon he can use to force the family to agree to the marriage. At the last moment, however, he decides not to use this weapon, and so he loses Claire. This is a story of revenge rather than romance, but revenge not taken.

Near the end of the novel, in chapter 25, Newman accidentally runs across Noémi Nioche, who has become the mistress of Lord Deepmere; she is accompanied by her father, who pretends that he is not colluding in and benefiting from her immorality. At the end, in chapter 26, Newman stands outside the walls of the convent where Claire de Cintré is now living; and finally he burns the note that is the evidence against Mme. de Cintré's family. The Meeting of Newman and Noémi Nioche at the Beginning is not a misstep, but one key to the structure of the plot. The central character of the novel as a whole is Christopher Newman, and the instability of the plot is finally resolved by his decision not to seek revenge; his final action is to destroy the evidence that could bring him that revenge. In addition, the novel tells parallel stories of two women, one at the very top of society, the other barely hanging on to her respectability. Mme. de Cintré is finally defeated by her family's perverted sense of honor; Mlle. Nioche defeats her father, who protests to the end against his daughter's lack of honor while he profits from it. Newman judges Mlle. Nioche's immorality very harshly, but the story itself passes judgment on Mme. de Cintré's virtue.

It must be admitted, however, that not every novel is well-organized; in fact not every great novel is well-organized. There are other narrative values, which may outweigh organization. The novel is a generous form, and readers of novels do not always demand formal perfection.

5
Complex Plot Forms, Part I

In an ideally simple narrative, the events would unfold in strict chronological order. This ideal form is probably never achieved, nor desired. Most novels establish a generally progressive chronology but then allow or require small or large deviations from the chronological sequence. In Gérard Genette's terminology, a deviation from chronological order is called an *anachrony;* a *prolepsis* is "any narrative maneuver that consists of narrating or evoking in advance an event that will take place later," while an *analepsis* is "any evocation after the fact of an event that took place earlier than the point in the story where we are at any given moment" (Genette 1980, 40). Anachronies can be as short as a subordinate clause or prepositional phrase, but some anachronies are large enough to play a role in the architecture of the plot. Although temporal shifts are sometimes considered a characteristic feature of modernism, they can be found in narratives of all periods and genres.

In book 2 of the *Iliad,* for instance, Homer lists and briefly describes many of the leading figures on the Achaian side of the war; many of these descriptions include references to the birth or the history or the fate of a hero; the whole of a person includes past, present, and future. In book 6 of the *Iliad* the Trojan hero Glaukos and the Achaian hero Diomedes meet on the battlefield. Each recounts a story of his ancestry; they discover that their fathers are guest-friends, and so they decide not to fight each other (*Iliad* 6:119–234); what happened in the past determines what happens in the present. In book 7 of the *Iliad* the Achaians build a great wall and a ditch to protect themselves against the Trojans. Poseidon complains to Zeus: he fears that men will forget the wall which he and Apollo once built around Troy; but Zeus promises to destroy this new wall once the war is over (*Iliad* 7:446–463); the present looks toward the future.

Small temporal shifts of this sort are a recognition that we do not live simply in the present; our lives are always interfused with references to the past and the future, and so are the stories we tell. Deviations from chronology are the rule, not the exception. A reader must track these temporal shifts in a story as part of the experience of reading, but these frequent small anachronies defy general description.

Certain large-scale temporal shifts, however, tend to occur in conventionalized positions. In the first three sections of this chapter I will discuss four types of temporal dislocations—Beginning with the Ending, the Second Chapter Retrospect, Ghosts from the Past, and Multiple Retrospects—and in chapter 6 I will discuss other aspects of the organization of time in narrative: the One-Year Novel, the One-Day Novel, Mirror Plots, Alternating Chapters, Simultaneous Narration, and Unnatural Chronology, as well as Non-narrative Elements in Narrative.

Beginning with the Ending

The events or situations which end the story may be brought forward to the beginning. C. S. Forester's *The General* opens: "Nowadays Lieutenant-General Sir Herbert Curzon, K.C.M.G., C.B., D.S.O., is just one of Bournemouth's seven generals, but with the distinction of his record and his social position as a Duke's son-in-law, he is really far more eminent than those bare words would imply. He is usually to be seen in his bathchair with Lady Emily, tall, raw-boned, tweed-skirted, striding behind" (2017, 1). The adverb "nowadays" is a clue that something is happening to the time of the story. After this opening, the novel recounts the story of Curzon's life and his promotions within the British army until he is badly wounded in battle. The book closes: "And now Lieutenant-General Sir Herbert Curzon and his wife, Lady Emily, are frequently to be seen on the promenade at Bournemouth, he in his bathchair with a plaid rug, she in tweeds striding behind. He smiles his old-maidish smile at his friends, and his friends are pleased with that distinction, although he plays such bad bridge and is a little inclined to irascibility when the east wind blows" (288). The adverb "now" picks up "nowadays" from the opening, to reinforce the ring.

V. S. Naipaul's *A House for Mr. Biswas* starts with a prologue that recounts the death of the title character, which is also recounted in the epilogue—the Beginning with the Ending creates a ring. The first chapter then recounts the birth of Mr. Biswas, so the story, in a sense, begins with the Death and Birth of the same character.

The forward impulse of a novel which Begins with the Ending may seem to be driven not so much by the question What will be the end? as by the question How will this ending come about? Most often, however, the Beginning does not give a complete account of the situation at the End, so a certain suspense can still obtain. The instability that gets the story going, however, may be situated in the question posed by the transposed Ending, rather than in any of the common Beginnings considered in the simple plot forms described in chapter 4.

Beginning with the Ending creates a ring that encloses the narrative which constitutes the middle of the ring. This kind of ring is usually quite different from the kind of ring created by Ending with the Beginning. Most often a Beginning with the Ending ring is created by a deviation from chronological order, while an Ending with the Beginning develops from the shape of the plot, without temporal deviation. Both kinds of rings are in a sense artificial, since they are created by the artifice of the author, but the Beginning with the Ending feels like the result of manipulation of the chronology.

A novel may begin with the narrator's present meditation on the past. L. P. Hartley's *The Go-Between* starts with a prologue, when the narrator, a man in his mid-sixties, finds his diary for the year 1900, when he was twelve. The middle of the book is an account of the events of the summer of 1900—tragic events which left the narrator emotionally injured. The Epilogue returns the reader to the time of the Prologue: "When I put down my pen, I meant to put away my memories. They had had days, weeks, months, to settle, but in the end they didn't, and that is how I came to write this epilogue" (2002, 306). The Epilogue then tells another story, a story of what the narrator did after he wrote the story we have just read, a story that attempts to bring to a close the issues left unresolved at the end of the main body of the book. The novel is not just the story of the events of the summer of 1900, but the events of the ring narrative in the 1950s as well.

John Knowles's *A Separate Peace* begins as the narrator returns on a rainy November day to his old prep school: "I went back to the Devon School not long ago, and found it looking oddly newer than when I was a student there fifteen years before" (2003, 9). "In the deep, tacit way in which feeling becomes stronger than thought, I had always felt that the Devon School came into existence the day I entered it, was vibrantly real while I was a student there, and then blinked out like a candle the day I left" (9–10). He is able to recognize in the present the fear that had dominated his feelings in the past: "Looking back now across fifteen years, I could see with great clarity the fear I had lived in, which must mean that in the interval I had succeeded in a very important undertaking: I must have made my escape from it" (10). He wants to revisit two places in particular: "Both were fearful sites, and that was why I wanted to see them" (10). The first of these places was a building, the First Academy Building, and in that building a marble flight of stairs. The second was a tree beside the river, which he is able to identify by characteristic scars along its trunk and by a particular configuration of branches: "This was the tree, and it seemed to me standing there to resemble those men, the giants of your childhood, whom you encounter years later and find that they are not merely smaller in relation to your growth, but that they are absolutely smaller, shrunken by age" (14). There is a gap of a few lines in the text, and when the narrative resumes we are back fifteen years, but standing at the same tree: "The tree was tremendous, an irate, steely black steeple beside the river. I was damned if I'd climb it. The hell with it. No one but Phineas could think up such a crazy idea" (14). Phineas—Finny—does climb the tree, and he jumps into the river. The narrator follows suit, and the whole of the plot, ending in Finny's death later that year, unfolds from this moment. The Beginning with the Ending does not reveal any of the events of the story, or indeed its tragic ending; but it places us in the narrator's mind as he comes to this place to remember and exorcise the past.

Another type of Beginning with the Ending can occur if the narrator is incarcerated. Günter Grass's *The Tin Drum* begins: "Granted: I am an inmate of a mental hospital; my keeper is watching me, he never lets me out of his sight; there's a peephole in the door, and my keeper's eye is the shade of brown that can never see through a blue-eyed type like me" (2010, 15). The narrator, we find out later, is named Oskar, and the keeper is named Bruno. On the second page of the novel, Oskar asks Bruno for a ream of blank paper, and on the third page, he begins to write: "For a time I weighed the hard, flexible ream in my hands; then I counted out ten sheets and stowed the rest in my bedside table. I found my fountain pen in the drawer beside the photograph album: it's full, ink is no problem, how shall I begin?" (17). He considers several different ways of starting a novel: you can start in the middle and then work backwards and forwards; in a modern style, you can start with no mention of time and distance and then proclaim that you have solved the space-time problem; you can start by saying that it's impossible to write a novel, and then write one anyway. But this is how he begins: "I shall begin far away from me; for no one ought to tell the story of his life who hasn't the patience to say a word or two about at least half of his grandparents before plunging into his own existence" (17–18). He begins, then, so he says, with his maternal grandmother, and the circumstances of the conception of his mother. But this is not really the beginning; he has already begun before the beginning, with the ending, when he situates himself in the mental hospital writing his story. Before the beginning the reader already knows the end—at the very end of the novel Oskar is taken into custody. The middle of the ring is the whole story, a long and complex tale with many repetitions and cross-references, of the sort we have examined in other novels, and the whole is neatly tied up in the Ending with the Beginning.

Ralph Ellison's *Invisible Man* is in a sense a story of self-incarceration. The novel begins with a prologue, in which the narrator tells us that "the end is in the beginning" (1980, 6). He has taken refuge in a basement which he has specially outfitted for himself, and from this refuge he tells his story, the story which compels him finally to take refuge. The novel ends with an epilogue that returns to the narrator in his basement refuge: "So there you have all of it that's important" (572).

Second Chapter Retrospects

In book 1 of the *Aeneid,* Aeneas and his companions are shipwrecked on the coast of Africa near Carthage. There they meet Queen Dido; she entertains them; and at the very end of book 1 she asks Aeneas to tell his story. In book 2 he tells the story of the destruction of Troy and in book 3 he recounts his travels thereafter. Book 4 returns us to the present time of the epic and recounts the tragic love affair between Aeneas and Dido; it ends with his departure and her death.

Here we find an early instance of what becomes a very common narrative structure, which I will call the Second Chapter Retrospect—with the understanding that the retrospect does not have to fall exactly in the second chapter. A simple Second Chapter Retrospect can be diagrammed BAC, where the events of A are earlier in the chronology but later in the presentation than the events of B. This diagram, however, fails to capture the progression of time within the sections. A better diagram might be

(C>D)(A>B)(D>E . . .), but really every instance needs its own diagram. Most often, the beginning of the story, figured as C in the diagram, is the beginning of the story time, and the retrospect (A>B) will turn back to a time before the story time begins. The use of a Second Chapter Retrospect often complicates the structure of a narrative, in particular the identification of the Beginning.

Thus, in the *Aeneid,* the retrospect allows a dramatic element of the story—the shipwreck and arrival—to stand at the opening, and then the narrative turns back to fill in the past, before picking the story up again after the retrospect. This Second Chapter Retrospect allows for what is often called a beginning *in medias res,* a beginning in the middle of the situation. The narrative of the *Aeneid* as it is presented begins with an Arrival and a Meeting, but the Beginning of the story as a whole is probably Aeneas's Departure from Troy, which sets up his search for a new home and his eventual Arrival in Italy. Virgil could have started his epic with the Fall of Troy, but he preferred to start with Aeneas's Arrival in Africa and his Meeting with Dido, which tends to emphasize the historical theme of the conflict between Rome and Carthage; the earlier events, including the Departure Beginning, are then folded back into the story in a retrospect.

The digression in books 2 and 3 of the *Aeneid* is modeled after the digression in books 9 through 12 of the *Odyssey.* If one were to omit from the *Odyssey* the initial four books, which deal with Telemachus rather than Odysseus, the resemblance between the retrospects in the two epics is even clearer. Indeed, some critics have speculated that some form of the Odysseus story predates the creation of the *Odyssey* as we have it, and the Telemachus sections were added later.

In book 5, Odysseus leaves the island of Calypso and he is wrecked on the shores of the land of the Phaiakians. In book 6 he meets Nausikäa, the princess of the Phaiakians, and in book 7 he is welcomed by Antinoös and Arete, the king and queen. Book 8 continues with their entertainment of Odysseus and ends as King Alkinoös asks Odysseus to tell his story, which he does, in books 9 through 12, and book 13 brings us back to the present time of the epic. Thus Odysseus arrives in a new land, meets the Princess, is entertained, and tells his story in a digression, just as Aeneas arrives in a new land, meets the Queen, is entertained, and tells his story. But the Beginning of this narrative of Odysseus does not begin with his Arrival in the land of the Phaiakians and his Meeting with Nausicäa, and there is no tragic love story; the Beginning is his Departure from the island of Calypso as the first stage of his final journey home, and all this is anticipated at the very opening of Homer's epic, when Athena appeals to Zeus for the release of Odysseus.

Brief retrospective passages of one sort or another are of course very common in narrative, and they can occur anywhere at all. The Second Chapter Retrospect, however, should be marked out as a particular structure with a particular function, or range of functions. All retrospective passages involve a turn back to the past, but the Second Chapter Retrospect has the particular function of selecting material to stand at the opening of the narration. Since the usual verb tense in narrative is past, the characteristic, but by no means obligatory, tense of a retrospect is the pluperfect. A Second Chapter Retrospect does not have to fall in the second chapter, but it should occur after some reasonably substantial opening section, and it must be reasonably substantial itself.

Exactly what counts as substantial is a matter of judgment. The retrospect in Nabokov's *King, Queen, Knave* is perhaps towards the short end of the scale. At the Beginning of the novel Franz takes the train to Berlin to meet his wealthy cousin, Dreyer, whom he does not know, in hopes of getting a job. He enters a compartment which happens to be occupied by his cousin and his cousin's wife, Martha.

> "I'm thirsty," said the man with a Berlin accent. "Too bad there's no fruit. Those strawberries were positively dying to be sampled."
>
> "It's your own fault," answered the lady in a displeased voice, adding a little later: "I still cannot get over it—it was such a silly thing to do." (1968, 6–7)

The silly thing was a visit Dreyer paid to his cousin Lina, Franz's mother. The visit led to Dreyer's promise to give Franz a job, a promise Martha thought was silly. The retrospective account of this visit takes two long paragraphs (full of pluperfect tenses in the English translation). Then the present time of the story resumes as Dreyer and Martha are boarding the train. He sees Lina, and because they want to avoid her he is unable to buy the fruit he wants for the trip to Berlin. Thus the retrospect—Dreyer's visit to his cousin—explains why Franz is on his way to Berlin. Like many retrospects, it is framed as a ring—by the words "strawberry" and "fruit," and also the repetition of "silly," which occurs at the beginning of the ring and then a paragraph after the ring has closed.

The retrospect in *King, Queen, Knave* is a convenient way of introducing antecedent action, but a retrospect can also include material which is essential to the structure and meaning of a novel. Willa Cather's *My Mortal Enemy* has a substantial Second Chapter Retrospect. The principal character of the novel is Myra Henshawe, who grew up in a small town in Illinois but ran away to New York when she was of an age to marry: "She and her runaway marriage were the theme of the most interesting, indeed, the only interesting, stories that were told in our family, on holidays or at family dinners" (1926, 9). The witness narrator of the story, Nellie Birdseye, is fifteen when Myra and her husband Oswald pay a visit to her hometown. The first chapter briefly introduces Myra and Oswald and the narrator, Nellie, at the beginning of the present time of the story.

The second chapter turns back to Myra's childhood. She was an orphan, brought up (but not adopted) by her wealthy great-uncle, John Driscoll, who rather spoiled her with "dresses and jewels, a fine riding horse, a Steinway piano" (19). She fell in love with Oswald Henshawe, the poor son of a poor schoolteacher. Driscoll opposed the relationship, partly because Oswald was poor, partly because he was an "Ulster Protestant," while Driscoll was Catholic. Oswald went to New York and had enough success to marry. He wrote to Driscoll asking for his permission, but Driscoll refused and told Myra that if she should marry Oswald he would write her out of his will and leave his money to the Church. Myra, with the connivance of her friends, ran off with Oswald, and they never returned to their hometown until after Driscoll's death. The end of the retrospect is a detailed description of Driscoll's elaborate Catholic funeral. The chapter, however, ends with a judgment and then with a return to the present time of the story: "After I went home from that first glimpse of the real Myra Henshawe, twenty-five years older than I had always imagined her, I could not help feeling a little disappointed. John Driscoll and his niece had suddenly changed places in my mind, and he had got, after all, the more romantic part. Was it not better to get out of the world with such pomp and dramatic splendour than to linger on in it, having to take account of shirts and railway trains, and getting a double chin into the bargain?" (27). In the final paragraph we learn that Nellie, with her Aunt Lydia, will spend the Christmas holidays with the Henshawes in New York, and the rest of part 1 is Nellie's story of her visit and her observation of the tensions in the Henshawes' far from romantically perfect marriage. Part 2 takes place ten years later, when Nellie, now a struggling young teacher, happens to meet the Henshawes, who have fallen on hard times, in a shabby apartment hotel. Myra is ill and mostly confined to a wheelchair. Oswald looks after her attentively, but she is bitter and hard on him.

One night when Nellie is helping Oswald nurse Myra, she hears her say to herself,

> "I could bear to suffer . . . so many have suffered. But why must it be like this? I have not deserved it. I have been true in friendship; I have faithfully nursed others in sickness. . . . Why must I die like this, alone with my mortal enemy?"
>
> Oswald was sitting on the sofa, his face shaded by his hand. I looked at him in affright, but he did not move or shudder. I felt my hands grow cold and my forehead grow moist with dread. I had never heard a human voice utter such a terrible judgment upon all one hopes for. (113)

At the end of the story Myra manages to take herself to a cliff looking over the seaside, where she dies, alone. Oswald moves to take another shabby job in Alaska, and a few years later he dies there. The novel ends: "Sometimes, when I have watched the bright beginning of a love story, when I have seen a common feeling exalted into beauty by imagination, generosity, and the flaming courage of youth, I have heard again that strange complaint breathed by a dying woman into the stillness of night, like a confession of the soul: 'Why must I die like this, alone with my mortal enemy!'" (122). The critics seem to agree that Myra's mortal enemy is Oswald, and there is support for this interpretation in the text—see, for instance, Myra's comment to Nellie, "People can be lovers and enemies at the same time, you know" (105). Nellie herself seems to share this interpretation at the moment when Myra makes her complaint.

And yet there is something strange in Myra's complaint, since Nellie is in the room at that moment and has been sharing nursing duties. Myra is not alone with Oswald. I wonder if perhaps Myra could be referring to her uncle. In her last days Myra has talked with Nellie about him (97–99); at least we can say that Cather wants to bring old Driscoll back to the reader's mind. Myra also returns to her Catholicism, and in her last note to Oswald she says, "Nellie knows where there is money for masses" (115). Ultimately the story is primarily about the failure of Myra's romantic elopement and about Nellie's disenchantment with romantic ideals. But surely the reader is meant to compare Myra's austere and lonely death with the death and funeral of her uncle, as described at the end of the Second Chapter Retrospect; we have, through Nellie, once already reassessed our judgments of Myra and old Driscoll, and the ending asks for a second reassessment, based on looking back into the Second Chapter Retrospect.

Nabokov's *Laughter in the Dark* has a double retrospect. The novel opens with what is a note from the author to the reader:

> Once upon a time there lived in Berlin, Germany, a man called Albinus. He was rich, respectable, happy; one day he abandoned his wife for the sake of a beautiful mistress; he loved; was not loved; and his life ended in disaster.
>
> This is the whole of the story and we might have left it at that had there not been profit and pleasure in the telling; and although there is plenty of space on a gravestone to contain, bound in moss, the abridged version of a man's life, detail is always welcome. (1978, 7)

The novel that follows is the detail. The first chapter explains, in a rather leisurely way, that Albinus had the idea that it might be interesting to animate the paintings of the great masters. He himself had no expertise in animation, but he discussed the idea with several film producers, who discouraged the idea as technically impossible or excessively expensive—except for one, Axel Rex. "Upon a certain day in March Albinus got a letter from him, but its arrival coincided with a sudden crisis in Albinus' private—very private—life" (10–11). This is the first hint we have of the story to come.

In a conversation at dinner, his brother-in-law encourages Albinus to pursue the idea, but Albinus finds that he has lost interest. "I'm going mad," he says to himself, "and nobody knows it. . . . Incredible" (13). And the first chapter ends: "No, you can't take a pistol and plug a girl you don't even know, simply because she attracts you" (13).

After this dramatic revelation, chapter 2 begins a retrospect, marked by the pluperfect tense: "Albinus had never been very lucky in affairs of the heart" (14). The chapter continues with an account of the unsuccessful and unfulfilling amours of his student days, his dull marriage to Elisabeth, then his chance meeting with a young woman working as an usher in a movie theater, and his increasing obsession with her. Then the retrospect returns in a ring to the present time of the narrative:

> After dinner he sat by his wife's side on the broad sofa, pecked at her with little kisses while she looked at gowns and things in a woman's magazine, and dully he thought to himself:
> "Damn it all, I'm happy, what more do I need? That creature gliding about in the dark. . . . Like to crush her beautiful throat. Well, she is dead anyway, since I shan't go there any more." (23)

Chapter 3 then begins: "She was called Margot Peters" (24); the rest of the chapter gives an account of Margot's childhood, her early jobs as an artist's model, and her drift into living as a kept woman, without much success, and her attempts to work as an actress. Finally she takes a job as an usher at a movie theater, where Albinus sees her, and this retrospect merges with the main story line. Here focalization works with the narrative structure.

Ghosts from the Past

A Ghost from the Past is the revelation near the end of a story of crucial information about the past that has been unknown to one of the characters in the story; the revelation should be a short narrative, rather than simply a fact; it should make a difference to that character's understanding of the events of the story; and it should make a difference to the understanding or actions of at least one character in the story. A Ghost from the Past is one variety of what Aristotle calls an *anagnorisis* (*Poetics,* chapters 10 and 11); this is usually translated "recognition," but "realization" or "revelation" might be better. Near the end of Sophocles' *Oedipus the King,* Oedipus realizes that he is the son of the man he has killed and the woman he has married: this realization is a classic Ghost from the Past.

We have already seen an example of a Ghost from the Past in Henry James's *The American:* almost at the end of the story, Christopher Newman is told by an old family servant that Claire de Cintré's mother had in effect killed her husband. Newman could have used this information to force Mme. de Cintré's family to allow him to marry her or at least to take revenge. He does not. His decision not to use this Ghost from the Past is the key action in the novel.

Another Ghost from the Past is found in James's *Portrait of a Lady,* as Isabel learns late in the story that Madame Merle has been Osmond's mistress and that Pansy is Madame Merle's daughter. James prepares this revelation carefully and gradually. The intimations begin in chapter 40, with an event marked by the narrator for the reader's attention: "One day, about a month after Ralph Touchett's arrival in Rome" (1964, 374) and then "On the day I speak of . . ." (375). Isabel has been out for a drive with Pansy. When Isabel returns home, she finds Osmond and Madame Merle together in one of the drawing rooms: "Just beyond the threshold of the drawing-room she stopped short, the reason for her doing so being that she had received an impression. The impression had, in strictness, nothing unprecedented; but she felt it as something new, and the soundlessness of her step gave her time to take in the scene before she interrupted it" (376). We note the emphatic repetition in anadiplosis of "impression." This impression is simply that Osmond is sitting while Madame Merle is standing, in "a sort of familiar silence." The casual familiarity of their postures is evidently unusual in terms of the etiquette of the time: "What struck Isabel first was that he was sitting while Madame Merle stood; there was an anomaly in this that arrested her." "Their relative position, their absorbed mutual gaze, struck her as something detected" (376). Detected, but not yet understood.

The hints are repeated in chapter 42, which recounts Isabel's great meditation on her situation, during which "her soul was haunted by terrors which crowded into the forefront of thought as quickly as a place was made for them. What had suddenly set them into livelier motion she hardly knew, unless it were the strange impression she had received in the afternoon of her husband and Madame Merle being in more direct communication than she suspected" (391). At the end of this chapter, at the end of this meditation, Isabel gets up to go to bed at four in the morning: "But even then she stopped again in the middle of the room, and stood there gazing at a remembered vision—that of her husband and Madame Merle, grouped unconsciously and familiarly" (401).

The hints keep coming. In chapter 47, Lord Warburton has left without proposing to Pansy; Madame Merle says to Isabel, "What on earth did you do with Lord Warburton?" And the narrator expresses Isabel's answering thought in free indirect discourse: "As if it were any business of hers!" (458).

But Madame Merle continues to make it her business. In chapter 49 she speaks with Isabel at some length about her hopes that Pansy would marry Lord Warburton. "Don't you know I had set my heart at it?" (473). "She had suffered a disappointment which excited our heroine's surprise—our heroine having no knowledge of her zealous interest in Pansy's marriage; and she betrayed it in a manner which quickened Mrs. Osmond's alarm" (474). Again she remembers "the manner in which Madame Merle and her own husband sat together in private." By the end of this paragraph, "a strange truth was filtering into her soul. Madame Merle's interest was identical with Osmond's. That was enough." A little later Madame Merle says to Isabel that she should not use her influence to keep Lord Warburton from marrying Pansy: "Let him off—let us have him!" (476). And Isabel asks her, "Who are you—what are you? [...] What have you to do with my husband?" (477). But Madame Merle does not tell her, and she does not yet guess.

It is the Countess Gemini, Osmond's sister, who finally tells Isabel the story. "In your place," she says to Isabel, "I should have guessed long ago. But have you never really suspected?"

> "I have guessed nothing. What should I have suspected? I don't know what you mean."
> "That's because you have got such a pure mind. I never saw a woman with such a pure mind!" cried the Countess.
> Isabel slowly got up. "You are going to tell me something horrible." (500–501)

The details don't matter here; the upshot is that Pansy was the child of an affair between Osmond and Madame Merle. When Pansy was born, Osmond's wife had only recently died, and it was possible—with the help of a change in residence from Naples to Rome—to sustain the fiction that the baby was her child.

All this the Countess explains to Isabel, but she is puzzled by Isabel's reaction. "You don't take it as I should have thought" (504). The reader may also be puzzled. Isabel seems to take this revelation almost in stride. "It's very strange. I suppose I ought to know, but I am sorry," Isabel said. "I am much obliged to you." And a little later she says again, "I am much obliged to you." She does not seem particularly upset or angry. But this knowledge does seem to give her the resolution to go to see her cousin Ralph, who is dying in England, in opposition to Osmond's objection to the journey. She also uses this knowledge to make a final break with Madame Merle (in chapter 52), but she never says anything about it to Osmond. I suspect, however, that the revelation of this Ghost from the Past is as much for the reader as it is for Isabel; it certainly enters into our total judgment of both Osmond and Madame Merle.

It is not always easy to decide if a revelation counts as a Ghost from the Past. I would say that a Ghost from the Past should come near the end of the story and it should reveal something from some years before the beginning of the story time. Thus in Jane Austen's *Emma*, the revelation that Frank Churchill and Jane Fairfax are engaged does not count as a Ghost from the Past—it comes near the end, but the event revealed is not from the distant past. In *Pride and Prejudice*, the revelation of Wickham's true character in Darcy's letter probably comes too early to count as a Ghost from the Past, while the revelation that it was Mr. Darcy who managed the wedding between Wickham and Lydia is too recent. The revelation in Charlotte Brönte's *Jane Eyre* of Mr. Rochester's first marriage comes well before the end of the story, but in every other way it has the characteristics of a Ghost from the Past.

Multiple Retrospects

References to the past are by no means restricted to these types—Beginning with the Ending, Second Chapter Retrospect, and Ghosts from the Past. Modernist narrative architecture in particular often includes frequent deviations from straightforward chronology, and these deviations have become a regular part of the novelist's toolkit. Here I will examine just one example, Richard Yates's *Revolutionary Road*. I begin with a very brief summary of some of the essential events of the plot and then continue with a more detailed examination of the retrospects in the novel.

The story is set in 1955. The two central characters are Frank and April Wheeler, a young couple who live in the suburbs of New York City, where Frank works at an unrewarding job. They have two children, whom they seem largely to ignore. The novel charts their unsatisfying lives and the difficulties in their deteriorating marriage. In the middle of the story they decide to throw it all up and move to France. But then Frank is promoted to a more interesting position and April discovers that she is pregnant; she tries to give herself an abortion and dies. Frank sends the children to live with his older brother's family and he moves back to New York. The action of the novel takes just a year.

The story begins *in medias res:* "The final dying sounds of their dress rehearsal left the Laurel Players with nothing to do but stand there, silent and helpless, blinking out over the floodlights of an empty auditorium" (2008, 3). As this opening continues, the director delivers an encouraging talk to the actors, who then buy a case of beer and sing songs until it's time to go home to get a good night's sleep before the performance. All of this takes four paragraphs, and then we have the first retrospect, which establishes the scene and the circumstances: "The year was 1955 and the place was a part of Western Connecticut where three swollen villages had lately been merged by a wide and clamorous highway called Route Twelve. The Laurel Players were an amateur company, but a costly and very serious one, carefully recruited from among the younger adults of all three towns, and this was to be their maiden production" (4).

This retrospect continues for a couple of pages, and then the narrative returns to the present time of the story: "And now tonight, with twenty-four hours to go, they had somehow managed to bring it off" (6). The boundaries of the retrospect are marked by pluperfect tenses at the beginning and the adverb "now" at the end. Most of the many retrospects throughout the story are clearly marked.

The first performance turns out to be a disaster. In chapter 2, the story comes to focus on the reactions of the female star, April Wheeler, and her husband, Frank Wheeler, who was not an actor but just in the audience; they become the central characters of the novel. Near the beginning of the chapter, after the play is over, he goes to comfort April in the dressing room, but he feels in need of comfort himself: "The trouble was that all afternoon in the city, stultified at what he liked to call 'the dullest job you can possibly imagine,' he had drawn strength from a mental projection of scenes to unfold tonight": scenes he imagined of delight and pride after what he anticipated would be April's triumphant performance in the play (13). This short retrospect, marked by pluperfect tenses ("had drawn strength," "had he foreseen," "had warned"), is an analepsis containing a prolepsis, as in the past he imagines a future which has become the present, but not as he imagined.

Frank goes to the dressing room and tries to reassure April that she at least was wonderful, even if the performance as a whole was a failure. She is not, however, willing to be comforted. As they leave the school to go home we are given another retrospect: "The smell of school in the darkness, pencils and apples and library paste, brought a sweet nostalgic pain to his eyes and he was fourteen again, and it was the year he'd lived in Chester, Pennsylvania—no, in Englewood, New Jersey—and spent all his free time in a plan for riding the rails to the West Coast" (18). The retrospect again ends with the adverb "now": "Walking now through the same smells and looking at the pale shape of April's profile as she walked beside him..." (19). Within the same paragraph there is another retrospect, this time focused on April, but mediated through Frank's thoughts: "The school smell made him think of one particular time she had told about, a morning in Rye Country Day when a menstrual flow of unusual suddenness and volume had taken her by surprise in the middle of class" (19). Again we see the pluperfect tense, and again the retrospect ends with "now": "Her face must have looked almost exactly the way it did now" (20).

As Frank and April drive home from the performance, Frank again has a retrospective memory, of the time after the Second World War, when he was a student at Columbia University: "In his very early twenties, wearing the proud mantles of 'veteran' and 'intellectual' as bravely as he wore his carefully aged tweed jacket and washed-out khakis, he had owned one of three keys to a one-room apartment..." (21); he and two other classmates at Columbia had scheduled their use of this apartment for their affairs. This retrospect, the most extensive so far, extends for several pages, and it includes the first meeting of Frank and April and the beginning of their affair, which eventually leads to their marriage. And this retrospect also ends with the temporal adverb "now" (25).

As Frank and April approach their house, we see another retrospect, an explanation of their first sight of the house they now live in: "This was the way they had first come, two years ago, as cordially nodding passengers in the station wagon of Mrs. Helen Givings, the real-estate broker. She had been polite but guarded over the phone..." (29). This retrospect continues for several pages, and ends with "now": "Now, as the house swam up close in the darkness with its cheerful blaze of kitchen and carport lights..."

(32). When they get home, they have a fight and Frank ends up sleeping on the couch.

Thus we see five retrospective passages in this chapter alone. In the following chapter there are, by my count, another four, and there are many more throughout the novel. Of these retrospects, none, I think, functions as a traditional Second Chapter Retrospect. We do get some idea of Frank's childhood, however, through one of the retrospects in chapter 2—the one which takes us back to his time in school (18–19)—and also through a retrospect in chapter 3, an account of his parents over several pages: "They had both been dead for several years now" (36). This sentence uses both retrospective markers, the pluperfect tense and the adverb "now." The first time Frank and April meet is narrated in a retrospect in chapter 2 of part 1. It is easy to see that this meeting has to be subordinated by its position in a retrospect rather than marked as the beginning of the story—this is not a Meeting/Marriage novel, but the story of a marriage in ruins.

Longer or shorter retrospects occur throughout the novel; a long retrospect in chapter 2 of part 2 is focalized through a friend, Sheppard Sears Campbell, who will turn out to be an important character towards the end of the story: "For years, boy and man, he had yearned above all to be insensitive and ill-bred, to hold his own among the sullen boys and men whose real or imagined jeers had haunted his childhood" (145). We note the pluperfect tense marker, "had yearned." This retrospect continues for several pages and then a temporal marker brings the narrative back to the present time of the story: "For Shepp, too, the past few years had been a time of comparative peace. Or so it seemed, at any rate, in the glowing dusk of this fine spring evening" (149).

Quite late in the story we see an extensive and important retrospective view of April's terrible childhood (though this is briefly anticipated in chapter 3 of part 1). Her parents had split up, and she was raised by her Aunt Claire. In the retrospect, she has just received a short and very unsatisfying visit from her mother, followed by an even shorter and less satisfying visit from her father. This retrospect comes in the penultimate chapter, just before she makes her fatal decision to try to abort her pregnancy. Clearly the position of this retrospect is strategic and significant. No doubt it is designed to explain April's emotional blockage throughout the story and more particularly her decision to attempt the abortion. It functions almost as a Ghost from the Past—almost but not quite: it is the reader rather than a character in the story who receives this revelation. Perhaps one shouldn't be too strict with definitions, especially when making them up. If this retrospect isn't a Ghost from the Past it surely has something of the same effect. In addition, I am sure that we are supposed to remember this retrospect when we find out at the end, after April's death, that the Wheelers' children will be raised by their uncle, with weekend visits from their father.

These extensive Multiple Retrospects are more than a narrative convenience; they are part of the overall meaning of the story. This novel shows the past and the present woven together, not in a simple straightforward chronological progression, but in a kind of web of time. The past is not just the past, it is inescapably part of the present—and we see that the past and the present will live on in the future.

6

Complex Plot Forms, Part II

One-Day Novels

One-day stories and One-day plays have been around for a very long time, but One-Day Novels are a more recent development. The earliest One-Day Novel I have found is Herman Melville's *The Confidence-Man,* first published in 1857. The action of the book takes place on an unspecified April Fools' Day on board a Mississippi steamboat. In a sense there is no story, just a sequence of encounters, which are too many and too complicated to summarize here. The date of the action is significant, since the point of the story is the unmasking of fools. Early in the novel, one of the characters delivers a general judgment: "'You fools!' cried he with the wooden leg, writhing himself loose and inflamedly turning upon the throng; 'you flock of fools, under this captain of fools, in this ship of fools!'" (1954, 21). I don't believe *The Confidence-Man* led to a tradition of other One-Day Novels. In a way the book is a dead end. It is also almost unreadable today, not least because of its treatment of race, which I think most readers would find disturbing.

Perhaps the most famous One-Day Novel is James Joyce's *Ulysses,* published in parts beginning in 1918 and completed in 1922. Like most One-Day Novels, it includes extensive anachronies, so that the story folds the events of many years into the single day of the narrative proper. As in many One-Day Novels, the day of the narration is felt as the culmination and fulfillment of everything which has gone before: the whole of a life is seen under the aspect of a single day.

Virginia Woolf's *Mrs. Dalloway* was published in 1925; according to Elizabeth Abel, "The narrative present [of *Mrs. Dalloway*], patterned as the sequence of a day, both recalls the structure of *Ulysses,* which Woolf completed reading as she began *Mrs. Dalloway,* and offers a female counterpart to Joyce's adaptation of an epic form" (1988, 106–07). Although the story in a sense takes just one day, in another sense it includes incidents from a span of many years, told in various kinds of anachronies. These begin on the very first page of the novel. The opening of the novel establishes the beginning of the story time, the day of the party:

> Mrs. Dalloway said she would buy the flowers herself.
> For Lucy had her work cut out for her. The doors would be taken off their hinges; Rumpelmayer's men were coming. And then, thought Clarissa Dalloway, what a morning—fresh as if issued to children on a beach. (1)

In the very next paragraph the story reaches back into the past: "What a lark! What a plunge! For so it had always seemed to her when, with a little squeak of the hinges, which she could hear now, she had burst open the French windows and plunged at Bourton into the open air. How fresh, how calm, stiller than this of course, the air was in the early morning; like the flap of a wave; the kiss of a wave" (1). The narrative moves between the present and the past throughout. In this novel, and in many other modernist novels, there is a sense that the present is interfused with the past; in earlier novels time tends to move in a more or less regular sequence of cause and effect.

Since *Ulysses* and *Mrs. Dalloway,* the One-Day Novel has become a frequent form; examples include *The Last Post* (Ford Madox Ford, first published in 1928); *The Circus of Dr. Lao* (Charles G. Finney, 1935); *The Erasers* (Alain Robbe-Grillet, 1953); *Seize the Day* (Saul Bellow, 1956); *The Floating Opera* (John Barth, 1956); *The Poorhouse Fair* (John Updike, 1959); *A Single Man* (Christopher Isherwood, 1964); *Do Androids Dream of Electric Sheep?* (Philip K. Dick, 1968). In addition, there are many one-day thrillers, in which time is a factor in the suspense.

Malcolm Lowry's *Under the Volcano* (first published in 1947) complicates the one-day structure. The main action of the novel, which is narrated in chapters 2 through 12, takes place on November 1, the Day of the Dead, 1938, in the Mexican village of Quauhnahuac. The central character of this story is Geoffrey Firmin, known as the Consul. On the day of the main action, Firmin's wife, Yvonne, returns to him after a year's separation. Two other major characters in the story are the Consul's half-brother, Hugh, and the Consul's friend and neighbor, Jacques Laruelle. Each of the chapters of the main action is primarily focused through the consciousness of a particular character: thus chapter 2 is focused through Yvonne, chapter 3 is focused through the Consul, chapter 4 is focused through Hugh, and so on. The novel ends with the death of the Consul at the hands of the local police. Chapter 1 takes place exactly one year later, November 1, 1939, as Laruelle remembers the events of the main story. The novel thus has a variation of Beginning with the Ending; its chapters are structured through shifting focalization; and it is both a One-Day Novel and a One-Year Novel.

One-Year Novels

In most One-Day Novels, the action is concentrated into a brief period of time. One-Year Novels, however, often emphasize a sense of some kind of rhythm of recurrence, sometimes linked to the seasons.

The cycle of recurrence is essential to Thomas Hardy's *The Return of the Native*. The main action of the story takes one year and one day (with an epilogue narrating later events). The following summary concentrates on the beginning and ending of that year and a day.

The story begins on Guy Fawkes' Day, the fifth of November, and the first eight chapters all take place on that day. On that evening Captain Vye meets Diggory Venn as he is bringing Thomasin Yeobright home from her failed wedding to Damon Wildeve. Then we see a solitary figure—we learn later that this is Eustacia Vye, Captain Vye's granddaughter—standing on the summit of a barrow; after a few moments the figure leaves. The townspeople gather at the top of the barrow and light a great bonfire to celebrate Guy Fawkes' Day, though Hardy makes it clear that "such blazes as this the heathmen were now enjoying are rather the lineal descendants from jumbled Druidical rites and Saxon ceremonies than the invention of popular feeling about Gunpowder Plot" (1974, 45), and he further links the ceremony to elemental resistance to the onset of winter. This seasonal recurrence of human response to nature is the background for the events of the story.

That same night, Eustacia Vye builds a fire of her own at the house where she lives with her grandfather, a signal fire to call her former lover Damon Wildeve to her. During their conversation, we learn that exactly one year earlier Eustacia had built a fire to summon him (88).

The plot unfolds with many complications over the course of the next year. In brief, Eustacia's affections shift to Clym Yeobright, Thomasin's cousin, who has returned from his career as a diamond merchant in Paris.

Wildeve marries Thomasin; Clym marries Eustacia, but after the death of Clym's mother, which Clym blames on Eustacia, they separate. Eustacia returns to her grandfather's house and sinks into despair, but she is cared for by a young boy from the neighborhood, Charley. On the fifth of November, Charley makes a plan to relieve her grief: "For two successive years his mistress had seemed to take pleasure in lighting a bonfire on the bank overlooking the valley; but this year she had apparently quite forgotten the day and the customary deed. He was careful not to remind her, and went on with his secret preparations for a cheerful surprise, the more zealously that he had been absent last time and unable to assist. At every vacant minute he hastened to gather furze-stumps, thorn-tree roots, and other solid materials from the adjacent slopes, hiding them from cursory view" (356). Charley calls Captain Vye and Eustacia out to see his bonfire; the Captain praises him and adds, "Ah, it was this time last year that I met with that man Venn, bringing home Thomasin Yeobright" (357).

Although Eustacia had not built the bonfire, Wildeve responds to it as if it had been her summons. When he comes to talk with her, she tells him that she is planning to leave and go to Paris, but she needs his help to take her to the port city of Budmouth; there is a suggestion that she may want him to go with her and a suggestion that he will. She asks him to watch out for her signal when she is ready to leave. In fact she decides to leave the next night, one year and one day after the beginning of the story, in the midst of a severe storm. I will skip over the details; it is enough to say that Eustacia falls into the river; Wildeve and Clym try to rescue her, but Eustacia and Wildeve drown. The main action of the story is followed by an epilogue, a book of four chapters titled "Aftercourses," in which Thomasin marries Diggory Venn and Clym finds his vocation as a preacher and lecturer.

Hardy places his story in three different dimensions of time—first, the geographical time and archaeological time of the heath and its ancient inhabitants; second, the time of the recurrence of the seasons; and third, the progress of human life across these other temporal dimensions. Many One-Year Novels mark the passage of the seasons through the year of the story through the contrast of linear and cyclical time. Further examples of more or less strict One-Year Novels are Ellen Glasgow's *The Romantic Comedians,* Willa Cather's *Shadows on the Rock,* also her *Lucy Gayheart,* Anthony Trollope's *Framley Parsonage,* Jane Austen's *Emma,* and Toni Morrison's *The Bluest Eye.*[1]

Mirror Plots

Anthony Burgess's *A Clockwork Orange* is constructed in three parts, with chapters 1 through 7 in part 1, chapters 1 through 7 in part 2, and chapters 1 through 7 in part 3—though part 3 is divided 6+1. (I have previously discussed the structure of *A Clockwork Orange* in Clark and Phelan 2020, 38–39.) In part 2 the narrator, Alex, is incarcerated and treated for his violent impulses; Part 1 tells what happens before his treatment; part 3 tells what happens afterward. In order to make the contrast particularly pointed, many of the events in part 1 are repeated in part 3. The repetitions of words and people and actions are extensive, and here I will note only some of the most obvious and most important. This analysis will leave out the progression of events and note only the correspondences, but of course these correspondences and repetitions are supposed to be read in the order determined by the author.

The novel begins with the narrator speaking to his friends: "What's it going to be then, eh?" The narrator explains to the reader, "There was me, that is Alex, and my three droogs, that is Pete, Georgie, and Dim, Dim being really dim . . ." (1986, 3). Alex and his friends are sitting in the Korova Milk Bar, and they are dressed "in the heighth of fashion, which in those days was a pair of black very tight tights" and so on (4). This is matched at the beginning of chapter 7 of part 3: the narrator says to his friends, "What's it going to be then, eh?" And he explains to the reader, "There was me, Your Humble Narrator, and my three droogs, that is, Len, Rick, and Bully, Bully being called Bully because of his bolshy big neck . . ." (200). Alex and his friends are sitting in the Korova Milk Bar and they are dressed "in the heighth of fashion, which in those days was these very wide trousers and a very loose leather like jerkin" and so on (201). More repetitions could be noted—the girls in the Milk Bar (5 and 202), the music playing (6 and 201), and so on.

Alex decides that he and his friends should go out—"Out out out out" (7), which is matched by "Out out out out" in part 3 (203). They meet a man coming out of the public library, carrying books about crystallography. They tear up the books and beat him up (7–10). In chapter 2 of part 3 Alex goes to the library and accidentally meets the same man, who this time raises a crowd against him, until the police are called.

In chapter 2 of part 1, Alex and his droogs run into a rival gang, Billyboy and his five droogs (18); they fight until the police come to break it up (20).

In chapter 3 of part 3 Alex runs into Billyboy again; he is now a policeman, one of the police called when Alex is being beaten in the library, and so is Alex's old comrade Dim (166); they take him outside the city, beat him up, and leave him in a field (169).

The most important incident in part 1 is also mirrored in part 3. In chapter 2 of part 1, Alex and his droogs go out of the city and find a country cottage with the name HOME on its gate. They talk their way into the cottage and find a young married couple. (The husband of the couple is writing a book titled "A Clockwork Orange.") The gang proceeds to beat the husband and rape the wife. In part 3, chapter 3, as I have mentioned above, Alex is beaten by Billyboy and Dim and left in a field outside the city. He gets up and looks for somewhere to go to get help, and he comes across the same country cottage, HOME (170). The people there take him in—including the husband he beat in part 1, who does not recognize him. (We find out a little later that his wife died from the rape.) These people are reformers, and they take Alex up as the symbol of the brutality of the social system.

The form of *A Clockwork Orange* is somewhat like a ring, where the middle of the novel, part 2, is ringed by the repetitions in parts 1 and 3. Almost everything that happens in part 1 also happens in part 3. The form asks the reader to compare Alex before his treatment to Alex afterwards. I propose to call this particular kind of composition Mirror Architecture, perhaps as a type of extended ring composition.

A rather different kind of Mirror Structure is found in Eric Ambler's thriller *Passage of Arms,* which is organized in blocks of focalization. The whole novel tells three stories with three different but overlapping sets of characters. These stories are arranged in a kind of ring: the A story comes first; then this is dropped and the B story starts; then this is dropped and the C story starts. After the C story ends, the B story comes back and comes to a conclusion, and then the conclusion of the A story ends the book as a whole. The basic form of the story is ABCBA, but there is an additional smaller move in the middle which creates the complete form: ABC(BAB)CBA.

In the A story, an Indian clerk, Girija Krishnan, who lives in Malaya, comes across a large stash of weapons abandoned by a terrorist group. He realizes that this stash could give him the money he needs to realize his life's ambition—to own and operate a bus service. The difficulty is finding a way to sell this contraband. All this is in chapter 1.

Eventually, in chapter 2, he approaches a Chinese businessman, Mr. Tan Siow Mong, in Kuala Pangkalan. This meeting begins the B section of the novel. In a carefully indirect conversation Mr. Krishnan offers the contraband to Mr. Tan. After consideration, Mr. Tan decides to hand the difficult and dangerous proposition over to his younger brother, Mr. Tan Yam Heng, who is based in Singapore. They agree that a middleman is needed, perhaps an American, who can act as a cover for the transaction. Mr. Tan Yam Heng then meets with Mr. Krishnan and they come to an initial agreement on prices and the logistics of delivering the illegal arms. All this is in chapter 2.

Chapter 3 introduces Greg and Dorothy Nilsen, a middle-aged American couple who are engaged in a sailing tour around the world. Their story takes up the central portion of the story, from chapter 3 to chapter 9, as they get entangled in the sale of these clandestine arms. In the middle of this section Mr. Tan and Mr. Krishnan work out the delivery of the arms and the payment, thus creating the interior BAB section. The C story, the story of Greg and Dorothy Nilsen, is the center of the story, but after they are off the scene, the narrative returns to Mr. Tam, in a short B section, and then to Mr. Krishnan. The sense of an ending comes as Mr. Krishnan achieves his ambition to own a bus service, thus closing off the A section that began the whole novel.

Other examples of Mirror Structure include Elizabeth von Arnim's *Mr. Skeffington*, in which the central character, Mrs. Skeffington, revisits the several lovers she enjoyed after her divorce before finally reuniting with her husband; and David Mitchell's *Cloud Atlas*, which consists of six nested stories with different characters in different times and places, in the pattern ABCDEFEDCBA.

Alternating Chapters

A narrative can be organized in more or less regularly alternating blocks; the principle of organization can be time, place, narrative voice, class, or what have you. In Ursula K. Le Guin's *The Dispossessed*, the story world and the narrative structure are matched. The world consists of a double planetary system—a large planet called Urras and a smaller one called Anarres. Both planets can sustain life, though Anarres is mostly desert. Urras is divided into several different competing capitalist nations, while Anarres has a single society organized in a form of anarchism. The two planets are hostile and barely communicate with each other. The central character of the story is a mathematical physicist named Shevek, a native of Anarres, who travels to Urras at the beginning of the story and returns to Anarres at the end. The shape of the plot is Departure+Arrival / Departure+Return.

The first chapter is a chapter of transition, as Shevek is taken in a spaceship from Anarres to Urras. The opening of the chapter is a brilliant meditation on the topology of walls:

> There was a wall. It did not look important. It was built of uncut rocks roughly mortared. An adult could look right over it, and even a child could climb it. Where it crossed the roadway, instead of having a gate it degenerated into mere geometry, a line, an idea of boundary. But the idea was real. It was important. For seven generations there had been nothing in the world more important than that wall.
>
> Like all walls it was ambiguous, two-faced. What was inside it and what was outside it depended upon which side of it you were on.
>
> Looked at from one side, the wall enclosed a barren sixty-acre field called the Port of Anarres. [. . .] It was in fact a quarantine. The wall shut in not only the landing field but also the ships that came down out of space, and the men that came on the ships, and the worlds they came from, and the rest of the universe. It enclosed the universe, leaving Anarres outside, free.
>
> Looked at from the other side, the wall enclosed Anarres: the whole planet was inside it, a great prison camp, cut off from other worlds and other men, in quarantine. (2014, 1–2)

This opening is a lesson that the reader must keep in mind throughout the book, a lesson in reading from both sides.

The rest of the chapter tells how Shevek comes to the Port, where a hostile crowd of Anarristi has gathered to chase him away, or to keep him from leaving, or even to kill him; he leaves Anarres on a spaceship and is greeted by a welcoming Committee on Urras. Eventually we learn that the people on Anarres are the descendants of an anarchistic faction which was more or less expelled from Urras and went to Anarres, where they barely survive in a strict egalitarian society. The two worlds stay in meager communication, but Shevek, who has become famous on Urras for his work in mathematics, is the first person in many years to move from one world to the other. Many of the people on his own world resent his fame and his independence of mind, both of which violate their sense of egalitarianism.

Chapter 2 puts the story back onto Anarres, back to Shevek's infancy and childhood. From then on, every even-numbered chapter is part of this timeline and plot line, a narration of Shevek's life on Anarres until he makes the decision to move to Urras. The odd-numbered chapters all take place on Urras and narrate Shevek's experiences living in a new and strange society. The final chapter is a second chapter of transition, as Shevek returns to Anarres. The general structure of the book can be diagrammed:

```
Transition   1                              13
Annares        2   4   6   8   10   12
Urras              3   5   7   9    11
```

The timeline of the Anarres sections moves from Shevek's childhood to the moment he decides to move to Urras; this moment, the end of chapter 12, links to the beginning of chapter 3, and the timeline of the Urras sections moves from his Arrival on Urras to his decision to Return to Anarres; the first and last chapters are a ring. There is obviously much more to be said about this novel: much to be said about its representation of an invented story world, about the characters, and about the meditation on politics and society that runs through the whole story; but here the point is the narrative structure and its contribution to the meaning of the whole.

Philip K. Dick's *Confessions of a Crap Artist* is organized by changes in narrative point of view. The plot form of the novel is straightforward: the Beginning is an Arrival, as Jack Isadore leaves Seville, California, and goes to live with his sister Fay and brother-in-law Charley in Point Reyes; there is a secondary Beginning, a Meeting, as Fay and Charley meet Gwen and Nat Anteil. By the end of the story, Charley has killed himself, Gwen and Nat have broken up, Nat and Fay are living together, and Jack goes back to Seville.

The first and second chapters of the novel are narrated in the first person by Jack. The third chapter is narrated by an external third-person narrator; the focal character of this chapter is Charley Hume, the husband of Jack's sister Fay. Chapter 4 is narrated by Fay herself, chapter 5 is in the third person, and so on. The whole pattern looks like this:

Jack: 1, 2, 7, 10, 12, 17, 18, 20
Third person: 3, 5, 8, 9, 11, 13, 14, 16, 19
Fay: 4, 6, 15

Or like this:

Jack:	1	2		7		10	12			17	18		20
Third Person:			3	5	8 9			11	13 14		16		19
Fay:					4	6						15	

The effect of this kind of multiple narration can't be charted; it is an experience of reading sequentially through the story. Clearly the architecture of *Confessions of a Crap Artist* does not have the symmetry of *The Dispossessed*. The order of the chapters is determined by the needs of the story telling—the needs as perceived by the author. Dick wants some parts of the story to be presented by Jack, with all of his personal quirks, some to be presented by Fay, with her quirks, and some to be presented by an external narrator. The external narrative is usually focused through one or another of the characters. Chapter 3, for instance, is focused through Charley, as he deals (badly) with the embarrassment of buying Tampax for his wife. But Charley never gets a chance to narrate in his own voice, as Jack and Fay do. Chapter 9 is focused through Nat Anteil; neither of the Anteils gets to narrate. The author's control of the narrative voice is an essential feature of the success of this novel. And Jack gets the first and last word.

Robert Graves's true-crime novel *They Hanged My Saintly Billy* is also organized primarily by narrative voices. The basis of the novel is the story of William Palmer, a surgeon and horseracing enthusiast, who was tried, convicted, and executed in London in the year 1856 for the murder of John Cook. The novel itself takes the form of the results of an investigation, though the identity of the investigator is unclear. The first chapter is narrated in the voice of the investigator, who is external to the events narrated but internal to the world of the narrative. The voice of this primary narrator continues on-and-off throughout the novel and presents the other narrative voices.

The second chapter begins with an account, in the voice of the primary narrator, of Palmer's family and their family home. Then the primary narrator introduces a secondary narrator: "The gardener, by name Littler, once top-sawyer at The Yard, knew the family well and is ready, for a pint of ale, and a half ounce of tobacco, to talk about them. Here is his account" (1989, 10). Then the reader sees the name "Robert Littler," all in caps, centered in the page, followed by Littler's narrative; this is clearly presented in Littler's voice, which is quite different from the primary narrator's voice. Littler's narrative, which takes up the whole of the rest of the chapter, details the early period of Palmer's life, his apprenticeship, and in particular his sexual entanglement with a conniving young woman, Jane Widnall.

Chapter 3 presents the narrative of Thomas Clewley; the primary narrator tells us, "Mr. Clewley is even less reluctant to discuss the 'Palmer affair' than old Littler, and equally positive about the Doctor's innocence. We have taken down the following from his lips, in shorthand" (23). Thus we are assured that the voice is really the voice of Mr. Clewley; presumably the other voices are similarly verbatim—verbatim within the world of the narrative, as reported by the principal narrator.

The narrations of these secondary narrators are arranged to give a chronological summary of Palmer's life and career from his childhood up to a few days before the time of the alleged murder. The principal narrator evidently was not a witness to Palmer's life, and so he hands the narrative over to these secondary narrators. He is clearly in charge; he selects the secondary narrators and he judges them. Each of these secondary narrators is used once and then discarded, though one might imagine that some of them might have had information relevant to more than one point in the chronology.

Beginning with chapter 14, however, the mode of narration changes, as these secondary narrators are dropped (with the exception of chapter 20). Chapter 14 includes part of the speech of the Attorney-General at the trial and part of the transcript of the trial. Chapter 15 then reports Cook's last illness and death; chapters 16, 17, and 18 report the events after Cook's death, the increasing suspicions of foul play, the inquest into the death, the eventual arrest of Dr. Palmer, and events between the arrest and the trial. Several witnesses are quoted, but no single witness is given the status of a secondary narrator.

The trial itself, concluding with the guilty verdict, is detailed in chapters 19 to 22; much of these chapters is presented in the form of transcripts.

Chapter 23 concerns the public efforts after the trial to overturn the verdict; this chapter includes a newspaper report of a public meeting called to demand a delay of the execution so that new evidence could be considered, as well as letters written to the newspapers in defense of Palmer. Chapter 24 recounts the execution. The last voice heard is the voice of Palmer's mother, sometime after the execution, talking to an artist hired to make sketches for an illustrated *Life of Wm Palmer;* she speaks for about two pages; here are the beginning and ending:

> "Bye the bye, I'm Dr. Palmer's mother, and not ashamed of it, neither. Yes, they hanged my saintly Billy! He was a bit of a scamp right enough, but a good son to me; the best of the brood, except Sarah, and no murderer. [. . .] There's been kind letters, too, and some strange ones, and the strangest of all came from a lady who signs herself 'Jane Smirke'—Jane Widnall, as was. She knew my Billy at Liverpool and Haywood, and feels guilty about leading him astray. He was a very good boy, she says, and now if she can be of any service to me in my affliction, etc. . . . But that letter I could not answer; my heart was too full; besides, she gave me no address . . ." (268–69)

And thus the story ends.

Simultaneous Narration

If an event in a story is narrated by or focalized through more than one character, we may say that the narration is simultaneous. A good example of simultaneous narration is found at the climax of *The Return of the Native.* Chapter 7 of the fifth book is titled "The Night of the Sixth of November," but the events of that night also take up chapter 8, "Rain, Darkness and Anxious Wanderers," and chapter 9, "Sights and Sounds draw the Wanderers together."

Chapter 7 of book 5 is focalized through Eustacia herself or through the reactions of others to her. After an initial paragraph describing her general state of mind at the time, the second paragraph focuses directly on her: "Towards evening on the sixth her determination to go away again revived" (1974, 367). In the next paragraph she leaves the house and passes by Susan Nunsuch's cottage: "A woman who was sitting inside the cottage had seen and recognized her. . . . Susan dropped the spoon, shook her fist at the vanished figure, and then proceeded with her work in a musing, absent way" (367–68); the point is not Susan, but Susan's perception of Eustacia.

The next two paragraphs return to Eustacia's point of view, and the next makes a transition to her grandfather: "Eustacia returned to the house. Supper having been got over she retired early, and sat in her bedroom waiting for the time to go by. The night being dark and threatening, Captain Vye had not strolled out . . ." (368). Captain Vye takes over as the actor in the next couple of pages, but all his thoughts and actions are directed towards Eustacia; about half-past eleven he hears her leave the house and he deliberates following her.

The time now shifts back a few minutes to describe Eustacia's departure: "At half-past eleven, finding that the house was silent, Eustacia had lighted her candle, put on some warm outer wrappings, taken the bag in her hand, and extinguishing the light again, descended the staircase" (370). "Eustacia opened her umbrella" (370); "Eustacia at length reached Rainbarrow" (371). The next paragraph begins with an imagined witness— "Any one who had stood by now would have pitied her" (371)—but then introduces Eustacia's impassioned soliloquy. At the end of the chapter Susan Nunsuch makes a doll representing Eustactia which she punctures with pins and melts in the fire. The whole of the chapter concentrates on Eustacia.

Chapter 8 moves from Eustacia to Clym: "While the effigy of Eustacia was melting to nothing, and the fair woman herself was standing on Rainbarrow, her soul in an abyss of desolation seldom plumbed by one so young, Yeobright sat lonely at Blooms-End" (375). He is waiting for Eustacia, but when he hears someone at the door he finds that his visitor is Thomasin, with her baby, who fears that Wildeve and Eustacia have run off together. Captain Vye then comes to tell them that Eustacia has gone. He and Clym leave together, Vye to return to Mistover, Clym to look for Eustacia and Wildeve. Thomasin is left by herself, but after a short while she takes the baby and leaves to return home. On her way she meets Diggory Venn, who undertakes to accompany her. The chapter thus begins with Clym as focalizer, moves to Thomasin, and ends with the joint focalization of Thomasin and Venn.

Chapter 9 shifts to Wildeve and shifts back in time: "Having seen Eustacia's signal from the hill at eight o'clock, Wildeve immediately prepared to assist her in her flight" (385). Wildeve is the subject of the next six paragraphs, which take us to a quarter past midnight as he waits for Eustacia to meet him. But the person who finally approaches is Clym. As they hesitate to speak to each other, they hear someone—Eustacia—fall into the river. They try to save her. At this moment Diggory and Thomasin approach, so at the end all the principals are in the same place at the same time. Each of the major figures in the story plays a part in and focalizes a part of this climactic episode—Eustacia, Clym, Thomasin, Diggory, and Wildeve. The artful arrangement of the narrative gives the reader—this reader, at least—a sense of closure because everyone has been heard from.

Unnatural Chronology

C. S. Forester's *The General* begins with the ending, but it is easy to reconstruct the underlying chronology. Henry James's *The Portrait of a Lady* has a Second Chapter Retrospect, but it is easy to reconstruct the underlying chronology. Ursula Le Guin's *The Dispossessed* is told in alternating chapters with different time schemes, but it is easy to reconstruct the underlying chronology.

Some novels, however, are told in a way that seeks to disrupt our sense of the orderly progression of time. Joseph Heller's *Catch-22* is told out of order. The narrative also tells a few incidents—particularly the death of Snowden—over and over and over again, in ever more vivid detail, as Yossarian and the reader have to repeat the trauma in order to recover from it. Although it is possible to reconstruct the chronology, I doubt that Heller wants the reader to go to the trouble of tracking the time, and the presentation of events outside of chronological order is surely an essential feature of the novel.

Time travel stories often create two different timelines: the ordinary chronological progression and the timeline of the time-traveler, which may jump forward or loop backwards. In Robert Heinlein's short story "All You Zombies," all the characters—the hero/heroine, the hero's mother and father and child—are just one person in a complex knot of overlapping timelines.

Martin Amis's *Time's Arrow* narrates its story as if time flowed backwards, moving from the main character's death to his birth. The topic of the novel is the Holocaust; the main character is a Nazi physician, Odilio Unverdorben, a perpetrator of war crimes, who managed to escape after the war, change his identity, and build a new and prosperous life in the U.S.

In this inverted chronology Unverdorben's victims are not killed by his actions, but brought back to life, The inverted chronology is an innovative way of speaking the unspeakable.²

Alain Robbe-Grillet's *Jealousy* (*Jalousie*) is the story of a man caught in his obsessive fear that his wife is having an affair. The story takes place in some unspecified tropical country; the principal characters are the unnamed owner of a banana plantation, his wife, who is simply called A..., and his neighbor, Franck, also the owner of a plantation. Elsewhere I have discussed the representation of subjectivity in this novel;³ there is also much to be said about the narrator's presentation of sensuosity; also much to be said about race and colonialism; here, however, I will discuss primarily the representation of time.

Jealousy, in its English translation, begins with the word "Now," and "*Maintenant*" is the first word in the French original: "Now the shadow of the column—the column which supports the southeast corner of the roof—divides the corresponding corner of the veranda into two equal parts" (1965, 39) ["Maintenant l'ombre du pilier—le pilier qui soutient l'angle sud-ouest du toit—divise en deux parties égales l'angle correspondant de la terrasse"]. The word "now" is a temporal shifter—that is, it takes its meaning from the context in which it is used—it means whatever time I say it: the meaning of the word shifts, depending on when it is said. Narrative, however, has a curious ability to freeze any given "now" into an unshifting moment. Thus, when "now" begins *Jealousy*, it does not refer to the reader's "now" as the reader happens to be reading the sentence, but to the "now" when the narrator is observing the shadow of the column.

This "now" of the beginning will be contrasted to many other "nows" within the novel. The second paragraph also begins "Now" ("*Maintenant*"), but this "now" is perhaps different from the first "now": "Now A... has come into the bedroom by the inside door opening onto the central hallway" (39). A few pages later "now" is clearly different: "Now the shadow of the column—the column which supports the southwest corner of the roof—lengthens across the flagstones of the central part of the veranda" (42). The column is the same, but the "now" is different.

The word "now" is used around forty times in the novel. Clearly nowness matters to the narrator. But he makes it impossible to place these nows in any sort of succession, order, or causal relationship to each other. The column could be the gnomon of a sundial, but the narrator makes no attempt to use this accidental sundial to track the times and relate them to each other. Each now is its own moment. When we read, "Now the shadow of the southwest column—at the corner of the veranda on the bedroom side—falls across the garden" (50), or "On the bare earth of the garden, the column's shadow now makes an angle of forty-five degrees with the perforated shadow of the balustrade, the western side of the veranda, and the gable end of the house" (124), or "Now the shadow of the column falls across the flagstones over this central part of the veranda in front of the bedroom" (134), we don't know which of these nows is before or after any other now.

The characters in the story don't do very much; when they do something, their actions are not linked in any kind of coherent sequence. Here are parts of two paragraphs in which the narrator describes his wife and what she is doing:

> A . . . is lying fully dressed on the bed. One of her legs rests on the satin spread; the other, bent at the knee, hangs half over the edge. [. . .] Her face is turned upward toward the ceiling. Her eyes are made still larger by the darkness.
>
> Near the bed, against the same wall, is the heavy chest. A . . . is standing in front of the open top drawer. . . . (92; see also 55)

There is no transition to link these two moments. They could be successive moments in the same period of time, or they could be two separate moments which are simply juxtaposed.

Most novels are a mixture of narration—the account of people acting in time—and description, which tends to stop the flow of time. The temporal cessation caused by an occasional brief description is, however, usually unnoticeable, or at least unnoticed. The descriptions in *Jealousy,* however, are both frequent and extensive. The narrator describes the layout of the banana plantation:

> The line of separation between the uncultivated zone and the banana plantation is not entirely straight. It is a zigzag line, with alternately protruding and receding angles, each belonging to a different patch of different age, but of a generally identical orientation.
>
> Just opposite the house, a clump of trees marks the highest point the cultivation reaches in this sector. The patch that ends here is a

rectangle. The ground is invisible, or virtually so, between the fronds. Still, the impeccable alignment of the boles shows that they have been planted only recently and that no stems have as yet been cut. (50–51)

And so on. This description, in which nothing happens and there is no person to do anything, continues for another ten paragraphs, over three pages. It is interrupted for a moment by the appearance of a person: "On the bridge that crosses the stream at the bottom edge of this patch, there is a man crouching: a native, wearing blue trousers and a colorless undershirt that leaves his shoulders bare. He is leaning toward the liquid surface, as if he were trying to see something of the bottom, which is scarcely possible, the water never being transparent enough despite its extreme shallowness" (52–53).

The man crouching on the bridge is just another object to be observed. The description of the plantation then resumes for another two pages. Then once again we see the man on the bridge: "The man is still motionless, bending over the water on the earth-covered log bridge. He has not moved an inch: crouching, head lowered, forearms resting on his thighs, hands hanging between his knees" (54). Finally A... appears and a little action begins: "The bedroom window—the one nearest the hallway—opens outward. The upper part of A...'s body is framed within it. She says 'Hello' in the playful tone of someone who has slept well and awakened in a good mood" (55). For five pages time has fundamentally come to a stop.

Conversely, the description of an action can be so detailed that it loses the quality of narration. Here the narrator describes his neighbor Franck eating:

> The right hand picks up the bread and raises it to the mouth, the right hand sets the bread down on the white cloth and picks up the knife, the left hand picks up the fork, the fork sinks into the meat, the knife cuts off a piece of meat, the right hand sets down the knife on the cloth, the left hand puts the fork in the right hand, which sinks the fork into the piece of meat, which approaches the mouth, which begins to chew with movements of contraction and extension which are reflected all over the face, in the cheekbones, the eyes, the ears, while the right hand again picks up the fork and puts it in the left hand, then picks up the bread, then the knife, then the fork.... (88–89)

Many events of the story repeat or else they are told repeatedly. On page 57, A . . . offers Franck a drink:

> "Is it cold enough?" A . . . asks him. "The bottles just came out of the refrigerator."
> Franck nods and drinks another mouthful.
> "There's ice if you want it," A . . . says. And without waiting for an answer she calls the boy.
> There is a silence, during which the boy should appear on the veranda at the corner of the house. But no one comes.
> Franck looks at A . . . , as if he expected her to call again, or stand up, or reach some decision. She makes a sudden face toward the balustrade.
> "He doesn't hear," she says. "One of us had better go."
> Neither she nor Franck moves. (57)

On page 86 A . . . again offers Franck a drink, or else the narrator describes this moment for a second time:

> This is when she asks if the usual ice cubes will be necessary, declaring that these bottles come out of the refrigerator, though only one of the two has frosted over upon contact with the air.
> She calls the boy. No one answers.
> "One of us had better go," she says.
> But neither she nor Franck moves. (86)

Several times Franck and A . . . discuss a short trip they plan to make to the port city on the coast.[4] A . . . brushes her hair several times, or else the narrator describes one instance several times.[5] The most important of the repetitions, I would suggest, is the killing of the centipede. The first reference to this action immediately places its temporal position into question: "Besides, she was no longer facing Franck at that moment. She had just moved her head back and was looking straight ahead of her down the table, toward the bare wall where a blackish spot marks the place where a centipede was squashed last week, at the beginning of the month, perhaps the month before, or later" (47). The stain of the centipede is mentioned again on pages 59 and (in somewhat more detail) on pages 61–62. On pages 64–65 the killing of the centipede is recounted at some length:

> On the light-colored paint of the partition opposite A . . . , a common Scutigera of average size (about as long as a finger) has appeared, easily seen despite the dim light. . . . The creature is easy to identify thanks to the development of its legs, especially on the posterior portion. . . .
>
> It is not unusual to encounter different kinds of centipedes after dark in this already old wooden house. And this kind is not one of the largest; it is far from being one of the most venomous. A . . . does her best, but does not manage to look away, not to smile at the joke about her aversion to centipedes.
>
> Franck, who has said nothing, is looking at A . . . again. Then he stands up, noiselessly, holding his napkin in his hand. He wads it into a ball and approaches the wall. . . .
>
> Suddenly the creature hunches its body and begins descending diagonally toward the ground as fast as its long legs can go, while the wadded napkin falls on it, faster still.
>
> The hand with the tapering fingers has clenched around the knife handle; but the features of the face have lost none of their rigidity. Franck lifts the napkin away from the wall and with his foot continues to squash something on the tiles, against the baseboard.
>
> About a yard higher, the paint is marked with a dark shape, a tiny arc twisted into a question mark, blurred on one side, in places surrounded by more tenuous signs, from which A . . . has still not taken her eyes. (64–65)

There are several further references to the centipede or the stain it leaves on the wall.[6] The last two repetitions are particularly interesting, because they link the centipede to A . . . 's hair. As the centipede dies its legs and mandibles make a faint noise; the paragraph ends, "It is possible for an ear close enough to hear the faint crackling they produce," and the next paragraph begins, "The sound is that of the comb in the long hair" (113). Then a little later the narrator imagines that Franck and A . . . have crashed their car on the way to the port:

> The blue sedan goes crashing into a roadside tree whose rigid foliage scarcely shivers under the impact, despite its violence.
>
> The car immediately bursts into flames. The whole brush is illu-

minated by the crackling, spreading fire. It is the sound the centipede makes, motionless again on the wall, in the center of the panel.

Listening to it more carefully, this sound is more like a breath than a crackling: the brush is now moving down the loosened hair. (113–14)

These and other repetitions tend to create a sense of suspended or cyclic time, rather than the progressive time more typical of novelistic narrative. Twice at least I see references within the text to this kind of time. At one point, A... is listening to one of the workers singing a repetitive song: "It is doubtless the same poem continuing. If the themes sometimes blur, they only recur somewhat later, all the more clearly, virtually identical. Yet these repetitions, these tiny variations, halts, regressions, can give rise to modifications—though barely perceptible—eventually moving quite far from the point of departure" (84). Then later, towards the end of the text, when A... returns from her trip to the port, she asks (whom does she ask?) if there is any news. "There is no news. There are only the trivial incidents of the work of cultivation which periodically recur in one patch or another, according to the cycle of operations. Since the patches are numerous, and the plantation managed so as to stagger the harvest through all twelve months of the year, all the elements of the cycle occur at the same time every day, and the periodical trivial incidents also repeat themselves simultaneously, here or there, daily" (132–33). The text of *Jealousy* presents a complex network of repetitions and associations that tend to defeat the forward progress of time in the narrative and any coherent chronological ordering of the events. The narrator is obsessed with time as he is with his wife's infidelity—and the two obsessions are surely linked. There is no progress from one event to another, no causal chain. Instead, an event in the story becomes a sore to be worried repeatedly, and the pain of the sore fills the consciousness of the absent but omnipresent narrator.

Non-Narrative Elements in Narrative

Almost all narratives include non-narrative elements. As I have noted above, a description, taken in itself, is not narrative. We would not ordinarily count a guidebook as a narrative—though I can imagine an unnatural narrative cast in the form of a guidebook. A psychological case study would probably not count as a narrative. But most narratives include descriptions and psychological portraits, which we usually take to be part of the narrative.

There are many other kinds of non-narrative elements in narratives. Titles, for instance, are not themselves narrative, but a title belongs to its book and can influence the readers' experience of the narrative. Some novels begin, before the beginning, with an author's disclaimer—something like "None of the characters in this novel are intended to represent real people." A few writers have used the disclaimer as a part of the narrative effect. Kurt Vonnegut begins *The Sirens of Titan* with this disclaimer—or perhaps one should call it a claimer: "All persons, places, and events in this book are real. Certain speeches and thoughts are necessarily constructions by the author. No names have been changed to protect the innocent, since God Almighty protects the innocent as a matter of Heavenly routine" (2004, 6).

Some nonfiction memoirs begin with what might be called an editorial authentication: a note by an editor or some other person with a claim to authority, who may justify the importance of the memoir or explain how the manuscript came to be published. Fictional authentications can be found at the very beginning of the tradition of the English novel, in Daniel Defoe's *Moll Flanders, Robinson Crusoe,* and *Roxana,* and they have continued to be used, for instance, by Vladimir Nabokov in *Lolita* and by John Barth in *Giles Goat-Boy.*

Many novels include more or less extensive footnotes. Some of these footnotes are used for more or less postmodern or metafictional effect, but footnotes are found in pre-postmodern fiction. I find one footnote in chapter 11 of Voltaire's *Candide.* An old woman who is telling her life's story begins by claiming to be the daughter of Pope Urban X and the Princess of Palestrine. The author adds this footnote: "Note the extreme discretion of the author; there has been up till the present no pope named Urbain X; he was afraid to give a bastard to a known pope. What circumspection! What delicacy of conscience!" (*"Voyons l'extrême discretion de l'auteur; il n'y est jusqu'à present aucun pape nommé Urbain X; il craint de donner une bâtarde à un pape connu. Quelle circomspection! Quelle délicatesse de conscience!"* [1961, 168].) One might suggest that this footnote does not break any realistic illusion, since the narrative does not create any illusion to be broken. Sir Walter Scott, however, in *Waverley,* surely does create a realistic illusion, for the most part, and yet he adds (at least in editions after the first edition of 1814) a number of authorial footnotes. There are footnotes also in H. Rider Haggard's *King Solomon's Mines* (1885) and *Allan Quartermain* (1887). The technique cannot be simply considered postmodern or metafictional. Other novels with footnotes include Herman Melville's *Moby-Dick* (first published in 1851), Edgar Rice Burrough's *A Princess of Mars* (serialized 1912, published as a book in 1917), Flann O'Brien's *The Third Policeman* (written in 1939–40; first published in 1967), Manuel Puig's *The Kiss of the Spider Woman* (1976), David Foster Wallace's *Infinite Jest* (1996), Junot Díaz's *The Brief Wondrous Life of Oscar Wao* (2007), and China Miéville's *The Last Days of New Paris* (2016); the footnotes in some of these do create a metafictional effect.

Charles G. Finney's *The Circus of Dr. Lao* (which I discussed briefly in the previous chapter) ends with a section titled "The Catalogue," and a note which says, "An explanation of the obvious which must be read to be appreciated" (2001, 136–54). This Catalogue, which is nearly twenty pages long, is divided into nine sections: I. The Male Characters; II. The Female Characters; III. The Child Characters; IV. The Animals; V. The Gods and Goddesses; VI. The Cities; VII. The Statuettes, Figurines, Icons, Artifacts, and Idols; VIII. The Questions and Contradictions and Obscurities; and IX. The Foodstuffs. The Catalogue should be read as a whole, but a few selected items will give some impression of its tone and effect.

The catalogue of Male Characters includes descriptions as long as a paragraph and also brief descriptions, such as "John Rogers: Learned the plumbing trade at fourteen, fifteen, sixteen, and seventeen. Never made a hell of a lot of money at it, however. A good union man." "Harry Martinez: His forefathers came to this country a little after Hernando Cortez. His foremothers, Mayans, Toltecs, and Aztecs, were already here." "Man Who Interrupted the High Priest: A lowborn, argumentative, vulgar, deceitful fellow." "Teddy Roosevelt: An American President." The Catalogue of Female Characters is similar: "Kate: A sad memory." "The Railroad Man's Wife: Martha. Calm, sad, insecure; sometimes she laughed; laughing, she wondered; wondering, she wanted to cry." "The Wife of the Plumber Rogers: Sarah. Loved her children, liked her husband, was content in Abalone, cooked good things to eat, kept a neat home, dreamed of no miracles, desired no victories, fretted when it was time to fret, laughed when it was time to laugh." Among the Catalogue of The Animals, we find "Crustaceans: Crawdads. Cornpaffies. You catch them when you are fishing for catfish sometimes. Dangling from your hook they wave their claws and feelers at you, and you wonder at the fantasies that dwell in muddy waters." And so on through the rest of the Catalogue. The final group, the Foodstuffs, is a lovely congeries: "Pork chops. Lettuce. Ham hocks. Lamb chops. Persimmons. Hay. Soda pop. Duck eggs. Garlic. Little fat brown boy. Candy. Onion seeds. Pie. Pelicans. Grapes. Proteins. Snails. Beer. Snow geese. Sea foods. Carbohydrates. Frigate bird. Butterfat. Chicken. Gooseliver. Fish. Vahine. Frogs. Bananas. Oysters. Brown boy's old pappy. Bugs. Plantain. Fishing worms. Little plants. Lizards. Grub worms. Hot dogs. Rattlesnakes. Noodles. Slop. Nuts" (154). Clearly this Catalogue is not just an appendage to the main story, but an essential element of the whole reading experience.

An entire novel may mimic a non-narrative form. Ursula K. Le Guin's *Always Coming Home* takes the form of the report of a time-traveling anthropologist who is studying a culture at some unspecified time in the far future: a short section at the very beginning titled "Towards an Archeology of the Future" is written, I think, in the voice of the author (1985, 3–5). The book has several narrative sections. The longest of these is an autobiographical account by a character named Stone Telling; this is divided into three parts (part 1: 7–42; part 2: 173–201; part 3: 340–76). The novel also includes four sections of unconnected shorter narratives (54–68; 96–111; 121–46; 263–304); an excerpt from a novel written by Woodriver of Talina-na (318–38); a section of dramatic works (202–38); four sections of short poems (69–82; 112–20; 255–62; 387–405); and so on. The novel ends with a long section titled "The Back of the Book," which includes descriptions of kinship (with charts of kin relationships); food; musical instruments; medical practices; writing and the alphabet. The last section of the novel is a Glossary. The novel is also lavishly illustrated with drawings by Margaret Chodos, and it was published with a companion cassette of music composed by Todd Barton. The book announces itself as a novel on the cover, but it certainly challenges our ideas of what a novel is.

7
Viet Thanh Nguyen's *The Sympathizer*

In this book and its companion, *How to Reread a Novel,* I have explored ways of reading and rereading a novel, with particular attention to reading as an experience and to the kinds of meaning that are created by narrative structures. In this final chapter I apply some of these ways of reading to Viet Thanh Nguyen's *The Sympathizer,* which was first published in 2015 and won the Pulitzer Prize the next year.[1] The novel really doesn't need interpretation—it stands on its own as an aesthetic experience—but analysis shows the intricacy of the composition and the complexity of meaning.

 Narrative analysis should acknowledge and respect the linear progression of the reader's experience. Reading does not proceed topic by topic; you don't find out everything about the narrative situation all at once; your sense of the style and its importance develops as you read; you gradually learn more about the characters; and you won't see the shape of the whole composition until you can see it whole. But narrative analysis is not limited to a line-by-line commentary. When we reread—and analysis is a kind of rereading—we note a key word the first time it occurs; we see a pattern when it is an unsprouted seed; we meet a character as already a friend—or already an enemy; and in general the temporal sequence of elements has been partly transformed into an atemporal overview.

 The analysis in this chapter is a hybrid that attempts to respect both the temporal experience of reading *The Sympathizer* and an atemporal overview made possible by rereading. The first section offers a brief summary of the story; the second section is a more detailed reading of the first three chapters. Section 3 treats Style and Rhetorical Figures, and the fourth section looks at one specific point of style, the use of names in the narrative. Section 5 deals with Links and Rings. Section 6 examines one of the key topics of the novel, as focused by the word "nothing," and the last section considers the ending of the novel.

All of these different topics are intertwined and dividing them into different sections is artificial. My discussion, therefore, will be more integrated than the division into sections might imply. Although I try to respect the temporal experience of reading, I will not pretend at the beginning of the analysis that we don't know the end of the story; I will feel free to jump around when jumping will be helpful.

An Overview of *The Sympathizer*

The Sympathizer is an incarceration novel—the narrator is a prisoner in a Vietnamese prison camp—and like many incarceration novels, it Begins with the Ending: we first meet the narrator in prison, and we gradually learn how he got there. We will see, however, that the end of the incarceration narrative is not the end of the novel.

The early chapters of the novel recount the narrator's Departure from Vietnam and Arrival in the United States. In chapter 17 the narrator Returns to Vietnam with a rag-tag army of refugees, and the end of the novel is his second Departure from Vietnam. The middle of the story is another Departure and Return, as the narrator goes to the Philippines to act as consultant for a movie about the war and then returns to the U.S. This episode is a sort of substitute Return to Vietnam, since the movie is about Vietnam and the movie set is a simulacrum of a Vietnamese village. The composition of the whole can be diagrammed: Departure > Arrival > [Departure > Arrival > Return] > Return > Departure.

The novel also can be divided into two major sections. The first and larger section consists of the narrator's confession to the commandant and the commissar at the reeducation camp; the second section is an account of his reeducation. The confession becomes a physical object in the world of the reeducation, as we see in the second paragraph of chapter 19: "The commandant sighed and laid the final sheet of my confession on top of the other 306 pages that preceded it, stacked on a table by his chair" (2015, 308). A little later the narrator again mentions the number of pages in his confession, "all 307 pages" (317). In chapter 23, the doctor who is treating the narrator, after he has been broken in interrogation, hands him a stack of papers. "Does this look familiar? Cautiously, I unfolded my arms and took the stack. I looked at the first page, then the second, and the third, slowly thumbing my way through the numbered sheaf of 307 pages" (372). The reader of the paperback edition may note that the confession does take exactly 307 pages, and the new narrative, the second confession, begins on page 308. But the reader of the hardcover edition will find that the confession takes 295 pages; also that the narrator refers to "all 295 pages" (304); and in chapter 23 the doctor hands him a stack of 295 pages (357). The numbers are adjusted to correspond with the pagination of the particular edition. One presumes that later editions with different paginations will also be appropriately adjusted. The effect is to make a point of the materiality of the confession as an object in the world of the narrative.

The story mostly proceeds in a chronological progression, covering several years, but there are also many retrospects, some of which are extremely important, including a Ghost from the Past, which I will discuss below. Because the narrative clock begins to tick just as the war finally ends, any events of the war itself and the narrator's experience in the war have to be told in retrospect.

There is a large cast of characters—twenty at least who attract the reader's attention to some degree. The central character is the narrator, who is a captain in the South Vietnamese Army, but also a secret agent of the North Vietnamese. We never learn his name. His superior is the General, who also is never named; the General's wife and eldest daughter also play important roles. The narrator was trained by an American CIA agent named Claude. The narrator's mother was a Vietnamese peasant, and his father was a French Catholic priest; both are dead by the time the story begins, but he talks about them often. The narrator has two close friends, Bon and Man, his blood brothers. These three form a set: Bon is fully committed to the cause of the Republic of Vietnam; Man is a devoted (but underground) communist; and the narrator can see both sides. Man, Bon, and the narrator became blood brothers when they are young, and their friendship is stronger than their political differences. At the end of the war, Man stays in Vietnam, Bon escapes to the United States, and Man sends the narrator along with him, ostensibly to have him act as a double agent among the refugees, but really to save him. When Bon decides to return to Vietnam, as part of a rag-tag army of refugees, the narrator goes along to protect him. At the end of the story, when Bon and the narrator are prisoners in the camp, Man, who is the commissar of the camp, protects them and arranges their final escape.

All these characters and a few more are introduced in the first chapter. In chapter 4 the narrator arrives in the U.S. (along with Bon, the General, and the General's family) and settles in Los Angeles. In chapter 6, Bon and the narrator are directed by the General to kill a fellow refugee, the crapulent major; the General suspects the major is a double agent—though it is the narrator himself who is the double agent. In chapter 9 the narrator goes to the Philippines, as a consultant for a movie about the war. In chapter 12 he returns to the U.S. In chapter 16, at the direction of the General, the narrator kills Sonny, a Vietnamese journalist living in Los Angeles. In chapter 17, the narrator and Bon return to Vietnam, as part of a little band of refugees, in a futile attempt to foment a rebellion against the communist regime there. At the end of chapter 18, most of the band is killed, but Bon and the narrator are captured. Chapters 19 through 23 recount the narrator's experience in a reeducation camp. The narrator's reeducation has two parts: first, under the direction of the commandant of the camp, he writes an extensive confession; once this confession is approved, he undergoes sensory deprivation and interrogation under the direction of the commissar. At the end of chapter 23 the narrator and Bon leave Vietnam again as refugees for a second time, presumably to return to the U.S.

Most of the narration is realistic—that is, the physical laws of the world of the novel are similar to the laws of our world—except that the narrator is haunted by the ghosts of the two people he murders, the crapulent major in chapter 6 and Sonny in chapter 16. Most likely these ghosts are embodiments of the narrator's guilt, but they are presented as real entities in the narrator's world; thus when the narrator is flying back to Vietnam he tells us that he shares his seat "with the crapulent major on one side and Sonny on the other" (280).[2] The two murders present the readers with a serious problem of moral evaluation. The reader may want to sympathize with the narrator, but the description of the murders and their relative lack of justification are a challenge. Perhaps the ghosts suggest that the murders present a moral problem for the narrator as well.

The Beginning of the Novel

With this much summary we can start with a close reading of the beginning of the novel. Here is the first paragraph:

I am a spy, a sleeper, a spook, a man of two faces. Perhaps not surprisingly, I am also a man of two minds. I am not some misunderstood mutant from a comic book or a horror movie, although some have treated me as such. I am simply able to see any issue from both sides. Sometimes I flatter myself that this is a talent, and although it is admittedly one of a minor nature, it is perhaps also the sole talent I possess. At other times, when I reflect on how I cannot help but observe the world in such a fashion, I wonder if what I have should even be called a talent. After all, a talent is something you use, not something that uses you. The talent you cannot *not* use, the talent that possesses you—that is a hazard, I must confess. But in the month when this confession begins, my way of seeing the world still seemed more of a virtue than a danger, which is how some dangers first appear. (1)

This first paragraph introduces the narrator, establishes his identity as a spy, and emphasizes his ability to see situations from both sides. In addition, however, it alludes to other first-person introductions, and in particular the opening of Dostoyevsky's *Notes from Underground:* "I'm a sick man. . . . I'm a spiteful man. I'm an unattractive man" (2009, 3), and of Ralph Ellison's *Invisible Man:* "I am an invisible man. No, I am not a spook like those who haunted Edgar Allan Poe; nor am I one of your Hollywood-movie ectoplasms. I am a man of substance, of flesh and bone, fiber and liquids—and I might even be said to possess a mind. I am invisible, understand, simply because people refuse to see me" (1980, 3). The narrator seems to be asking the reader to compare him to the protagonists of these other narratives. The story is told in first-person throughout, though at the end, as we will see, there is a very important shift in the way the first-person narrator refers to himself. The book is written without quotation marks, so the reader has to figure out when any character's speech begins and ends.

The second paragraph begins with another clear allusion:

> The month in question was April, the cruelest month. It was the month in which a war that had run on for a very long time would lose its limbs, as is the way of wars. It was a month that meant everything to all the people in our small part of the world and nothing to most people in the rest of the world. It was a month that was both an end of a war and the beginning of . . . well, "peace" is not the right word, is it my dear

Commandant? It was a month when I awaited the end behind the walls of a villa where I had lived for the previous five years, the villa's walls glittering with broken brown glass and crowned with rusted barbed wire. I had my own room at the villa, much like I have my own room in your camp, Commandant. Of course, the proper term for my room is an "isolation cell," and instead of a housekeeper who comes to clean every day, you have provided me with a baby-faced guard who does not clean at all. But I am not complaining. Privacy, not cleanliness, is my only prerequisite for writing this confession. (1–2)

The first sentence of this paragraph alludes to one of the most famous lines in twentieth-century literature, the first line of T. S. Eliot's *The Waste Land*—"April is the cruelest month"—which in turn alludes to the first line of Geoffrey Chaucer's *Canterbury Tales*. (George Orwell's *1984* also begins in April.) The Fall of Saigon did occur in April; Nguyen did not have to rearrange reality to make his point but he did take advantage of it. There are further allusive references in the novel, direct and indirect—to Graham Greene's *The Quiet American* and to Francis Ford Coppola's *Apocalypse Now*, and brief allusions to Emerson (12), Hegel (191), William Blake (323), and others. The narrator also frequently refers to and quotes from a book titled *Asian Communism and the Oriental Mode of Destruction*, by Richard Hedd. This book and author, however, are inventions of the author.

An allusion has a meaning in its immediate context but it also creates a larger context and a larger meaning. In addition to saying that his narrator is a spy and that the story begins in April, Nguyen is making a claim that his work belongs with *The Canterbury Tales* and *The Waste Land,* just as the first paragraph claimed that it belongs with *Notes from Underground* and *Invisible Man*. The allusion to *The Waste Land* also, in a way, issues a challenge to Eliot—I see your cruel April, and I raise you my cruel April. These allusions also ask for a reader who will get the allusions. Some readers will, some won't, and even those who get them may be put off by what could seem to be a sort of cultural arrogance, especially in a time when the canon is in question. These allusions to the Western canon come at the beginning of a story situated at one of the fault lines of postcolonial history. The situating of the story in the Western canon through allusion and style takes on thematic importance at the end of the story.

This second paragraph adds to our knowledge of the narrator and the moment of narration. We learn that he is a prisoner in a camp and that he is in an isolation cell, though previously he had lived in a villa and had a housekeeper to do his cleaning. He must have been in a position of some privilege. The first paragraph may seem to be addressed to the flesh-and-blood reader or perhaps to an implied reader, as *Notes from Underground* or *Invisible Man* are addressed to implied readers, but in the second paragraph we learn that the narrative is addressed to the commandant of the camp, who is an internal reader, a narratee. (A little later we will find that there is another internal reader, the commissar, who is almost hidden for most of the novel.) Perhaps the narrative is addressed to two audiences at the same time: the implied author is addressing the implied reader and the narrator is addressing the commandant. The first two paragraphs establish the four fundamental narrative positions: at one level, the narrator, an incarcerated spy, is addressing the narratee, the commandant of the prison camp; on another level the implied author is addressing the implied reader.

The first two paragraphs are linked by the word "month" and by the word "confession." In the first paragraph, the word "confession" could simply be a general designation for a kind of narrative; in the second paragraph it means the confession of a prisoner. The first meaning is part of the communication addressed by the implied author to the implied reader; the second meaning is part of the communication addressed by the narrator to the narratee. When the narrator addresses the commandant, I would assume that he writes in Vietnamese; but when the implied author addresses the implied reader, he writes in English—a very sophisticated, stylish, and idiomatic English. The implied author may be creating a kind of illusion here, the illusion of a text in Vietnamese presented in English. Occasionally, however, the narrator inserts a Vietnamese word or phrase as if in an English text (167, 238). If an illusion was intended, these passages may break it. Perhaps the reader is not supposed to notice or to ask awkward questions.

Style and Rhetorical Figures
Near the end of the novel the style of the narration will become thematically important, as we will see below, and so it is worth close attention throughout. The elegant (English) style belongs to both the narrator and the implied author.

The first sentence ("I am a spy, a sleeper, a spook, a man of two faces") has asyndeton as well as mild alliteration. The first paragraph creates a kind of antithetical opposition of "talent" and "virtue" on the one hand and "danger" on the other; this antithesis is coupled with the antithesis of "something you use" and "something that uses you." The second paragraph has more antitheses: "everything to all the people in our small part of the world" and "nothing to most people in the rest of the world" and "It was a month that was both an end of a war and the beginning of . . . well, 'peace' is not the right word" (1). I will have more to say about antithesis below.

The careful composition of sentences and paragraphs continues throughout this first chapter and throughout the whole novel. Overall the language is reasonably transparent—that is, it represents the people and places of the fictional world (though we will see that the problem of representation is a theme of the narrative). The narrative is not abundantly furnished with objects, in the manner of Dickens or Balzac, but when objects are mentioned we understand that they are part of a fictional world that corresponds more or less to our own—as in the third paragraph of the first chapter, which describes a typical morning in the General's villa: "In the mornings, before I chauffeured him the short distance to the office, we would breakfast together, parsing dispatches at one end of the teak dining table while his wife oversaw a well-disciplined quartet of children at the other, ages eighteen, sixteen, fourteen, and twelve, with one seat empty for the daughter studying in America" (2). In a description like this, the language does not interpose itself as an object of observation obscuring the teak table or the General's family. A little later in the same paragraph, however, the narrator describes the General: "He was an epicurean and a Christian, in that order, a man of faith who believed in gastronomy and God; his wife and his children; and the French and the Americans" (2). This sentence tells us something about the General, but it also shows us something about the mind of the narrator as he carefully deploys his thoughts and his language; the language to some extent is an object in itself. The style rarely overshadows the world and the events described—the signifier rarely dominates the signified—but there are some notably florid passages, particularly at moments of high emotion.

The narrator uses many figures: anaphora, antithesis, palilogia and local palilogia, epistrope, correctio, tricolon, paradox, anadiplosis, epizeuxis and extended epizeuxis, epitheton, asyndeton and polysyndeton, chiasmus, congeries, apostrophe, equivocation, homoioteleuton, paronomasia, litotes, epimone, pysma, zeugma, and polyptoton. The figures are not so frequent as to be overwhelming, but there are enough to give the reader a sense that the writer—either the narrator or the implied author—cares about the language he uses. Some, however, are frequent enough or prominent enough to stand out.

The narrator occasionally uses a somewhat elevated vocabulary: crapulent (13), amniotic (13), phrenological (14), proscenium (23), steganography (55), ferric (125), glabrous (128), susurrus (139), apsara (245), palimpsest (264), chiaroscuro (264), pheromone (278), hematoma (279). These words are used precisely: steganography, for instance, is the hiding of one message inside another, and that is exactly how the narrator, once in the United States, communicates with his superiors back in Vietnam: he writes a letter to his "aunt" in Paris, and between the lines adds a message in invisible ink. "Glabrous" means "free from hair, smooth"; the narrator talks about his own "relative hairlessness, my chest (and stomach and buttocks) as streamlined and glabrous as a Ken doll." He could have said "smooth"; the word "glabrous" is used for effect, though it is not easy to say what that effect is. Words like these call attention to the writing as writing, and perhaps to the writing as English rather than Vietnamese.

The narrator is fond of similes and metaphors. A few examples will suffice. "His singing partner was an equally long-haired woman of dulcet voice, her slim figure outlined by a silk ao dai the same shade as a virgin's blush" (16); "we heeded the call of the Katyusha rockets, hissing in the distance like librarians demanding silence" (35); "So it was that we soaped ourselves in sadness and we rinsed ourselves with hope" (71); "I was finally left with nothing but myself and my thoughts, devious cabdrivers that took me where I did not want to go" (186); "How could I forget that every truth meant at least two things, that slogans were empty suits draped on the corpse of an idea?" (371).

Antithesis is frequent—and fitting to the situation of the narrator, who is himself a sort of embodied antithesis, a double agent of mixed race. Here are a few examples: "It is always better to admire the best among our foes rather than the worst among our friends" (32); "A mid-ranking apparatchik in the ministry of the interior, he was neither too tall nor too short, too thin nor too wide, too pale nor too dark, too smart nor too dumb" (42); "passions running hot and food getting cold" (93); "while he was an expert by necessity, I was a novice by choice" (98); "America, where even whites played jazz and even blacks sang in the opera" (187). Several of these contrast life and death: "It was here that the living went to sleep but the undead awoke" (175); "What am I dying for? he cried back. I'm dying because this world I'm living in isn't worth dying for! If something is worth dying for then you've got a reason to live" (224); "Bon, having decided to die, was finally showing signs of life" (232); "To live was to be haunted by the inevitability of one's own decay, and to be dead was to be haunted by the memory of living" (305).³

Chiasmus is another figure appropriate to the narrator's dual character. The first chapter ends with a particularly marked example: "My mother was native, my father was foreign, and strangers and acquaintances had enjoyed reminding me of this ever since my childhood, spitting on me and calling me bastard, although sometimes, for variety, they called me bastard before they spit on me" (19). The verbal inversions can suggest a kind of complexity of emotion: "In short, I was in a familiar place, the place of feeling unfamiliar" (156); "The cinematographer got especially close to capture the look in Bihn's eyes, which I could not see from where I was watching, but which I assumed to be some saintly mix of ecstatic pain and painful ecstasy" (171); "To them he's one of us, and to us he's one of them" (214).⁴

The narrator is particularly fond of congeries; I have counted twelve instances.⁵ Several of these also involve parallelism and anaphora. Congeries by its nature is a long figure, so I will cite just one:

> If allowed to stay together, I told my aunt, we could have incorporated ourselves into a respectably sized, self-sufficient colony, a pimple on the buttocks of the American body politic, with ready-made politicians, police officers, and soldiers, with our own bankers, salesmen and engineers, with doctors, lawyers, and accountants, with cooks, cleaners, and maids, with factory owners, mechanics, and clerks, with thieves, prostitutes, and murderers, with writers, singers, and actors, with geniuses, teachers, and the insane, with priests, nuns, and monks, with Buddhists, Catholics, and the Cao Dai, with people from the north, the center, and the south, with the talented, the mediocre, and the stupid, with patriots, traitors, and neutralists, with the honest, the corrupt, and the indifferent, sufficiently collective to elect our own

representative to the Congress and have a voice in our America, a Little Saigon as delightful, delirious, and dysfunctional as the original, which was exactly why we were not allowed to stay together but were instead dispersed by bureaucratic fiat to all the longitudes and latitudes of our new world. (69)

The most important instance of congeries comes at the very end of chapter 21, after the narrator under interrogation has recounted the rape of a North Vietnamese agent; this passage, a single periodic sentence, extends in a series of forty-seven clauses, each the protasis of a conditional construction, ending with a single emphatic apodosis in the form of an appeal: "if you would please just turn off the lights, if you would please just turn off the telephone [. . .] and if I saw no more of these visions, please could you please just let me sleep" (353–54). The figuration of the language shows the strength of the emotion.

There are several figures of repetition. I begin with epimone, the frequent repetition of a phrase—in this case Marx's phrase "They cannot represent themselves; they must be represented," either in these words or in some variation (144).[6] Representation is particularly important in the center of the story, when the narrator gets a job as consultant for a movie, *The Hamlet*, about the War. The movie is filmed in the Philippines, which represents Vietnam, because Vietnam cannot represent itself. The three actors who play the only Vietnamese characters with speaking parts are a Filipino boy, a Chinese man, and a mixed-race woman of British and Chinese parents; as the director's assistant explains, "there just weren't any qualified Vietnamese actors" (157); the Vietnamese were unable to represent themselves. The extras without speaking parts, however, were Vietnamese refugees; their cinematic function was to be killed, without having spoken.

The production designer has created the representation of a village in the Central Highlands: "The dusty lanes, the thatched roofs, the earthen floors of the cottages and their simple bamboo furniture, the piggeries with real pigs already snorting softly in the night, the warble of the innocent chickens, the soupy air, the bite of the mosquitoes, the plop of my unsuspecting foot into a mushy cake of buffalo dung—all of it left me dizzy with the vertigo of sadness and longing" (153). The designer has also built a representation of the village's cemetery:

> When I had seen this field of stones, I had asked to have the biggest tomb for my own use. On the tombstone I had pasted a reproduction of my mother's black-and-white picture that I carried in my wallet.... On the gray face of the tombstone I painted her name and her dates in red.... Tombstone and tomb were cast from adobe rather than carved from marble, but I took comfort in knowing no one would be able to tell on film. At least in this cinematic life she would have a resting place fit for a mandarin's wife, an ersatz but perhaps fitting grave for a woman who was never more than an extra to anyone but me. (154)

The climactic scene of the movie is the destruction of the fake town, as if by American bombers. "It was only a fake cemetery with its fake tomb for my mother, but the eradication of this creation, in its wantonness and its whimsy, hurt me with unexpected severity" (180). The narrator goes to the cemetery to take one last look at the imitation of his mother's tombstone, but the timing of the scene is off, and the explosions begin while the narrator is alone on the set; his injuries put him in the hospital.

Representation is a topic throughout the book, as we see from the frequent repetition of Marx's phrase or of the single word "representation." The novel itself is a representation. Every novel is a representation of some kind, but this novel is a representation within a representation: it represents the war in Vietnam mostly after the war and outside Vietnam. The movie is a representation within this representation of a representation. According to the director of the movie, the Auteur, "A great work of art is something as real as reality itself, and sometimes even more real than the real" (178). "I had no doubt that in the Auteur's egomaniacal imagination he meant that his work of art, now, was more important than the three or four or six million dead who composed the real meaning of the war. *They cannot represent themselves; they must be represented*" (179). The narrator turns this critique against himself and his role in authenticating the movie's representation:

> For I had an encroaching sense of the meanness of my accomplishment, that I had been deluded in thinking I could effect a change in how we were represented.... I was no more than the garment worker who made sure that the stitching was correct in an outfit designed, produced and consumed by the wealthy white people of the world. They owned the means of production, and therefore the means of representation.

> ... The Movie was just a sequel to our war and a prequel to the next one that America was destined to wage. Killing the extras was either a reenactment of what had happened to us natives or a dress rehearsal for the next such episode. (179)

The narrator's critique of the movie as representation is also implicitly a critique of the novel as representation.

Local palilogia occurs here and there; two instances are worth some attention. The General has been trying to organize a small military force of refugees to return to fight in Vietnam. The narrator is driving the General to a meeting with potential donors to this cause. He mumbles something under his breath, and the General tells him to stop talking to himself. But as the narrator tells us: "The only problem with not talking to oneself was that oneself was the most fascinating conversational partner one could imagine. Nobody had more patience in listening to one than oneself, and while nobody knew one better than oneself, nobody misunderstood one more than oneself" (248). This is lovely writing, and worth enjoying just for itself, but it also contributes to the question of identity that runs through the novel and comes to a head at the end, as we will see below.

The meeting of potential donors has been convened by a congressman friendly to their cause, and the guest of honor is Richard Hedd (Dick Head?), the author of *Asian Communism and the Oriental Mode of Destruction*. During their meal, Hedd and the narrator get into a long discussion of the phrase "life, liberty, and the pursuit of happiness," focusing particularly on the word "happiness." The passage is too long to quote, but the word "happy" and its forms occur twenty-one times in two pages (254–55), and the word returns, to form a ring, twice more at the end of the chapter, when Dr. Hedd asks if he may use one of the narrator's phrases in his next book: "Nothing could make me happier, I said, though I was, for reasons unspeakable in this company, quite unhappy" (263).

In addition to these instances of local palilogia, there are two instances of thematically important long-range palilogia—repetitions that recur, sometimes in clumps, at greater distances in the text. In the midsection of the novel, the narrator goes to the Philippines to act as consultant to the movie. Just at the end of the filming, he is injured in an accident, which is perhaps not an accident, and he spends some time recovering in a hospital.[7] In this section, the word "white" is used over and over. "I was in a bed shielded by a white curtain, pressed beneath a white sheet." "A man in a white coat stood at the foot of my bed." "Above me the ceiling was white. My sheets, white. My hospital gown, white. I must be fine if everything was all white but I was not. I hated white rooms, but now I was alone in one with nothing to distract me" (183–84).

The repetitions continue a few pages later, in a retrospective account of the narrator's interrogation of a North Vietnamese agent known as the Watchman, because he builds bombs with watches as detonators. The narrator and the Watchman are of course on the same side, but the narrator can't let on, even to the Watchman, or he will blow his own cover. This retrospective memory, which is one of the key episodes in the story, begins as the lights are turned out in the narrator's hospital room. "Now that the room was dark, all I could see was the only other all-white room I had been in, at the National Interrogation Center back in Saigon, working my first assignment under Claude's supervision." "Every inch [of the room] had been painted white." "The idea for the all-white room was Claude's." (186). There are ten uses of the word "white" on this page, another four on the next, where it contrasts as a racial designation with "black," then nine more on the following four pages. At the end of the interrogation the Watchman manages to kill himself by choking on a white hardboiled egg. The end of this retrospect returns to the present time of the narrative:

> Time had stopped for the Watchman. What I did not realize until I woke up in my own white room was that time had stopped for me, too. I could see that other white room with utter clarity from my own, my eye peering through a camera in the corner, watching Claude and myself standing over the Watchman. It's not your fault, said Claude. Even I didn't think about this. He patted my shoulder reassuringly but I said nothing, the smell of sulfur driving everything out of my mind except for the fact that I was not a bastard. I was not a bastard, I was not, I was not, I was not, unless, somehow, I was. (193)

This passage leads to a consideration of the key word "bastard," which I will have to delay for a moment while I complete my discussion of "white." The word "white" is used again shortly after the repetitions I have already noted. While the narrator is still in the hospital, he has two visitors, Violet, who is the assistant to the director of the film, and "a tall, thin white man in a powder-blue suit." Violet asks the narrator how he feels: "All white, I whispered although I could speak perfectly fine" (200). Later, during the General's meeting with potential donors, Richard Hedd remarks that "only the pursuit of happiness is promised to all Americans, unhappiness is guaranteed for many." As the narrator writes, "The unspeakable had been spoken, which people like myself and the General could never have uttered in polite white company without rendering ourselves beyond the pale" (255). I wonder if "pale" here is a pun. Then later in the same conversation, there is a flurry of repetitions: "The General furrowed his brow just a bit to show his concern and his understanding. As a nonwhite person, the General, like myself, knew he must be patient with white people, who were easily scared by the nonwhite. Even with liberal white people, one could go only so far, and with average white people one could barely go anywhere. The General was deeply familiar with the nature, nuances, and internal differences of white people, as was every nonwhite person who had lived here a good number of years" (258). There are three more uses of the word on the same page. The narrator, or perhaps the implied author, seems to be playing on two senses of the word: "white" as the designation of a color and "white" as the designation of a race.

The word returns at the end of the story, when the narrator is being interrogated by the commandant and the commissar. In this episode, the narrator speaks of himself in the third person, in a sort of dissociation. He has been gagged so he cannot talk, a hood has been placed over his head so he cannot see, his ears have been plugged so he cannot hear, and he has been kept awake for some indeterminate length of time. Then, suddenly, the gag and the hood and the earplugs are removed: "Light! He could see, but just as quickly he had to shut his eyes. Suspended over him were dozens—no, hundreds of light bulbs, planted in the ceiling and blinding him with their collective wattage" (340). The intense light showed that the examination room was all white—the walls, the ceiling, the floor, and even the iron door, and his three interrogators are all dressed in white lab coats.

The final return of the word comes at the end of the interrogation, when the narrator is alone with the commissar, who has been revealed to be his blood brother Man, terribly disfigured by napalm on the day of the Fall of Saigon. "He smiled through his tears. I recognized the smile, too, the whitest I had ever seen among any of my people.... What had changed was not the smile but the face, or the lack of it, so that this white smile floated in a void, the terrible grin of a Cheshire cat" (362). The word "white" certainly has a complex of meanings, some simply realistic, some symbolic; the word is also used to link several key scenes. (I suspect that the light bulbs in the final interrogation were borrowed from Ellison's *Invisible Man*.)

Another repeated key word of the novel is "bastard." The narrator is, of course, literally a bastard child, and sometimes the word just has its literal meaning—though the meaning of "bastard" is never simply literal but always carries a judgment—but at times it is used simply as an insult without reference to the narrator's parentage.

The first use of the word comes toward the end of the first chapter. The narrator and his friends Man and Bon run into "a trio of hydrocephalic marines" who are drunk and argumentative. One of them calls the narrator a bastard and the two others repeat the insult. The argument almost turns violent, but just then the bombardment of the city begins and cuts it off. At the very end of the chapter the narrator comments on the incident: "One did not depend on marines for good table manners. One depended on them to have the right instincts when it came to matters of life and death. As for the name they had called me, it upset me less than my reaction to it. I should have been used to that misbegotten name by now, but somehow I was not. My mother was native, my father was foreign, and strangers and acquaintances had enjoyed reminding me of this ever since my childhood, spitting on me and calling me bastard, although sometimes, for variety, they called me bastard before they spit on me" (19). The next chapter begins with a link: "Even now, the baby-faced guard who comes to check on me every day calls me a bastard when he feels like it" (20). The placement of the word at the end of one chapter and then at the beginning of the next is quite emphatic. It seems that the narrator's status is the same before the revolution and after.

The narrator is not just a bastard, he is also of mixed race, and these two characteristics are equated. As chapter 2 continues, the narrator suggests that the baby-faced guard in the prison could have called him mongrel or half-breed, or métis or Eurasian, or even Amerasian: "Although a misnomer when applied to me, I could hardly blame Americans for mistaking me as one of their own, since a small nation could be founded from the tropical offspring of the American GI" (21). He then adds the terms "natural child" or "illegitimate son." "My mother called me her love child, but I do not like to dwell on that. In the end, my father had it right. He called me nothing at all" (21). At the very end of the book the word "nothing" becomes a key word; I will discuss this below.

At the beginning of chapter 3 the narrator returns to the word "bastard": "My weakness for sympathizing with others has much to do with my status as a bastard, which is not to say that being a bastard naturally predisposes one to sympathy. Many bastards behave like bastards" (36); we note the equivocation of the term "bastard."

The word also comes at a climax in the important episode of the interrogation of the Watchman, the underground bomb maker for the North Vietnamese (186–91). This episode brings out the moral dilemma of the narrator's role. As himself an agent of the North Vietnamese, he is on the same side as the Watchmaker, but as a member of the national police, he is the Watchmaker's interrogator: "I was thankful for the air-conditioning. Otherwise I would have been sweating, trying to figure out how to be both enemy and friend to the Watchman" (189). So far as the Watchman knows, the narrator is simply his enemy.

At the beginning of the interrogation, the Watchman insults the narrator: "you're not as smart as you think you are.... You're a bastard, and like all hybrids you are defective" (190). The narrator determines to prove that he is smarter than the Watchman: "Between the two of us, only one could be the master. The other had to be the slave" (190). We note the echo of Hegel's parable of the master and the slave.

The narrator writes a confession for the Watchman, which includes the (false) admission that the Watchman is homosexual. He confronts the Watchman with this confession, which he threatens to publish in the newspapers. After such a confession, the narrator tells the Watchman, he will be condemned by the revolutionaries and by his family.

> You'll be a man who has sacrificed everything for nothing. You will not even be a memory to your comrades or your family.... Think about it. He said nothing and did nothing except stare at his confession. I paused at the door. Still think I'm a bastard?
>
> No, he said tonelessly. You're just an asshole. (191)

A few days later, as we have seen, the Watchman kills himself by choking on a hard-boiled egg. "It's not your fault," Claude tells the narrator. "He patted my shoulder reassuringly but I said nothing, the smell of sulfur driving everything out of my mind except for the thought that I was not a bastard. I was not a bastard, I was not, I was not, unless, somehow, I was" (193). There are another ten instances, all of which are worth attention, but these demonstrate the importance of the word in the narrator's conception of himself and his situation; as he says, "While I chose to live two lives and be a man of two minds, it was hard not to, given how people had always called me a bastard. Our country itself was cursed, bastardized, partitioned into north and south . . ." (361).[8]

The narrator links his illegitimacy to his mixed parentage: he is a "mongrel or half-breed, or métis or Eurasian, or even Amerasian" (21). As a hybrid, he can see both sides; he can see the attractions of the East and the West. He had spent six years at college in the U.S.—at the aptly named Occidental College—and learned both the high culture and the popular culture of the West. Early in the novel he notes his ability to discuss "baseball standings, the awfulness of Jane Fonda, or the merits of the Rolling Stones versus the Beatles" (7). A couple of pages later, as he is working on plans to evacuate Saigon, he listens to American music: "The songs of the Temptations and Janis Joplin and Marvin Gaye usually made bad things bearable and good things wonderful" (9). Man, the narrator's handler (and blood brother), also has a taste for Western culture. When the narrator is packing to evacuate, he has to decide what few things he will be able to take along: "I had no room for Elvis or Dylan, Faulkner or Twain, and while I could replace them, my spirit was still heavy when I wrote Man's name on the box of books and records. They were too much to bear, as was my guitar, displaying its full, reproachful hips on my bed as I left" (14). We see these again near the end of the story, when the narrator first goes to Man's quarters in the reeducation camp: "Leaning against one of the chairs was a guitar with familiar curvaceous hips and at one end of the long table was a record player that looked like the one I had left behind at the General's villa" (323).

The flesh-and-blood reader of the novel may admire the narrator's style, but the reader of the confession inside the narrative, the commandant, does not like it: "Confessions," he says, "are as much about style as content, as the Red Guards have shown us" (312). The narrator knows that his confession should have included the slogans of the Revolution, such as "*Long live the Party and the State. Follow Ho Chi Minh's glorious example. Let's build a beautiful and perfect society!*," and he grants that he believes in the slogans, but he is unable to write them. "It seemed as much of a crime to commit a cliché to paper as to kill a man, an act I had acknowledged rather than confessed, for killing Sonny and the crapulent major were not crimes in the commandant's eyes. . . . My resistance to the appropriate confessional style irritated the commandant": "You are a communist only in name. In practice you are a bourgeois intellectual" (318). "The good news is that you show glimmers of collective revolutionary consciousness. The bad news is that your language betrays you. . . . It is the language of the elite" (319).[9]

Names and Epithets

Many characters in the novel are never named; some of these are given epithets. The crapulent major first appears in chapter 1 and then plays an important secondary role in the rest of the story. The three marines who insult the narrator at the end of Chapter 1 are not named; when they reappear at the end of the confession they are identified as the dark marine, the darker marine, and the darkest marine. The affectless lieutenant and the grizzled captain appear first in Chapter 13, as the General is assembling his little army of refugees, and then again at the end of the confession, along with the philosophical medic. Other characters are identified by title—the Commandant, the General, the Chair, the Congressman. Some others are identified by some characteristic role in the story—the Auteur, the Thespian, the Idol, the Poet, the Admiral. The narrator himself is never named, nor are his mother and father.[10]

One of the named characters is Ms. Sofia Mori, the secretary in the Department of Oriental Studies, who is introduced in chapter 4 (61). She and the narrator have an affair, which begins in chapter 5 (73). The narrator always calls her Ms. Mori, and she always insists that he call her Sofia. "Ms. Mori, I said, I am shocked by what I am hearing. I'll bet, she said. Call me Sofia, for Chrissakes" (75). When the narrator goes to the Philippines, Ms. Mori starts up an affair with Sonny, who always calls her Sofia (211).[11]

The commissar at first is unnamed. He is mentioned at the beginning of Chapter 3—"Thank you, dear Commandant, for the notes that you and the commissar have given me on my confession" (36); he is mentioned again at the beginning of chapter 15—"A great deal of what I have confessed so far may seem foreign to you, dear Commandant, and to this mysterious, faceless commissar of yours whom I have heard so much about" (244); and again at the very end of the confession—"Somewhere on the other side you were waiting for me, Commandant, as well as the faceless man who is the commissar" (304). The narrator does not at this point explain why the commissar is known as the faceless man.

In the reeducation section of the novel the commissar becomes an important character. In chapter 19, after the end of the confession and at the beginning of the reeducation, the commandant tells the narrator, "You are a special case. [...] You are a guest of myself and the commissar" (309). The commandant explains that the narrator is about to enter the last stage of his reeducation: "In short, the commissar believes you ready to be cured. He does? I had yet even to meet the faceless man, otherwise known as the commissar" (310). A little later the commandant says "I agree with the commissar about the state of your reeducation. I was just talking about you with *him* the other day. He's remarkably tolerant of you. He didn't even object to being called the faceless man. No, I understand, you are not mocking him, merely describing the obvious, but he's quite sensitive about his... condition" (316; see also 321).

At the end of chapter 19, the narrator is taken by the guards to meet the commissar; the guards knock, and the commissar says "Come in." The narrator says—to himself or to the reader—"That voice..." (323). The commissar comes forward from behind a netting:

> A hand parted the netting, its skin burned red, and he emerged from the bed's recesses, a visage of fearful asymmetry. I looked away. Come now, the commissar said. Am I really so horrible that you do not recognize me, my friend? I look back to see lips scorched away to reveal perfect teeth, eyes bulging from withered sockets, nostrils reduced to holes without a nose, the hairless, earless skull one massive keloid scar, leaving the head to resemble one of those dried, decapitated trophies swung on a string by an ebullient headhunter. He coughed, and a marble rattled in his throat.
>
> Didn't I tell you, Man said, not to return? (323)

Chapter 20 begins, "*He* was the commissar?" (324). The narrator's recognition that the commissar is actually his blood brother Man is one of the crucial turns in the story. The effect of this sudden revelation depends in part on the pattern of non-naming we have seen throughout the confession.

The most important unnamed character is the narrator. He goes to some trouble to leave himself unnamed, even in situations where it would be easy and natural for his name to be used. Once back in the United States he gets a job in the Department of Oriental Studies: "My job was to serve as the first line of defense against students who sought audiences with the secretary or the Department Chair, some addressing me by name though we had never met" (60). The students address him by name, but the reader cannot. When the narrator is asked to be an adviser for the movie, the director's assistant sends the narrator a copy of the script, "the thickish manila envelope arriving with my name misspelled in a beautifully cursive hand" (126; see also 262, 288). At the end of the story the narrator is subjected to sensory deprivation and interrogation (at this point of the story, the narrator refers to himself in the third person); he is asked his name:

> An easy question, or so he thought. He opened his mouth, but when his tongue would not move, he shrank in fright. Had he forgotten his name? No, impossible! He had given himself his American name. As for his native name, his mother, the only one who understood him, had given it to him, his father no help, his father who had never called him son or by his name even in class simply calling him *you*. No, he could never forget his name, and when at last it came to him, he freed his tongue from its gummy bed and said it aloud.
> The commissar said, He can't even get his name right. (341–42)

Here we should remember a passage from early in the book: "My mother called me her love child, but I do not like to dwell on that. In the end, my father got it right. He called me nothing at all" (21).

Links and Rings

The first and second paragraphs of the novel are linked, by the words "month" and "confession." The second and third paragraphs are also linked, by the word "privacy." The fourth paragraph is linked back to the first and second by the word "April," which also links the fifth paragraph. The fifth and sixth paragraphs are linked by the name "Claude"—and so on. Not all paragraphs are linked, but linkage is quite common, and no doubt it adds to the smooth flow of the narrative.

The end of the first chapter is emphatically linked to the beginning of the second, with the key word "bastard." Chapter 3 is not linked to chapter

2, but chapter 3 is linked back to the end of chapter 1 with the word "bastard." Chapter 3 is continuous with chapter 4, but without a specific link. Most of the chapters are not linked; many, but not all, are continuous. The next strongly marked link comes between chapter 18 and chapter 19. The end of chapter 18 is the end of the confession; the rag-tag army of refugees has been ambushed and most of them have been killed, but the narrator manages to save Bon, and the chapter ends: "The mission was over, he was alive, and my plot had worked, no matter how clumsily or inadvertently. I had succeeded in saving him, but only, as it turned out, from death." Chapter 19 then begins, "Only from death? The Commandant appeared genuinely wounded, his finger resting on the last words of my confession" (308). The confession which we have been reading is now a stack of pages in the world of a new narrative, and the commandant, who has been a narratee addressed within the confession, is now a character within this new narrative; he moves from the second person to the third. This new narrative will have to establish its own motive for telling and its own narratee. The two chapters are linked but they are discontinuous, not just in time or place or action, but in their fundamental narrative status.

At the beginning of chapter 21 the narrator begins to refer to himself in the third person. Chapter 20 ends in the first person: "The chair scraped again and I smelled the distinct, gamy odor of the baby-faced guard and I trembled. Please, Comrade, I said. Just let me sleep. The baby-faced guard snorted, nudged me once more with his horny foot, and said, I'm not your comrade" (338). Chapter 21 then begins immediately in the third person: "The prisoner had never known that he needed a respite from history, he who had committed his adult life to its hot pursuit" (339). The first person resumes later in the chapter (349), as the prisoner, the narrator, listens to a tape-recording of the torture of the North Vietnamese agent; I will return to this important episode later. Chapter 21 ends with the long congeries noted above; the last words of the chapter are "could you please just let me sleep?" (354), and chapter 22 begins, "Of course you cannot sleep" (355).

Chapter 22 ends with the narrator's realization of the crime he has committed: "*Somebody was screaming and I knew who it was*. It was me, screaming the one word that had dangled before me since the question was first asked—nothing—the answer that I could neither see nor hear until now—nothing—the answer I screamed again and again and again—*nothing!*—because I was, at last, enlightened" (368).[12] Chapter 23 (the last chapter in the novel) begins, "With that one word, I completed my reeducation" (369). Thus we see that most of the chapters in the first part of the novel, the confession, are not linked, with the notable exception of the emphatic "bastard" linking chapter 1 and chapter 2, but all of the chapters in the second part, the reeducation, are strongly linked. Perhaps the links in the reeducation increase the intensity of the narrative.

The overall structure of the plot is a ring: the story begins and ends with a departure from Vietnam. There are several small rings—for instance, from page 26 to page 30, joined by the ring word "basilica," and from page 254 to page 263, joined by the ring word "happiness." Two large rings are structurally and thematically important. In chapter 1, the narrator has a run-in with three marines, who call him a bastard (18); this is the first use of the key word in the novel. These same marines show up towards the end of the confession, as part of the band of refugees returning to Vietnam. Two of them are killed, but one is still alive when the narrator and Bon leave the prison camp, and he says "I knew you bastards would get out of here first. Good luck to you" (377). Thus the first and the last usages of the key word "bastard" are spoken by the same character, at the beginning and at the end of the novel, but with very different tones.

The most important ring joins chapter 1 to the crucial moment in the narrator's reeducation. In a retrospect in chapter 1 the narrator recalls the arrest of a communist agent. She is another of the unnamed characters, but she is the bearer of names:

> All of our names, from the lowest officer to the General, had been found on a list being crammed into its owner's mouth as we broke down her door three years ago. The warning I had sent to Man had not gotten to her in time.... I could not have risked my cover by telling her that I was on her side.... I kept her folder on my desk, a reminder of my failure to save her. It was my fault, too, Man had said. When the day of liberation comes, I'll be the one unlocking her cell. (9–10)

This agent disappears from the story, except for brief references, until late in the novel, in the reeducation, as we will see in the next section.

Nothing
After the narrator has completed his written confession, the commissar

takes over the narrator's reeducation, which he calls the final revision of the confession (336). The narrator protests that he has nothing left to confess, but the commissar answers, "There is always something. That is confession's nature" (336). The commissar then reads the narrator an early part of the narrator's confession, where the narrator tells about arresting the agent. "You mention her four more times in your confession. We learn that you pulled this list from her mouth and that she looked at you with mortal hatred, but we don't learn her fate. You must tell us what you did to her. We demand to know!" (336). And the narrator answers, "But, I said, I did nothing to her" (336).

> Nothing! Do you think her fate is the thing you have forgotten that you have forgotten? But how is her tragedy possible to forget? Her fate is so clear. Was there ever any fate for her that could differ from what a reader might imagine, seeing her in your confession?
> But I did nothing to her!
> Exactly! Don't you see how everything in need of confession is already known? You indeed did nothing. That is the crime that you must acknowledge and to which you must confess. (336–37)

It is in the next chapter, chapter 21, that the narrator begins to refer to himself in the third person: "The prisoner had never known that he needed a respite from history, he who had committed his adult life to its hot pursuit" (339). This change may be explained a few pages later, in the words of one of the interrogators: "As we can neither see nor touch his mind, all we can do is help the patient see his own mind by keeping him awake, until he can observe himself as someone else" (342).

The narrator is taken for further interrogation to a room all white—like the room where the Watchman was interrogated, and like the narrator's hospital room in the Philippines—with hundreds of lightbulbs. This section of the story is worth extensive close reading. Some passages I have already discussed, and I invite the reader to remember those previous discussions—passages about the narrator's name, for example (341–42).

For this part of the interrogation, the narrator—the prisoner, the pupil, the patient (340)—is left alone with the commissar, that is, with his blood brother Man, who had once been his instructor in their Marxist study groups. The point of the interrogation is to force the narrator to remember, and to tell the reader, about the interrogation of the communist agent—the memory of an interrogation within an interrogation. The details emerge gradually. The interrogation of the communist agent took place in a room called the movie theater. (The reader may remember that the narrator first saw the rape scene in *The Hamlet* in a movie theater in Bangkok.) The officer in charge was the crapulent major (whom the narrator kills in chapter 6).

The commissar asks the narrator who was in the theater, and the narrator names everyone except the communist agent, until the commissar prompts him. "How could he have forgotten the agent with the papier-maché evidence in her mouth. His own name was written on the list of policemen she had been trying to swallow when she was caught. Watching her in the movie theatre, he was certain that she was unaware of his true identity, even though he was the one who had passed the list to Man. But the agent, being Man's courier, knew who Man was" (348).

The narrator continues to describe in detail the brutal rape of the communist agent by three interrogators. This retrospective narrative is a gruesome Ghost from the Past. The chapter ends with the extensive congeries in parallel construction quoted in the third section above. At the beginning of chapter 22 the narrator once again refers to himself in the first person, but as a split self: "I was divided, tormented body below, placid consciousness floating high above.... Seen from this altitude, the vivisection being done to me was actually very interesting, leaving my wobbly body's yolk shimmering beneath my viscous white mind" (355). As the interrogation continues, the narrator repeats, "But I've done nothing!" and the commandant replies, "You simply weren't willing to sacrifice yourself to save the agent, though she was willing to sacrifice her life to save the commissar's" (356). The narrator observes: "I saw myself admit it then. I heard myself acknowledge that I was not being punished or reeducated for the things I had done, but for the thing I had not done. I wept and cried without shame for the shame I felt. I was guilty of the crime of doing nothing. I was the man to whom things are done because he had done nothing" (356–57). As the interrogation continues, the commandant reminds the narrator of a letter he wrote to Man during his first time in the U.S.: "Did I not remember what I had written to Man about my father? *I wish he were dead.*" The narrator protests that he didn't mean it, but the Commissar, Man, rebuts this protest: "Of course you did! Who did you think you were writing to?" (358).

> I was writing to the revolutionary who was on a powerful committee and who knew, even then, that he might one day be a commissar; I was writing to a political cadre already learning the plastic art of making over the souls and minds of men; I was writing to a friend who would do whatever I asked; I was writing to a writer who valued the force of a sentence and the weight of the word; I was writing to a brother who knew what I wanted more than I knew it myself. (358–59)

Indeed, Man arranged for the killing, through his agent—presumably the agent who was raped in the theater.

The commandant and the doctor leave the room, leaving the narrator alone with the commissar. The narrator exclaims, "I wish I was dead!" The commissar draws his pistol, and as the narrator expects to die he contemplates his own divided self, which he compares to the division of his country. "Now my friend would release me from this small world with its small-minded people, those mobs who treated a man with two minds and two faces as freak, who wanted only one answer for any question" (361). But it turns out that Man wants to die, he wants the narrator to kill him, as a release from the pain of his injuries. But the narrator cannot kill his friend. Man leaves the narrator alone, and the narrator begins to hear a tape-recording of a baby screaming. This leads to a long meditation on time and identity. This meditation is punctuated by a series of comments in italics: "*Somebody was screaming and it was not the baby.*" "*Somebody was screaming and it was the agent.*" "*Somebody was screaming and it was my mother.*" "*Somebody was screaming and I did not know who it was.*" And finally, "*Somebody was screaming and I knew who it was.* It was me, screaming the one word that had dangled before me since the question was first asked—nothing—the answer that I could neither see nor hear until now—nothing!—the answer I screamed again and again and again—*nothing!*—because I was, at last, enlightened" (368). This beginning of chapter 23 is linked to the end of chapter 22: "With that one word, I completed my re-education. All the remains to be told is how I glued myself back together" (369). Also remaining, however, is some explanation of what the narrator has learned in his enlightenment.

Enlightenment is often—perhaps always—to some degree ineffable; so the narrator himself says, as he is finally leaving the prison camp: "Nothing was truly unspeakable" (378). This gnomic statement could mean that everything is speakable—or that nothingness cannot be spoken. An explanation of enlightenment is like the explanation of a joke—if you have to have it explained, then you miss the essential flash of understanding. This flash is an experience—and an experience can only be experienced, not explained. Perhaps that experience can come through narrative.

One element of the narrator's enlightenment, and perhaps the reader's, is a double interpretation of nothing. We may say that the narrator understands nothing, or we may say that he understands "nothing." The narrator has learned "nothing," and "nothing" was the answer to the questions. At the end of the interrogation, the commissar comforts the narrator: "There, there, he said in the dark examination room, silent at last except for my sobbing. Now you know what I know, don't you? Yes, I said, sobbing still. I get it. I get it!" (370).

> What was it that I got? *The joke.* Nothing was the punch line, and if part of me was rather hurt at being punched—by nothing, no less!—the other part of me thought it was hilarious. That was why, as I shook and shuddered in that dark examination room, my wailing and sobbing turned to howls of laughter. I laughed so hard that eventually the babyfaced guard and the commandant came to investigate the cause of the commotion. What's so funny? The commandant demanded. Nothing! I cried. I was, at last, broken. I had, at last, spoken. Don't you get it? I cried. The answer is nothing! Nothing, nothing, *nothing!* (370)

The commandant, unlike the narrator and the commissar, cannot get the joke and cannot understand the answer. "He saw only one meaning in nothing—the negative, the absence, as in *there's nothing there.* The positive meaning eluded him, the paradoxical fact that nothing is, indeed, something.... People who do not get the joke are dangerous people indeed. They are the ones who say nothing with great piousness, who ask everyone else to die for nothing, who revere nothing. Such a man could not tolerate someone who laughed at nothing" (371). The rest of the novel is a coda to this enlightenment. The narrator has been broken. He is moved back to his cell, which is now unlocked, but he huddles in the corners. Finally the doctor devises a plan to rehabilitate him. The doctor brings him a pile of blank paper and he sets him the task of recopying his confession.

As the narrator recopies his confession he develops "a growing sympathy for the man in the pages, the intelligence operative of doubtful intelligence. Was he a fool or too smart for his own good? Had he chosen the right or the wrong side of history? And were not these the questions we should all ask ourselves? Or was it only me and myself who should be so concerned?" (372).

The narrator then decides to write a new document, a narrative of the events following his confession. He feels sorry for the man with two minds, for himself, but he also poses questions for and about himself. "How dare a man with two minds think he could represent himself much less anyone else, including his own recalcitrant people? They would never in the end be representable at all, regardless of what their representatives claimed" (373). He also develops sympathy for the commissar, for his friend Man, and he asks to see him. "As I sat watching him from my bamboo chair, still bisected into myself and another, I detected a similar division in him.... He was the commissar but he was also Man; he was my interrogator but also my only confidant; he was the fiend who had tortured me but also my friend. Some might say I was seeing things, but the true optical illusion was in seeing others and oneself as undivided and whole, as if being in focus was more real than being out of focus" (374). Man has arranged for the narrator and Bon to leave the camp and the country. He has bribed the proper officials to guarantee their safe escape. "Am I still the friend you recognize and love? He was the faceless man who had tortured me, for my own good, for the sake of nothing. But I could still recognize him, for who but a man with two minds could understand a man with no face?" (375). But Man will not leave, he will not escape; he will stay behind with his pain and facelessness. "The only benefit from his condition was that he could see what others could not, or what they might have seen and disavowed, for when he looked into the mirror and saw the void he understood the meaning of nothing" (375).

Sympathy for the Sympathizer

No aspect of a novel is more important than the reader's feelings about the characters. The naïve notion that the reader identifies with the hero hardly begins to do justice to the complexity of this relationship. Perhaps I have some wish-fulfillment identification with Frodo Baggins, with Randal Patrick McMurphy, or Philip Marlowe. I don't think that I identify with Emma Woodhouse, though I certainly wish her well. I don't care for Frank and April Wheeler, the main characters of *Revolutionary Road,* and I thoroughly dislike all the characters in *The Great Gatsby.* Even a character I like and hope for will likely make mistakes, sometimes serious mistakes, and I will want to see the hero correct his or her errors. Achilles was probably wrong to abandon his friends in the Greek army and almost certainly wrong to reject the appeal of the ambassadors in book 9; his final realization of a deeper morality is even more appealing because he was so wrong before.

What then does the reader feel about the narrator of *The Sympathizer?* I hesitate to make general statements about readers' responses, simply because readers are so various. It may be possible, however, to investigate how the author, or the implied author, guides the readers' feelings. The author of *The Sympathizer* makes it difficult for the reader to approve of the narrator—difficult but not impossible. Perhaps the reader will come to sympathize without approving. The word "sympathy" and its forms are key words in the text, and of course the reader is primed to notice a word which is the title of the book.[13]

The narrator introduces himself in the first sentence as a spy. I don't suppose spies are automatically unsympathetic, though we often recognize the ambiguous moral status even of spies we like—George Smiley, for instance. But the narrator is a spy for the communists. Readers will differ, but Nguyen can't expect a large part of his readership to think well of a communist spy. We see some details of the narrator's practice as a spy as early as the third page, as he surreptitiously photographs government reports about Vietnamese soldiers shooting Vietnamese civilians in the back as the regime crumbles, but we also see evidence of his ability to see both sides, which may mitigate the reader's judgment: "I could not help but feel moved by the plight of these poor people. Perhaps it was not correct, politically speaking, for me to feel sympathy for them, but my mother would have been one of them if she were alive" (3). The narrator thinks that he is wrong to be moved by the plight of the poor Vietnamese civilians, but he does so anyway. This is an instance of what James Phelan calls "bonding unreliability," that is "unreliability that reduces the distance between the narrator and the reader" (Phelan 2007, 222–23). The narrator thinks that his sympathy is bad, but the reader thinks it is good.

The author sets several challenges to the reader's evaluation of the narrator's moral judgment—the interrogation of the communist agent, the interrogation of the Watchman, the murder of the crapulent major, and the murder of Sonny. I have already discussed the interrogation of the Watchman; in this section I consider the other three challenges.

In the first chapter the narrator mentions for the first time the incident of the communist agent, one of Man's agents, found with the list of names of the members of the Special Branch. He knows that she will be imprisoned and tortured. "Even had I a moment to be alone with her, I could not have risked my cover by telling her that I was on her side" (90). The narrator keeps her folder on his desk, "a reminder of my failure to save her" (10). The narrator is caught on the horns of a moral dilemma. If he had revealed his position to the agent he could have endangered himself and Man as well, probably without saving the agent. Perhaps this kind of moral dilemma is just part of the job of being a spy. Clearly the narrator is troubled by his inability or unwillingness to endanger himself; the reader may be reassured by this sign of the narrator's bad conscience. Because the narrator blames himself, the reader may blame him less.

The author takes care to keep the communist agent in the reader's mind by mentioning her from time to time (31, 45, 170). Then at the end of the story, at the climax of his reeducation, Man forces the narrator to remember the gruesome details of the interrogation and rape of the agent, which the narrator witnessed and did nothing to stop. This ring is carefully arranged to make the reader reevaluate the narrator's action and inaction. Again, the narrator's feelings of guilt enter into the reevaluation, but there is no suggestion that the narrator should be forgiven. I am reminded of the moral dilemma set by Camus in *The Fall;* neither Camus nor Nguyen offers a solution.

Near the beginning of the novel, when the refugees reach California, the General fears that there is a double agent among them. In order to distract attention from himself, the narrator suggests to the General that the culprit could be the crapulent major. The General is convinced and he orders the narrator to kill the major. The narrator enlists Bon, who is an experienced killer, and in chapter 6 the killing is described in some detail: "The major turned around, gift in one hand, lunch box in the other. I stepped to one side and heard him start to say a word when he saw Bon, and then Bon shot him. The report echoed in the carport, hurting my ears. The major's skull cracked when his head hit the pavement, and if the bullet had not already killed him, perhaps the fall did. He lay flat on his back, the bullet hole in his forehead a third eye, weeping blood" (109). The narrator tells the commandant how he feels about the killing: "I confess that that the major's death troubled me greatly, Commandant, even if it does not trouble you. He was a relatively innocent man, which was the best one could hope for in this world" (111). The author provides the major with a wife and two children: "They were innocents to whom wrong had been done, as I had once been an innocent child to whom wrong was done" (140). The passive voice here is strategic: the narrator elides his own agency, so he can create a false parallelism between the wrong done to him and the wrong done to them, as if he had done no wrong.

When the narrator returns from the Philippines (in chapter 12), he visits the major's widow, who serves him tea and ladyfingers. He gives her half of the money he received as compensation for his accident on the movie set. She takes him into the children's bedroom to look at them sleeping. "They're my joy, she whispered as we gazed down at the twins. They're keeping me alive in these difficult days, Captain. Thinking about them I don't think about myself so much, or my dear, beloved husband" (206).

Clearly the author has created a situation designed to elicit the reader's judgment. Towards the end of the novel, however, the narrator reveals a new twist, which the author has deliberately kept hidden. When the commissar, Man, is forcing the narrator to remember and recount the torture of the communist agent, the reader learns that the officer in charge of the interrogation was the crapulent major, though he has turned over his responsibilities to the three policemen who carry out the torture (348). We must always remember that the facts of a story are the inventions of the author, and we must always ask why the author made the story just so. Nothing in reality required the major to be in charge, and nothing required the author to keep this point hidden from the reader until now. The narrator, just after the murder, had noted that the major was relatively innocent, but now we see that he was not innocent at all; even if he was not directly in charge of this interrogation, it was his responsibility, and no doubt he had participated in other interrogations.

Just after the narrator visits the major's wife, he goes to see Ms. Mori and there he finds Sonny, the Vietnamese journalist, who has evidently replaced the narrator in Ms. Mori's affections. Their interaction is tense, to say the least, and the narrator leaves knowing that he has lost this battle to Sonny.

Immediately after this little incident, the General takes the narrator to inspect the little army he has organized to return to Vietnam. Bon has decided to join this army, and the narrator wants to go along to protect him, his blood brother. But Sonny has also learned about this little army, and he publishes a story about it in his Vietnamese newspaper, with the headline "Move On, War Over" (227). The General is incensed. "Someone's been feeding this man some reliable information, Captain" (230). "And this newsman is peddling this leftist propaganda to poor people who are desperate for any kind of hope. He's getting more troublesome, don't you think?" (231).

> How do we know he's just a newsman? Half the newsmen in Saigon were communist sympathizers, and a good number were just communists. How do we know the communists didn't send him here years ago with exactly this plan in mind, to spy on any of us who made it here and undermine us? You knew him in college. Did he display these sympathies back then? . . . Why didn't you warn me of this when I met him? . . . Do you know what your problem is, Captain? I had rather a long list of my problems, but it was better to simply say I had no idea. You're too sympathetic, the General said. You didn't see the danger in the major because he was fat and you took pity on him for that. Now the evidence shows you've been willfully blind to the fact that Sonny is not only a left-wing radical but potentially a communist sleeper agent. . . . Something needs to be done, Captain. Don't you agree? (231)

Once again the General has charged an innocent man with the narrator's crime and has implicitly ordered the narrator to do something about it. The order becomes more explicit when the General makes the murder of Sonny a precondition for allowing the narrator to go back to Vietnam with the little army. "If what needs to be done is done, then you can return to our homeland" (265).

The narrator goes to Sonny's apartment and confronts him. Sonny believes that the narrator is angry because of Ms. Mori, and the reader may suspect that the narrator's motives are mixed. The narrator shoots Sonny several times; the description of the murder and its aftermath is detailed and vivid (276–78). This murder poses a great challenge for the reader, greater than the murder of the crapulent major, because there is no justification for it at all, except that it removes an obstacle in the way of the narrator's return to Vietnam. Sonny's death is collateral damage.

In a way, Sonny and the narrator are complementary characters. Both were born in Vietnam and came to the U.S. to study. They went to the same school, Occidental College, where the narrator maintained his cover of being a supporter of the South Vietnamese regime and Sonny was known as a campus leftist. The narrator returned to Vietnam, but Sonny stayed in the U.S. to avoid being drafted into the South Vietnamese army. When the narrator returns to the U.S., he maintains his cover, while Sonny has become a liberal journalist. And of course Sonny replaces the narrator in the affections of Ms. Mori. By killing Sonny, the narrator may be getting rid of what he might have been.

The Ending of *The Sympathizer*
In a sense this novel offers its own interpretation of itself. At the end of the story, when the narrator has his epiphany and realizes that the key was the meaning of nothing, he then asks, "But what was this meaning? What had I intuited at last? Namely this: while nothing is more precious than independence and freedom, *nothing is also more precious than independence and freedom!*" (375; see also 27). The first of these slogans, he says, is Ho Chi Minh's empty suit. "The second one was the tricky one, the joke. It was Uncle Ho's empty suit turned inside out" (375–76).

The narrator's interpretation of the story can be seen from several perspectives. The narrator's interpretation has an element of some kind of nihilism; as the narrator says, the question is a joke, with a punch line: "The answer is nothing! Nothing, nothing, *nothing!*" From this perspective, the answer is almost a Zen koan, which defeats logical understanding. From a different perspective, the answer depends on a kind of equivocation. The word "nothing" has two meanings. Nothing is both the absence of something and also something in itself. The narrator is talking about nothing, but he is also talking about "nothing." The commandant can see only the negative nothing, while the commissar and the narrator can see the positive nothing. That positive nothing, however, is also the void which the commissar sees as he looks in a mirror and sees the absence of his face. As he sees the void he understands the meaning of nothing—I presume he understands the meaning of "nothing." The play on the word "nothing" begins early in the story—"My mother called me her love child, but I do not like to dwell on that. In the end, my father got it right. He called me nothing at all" (21). From the perspective of the end of the novel, the narrator could mean "He didn't call me anything" or "He called me 'nothing.'"

The narrator's interpretation of "nothing" is also specifically applied to the Vietnamese revolution. Throughout the novel the narrator has criticized American imperialism, but he is someone who can see both sides; now he sees the failure of the Vietnamese revolution, as it has moved from "the vanguard of political change" to "the rearguard of hoarding power" (376). But all revolutions have similarly failed. "Having liberated ourselves in the name of independence and freedom—I was so tired of saying these words!—we then deprived our defeated brethren of the same" (376).

The revolution has no place for revolutionaries like him. Only the commissar, a man with no face, and the narrator, a man with two minds, can get the joke. "I was that man of two minds, me and myself. We had been through so much, me and myself" (376). He does not reject the revolution, but he questions it: "What do those who struggle against power do when they seize power? [...] Why do those who call for independence and freedom take away the independence and freedom of others? [...] Our life and our death have taught us always to sympathize with the undesirables among the undesirables" (381). "Yet we are not cynical. Despite it all—yes, despite everything, in the face of *nothing*—we still consider ourselves revolutionary. We remain that most hopeful of creatures, a revolutionary in search of a revolution" (382). The book ends on a note of hope:

> We lie in wait for the right moment and the just cause, which, at this moment, is simply wanting to live. And even as we write this final sentence, the sentence that will not be revised, we confess to being certain of one and only one thing—we swear to keep, on penalty of death, this one promise:
> *We will live!* (382)

I hardly know how to respond to this ending. On the one hand, it seems to call out for a political response. Different readers, no doubt, will have different political responses. Perhaps I should not leave mine unspoken. This novel is a work of art, after all, in my opinion a considerable work of art, and not a political tract. I do not believe, however, that art should be sealed off from the world. Novels, epics, plays, movies, these all come into existence in a world, a human world, and the human world is inevitably political. Some novels ask for more engagement, some for less, but none can escape that engagement entirely. This novel certainly does not ask to be read in some nonpolitical world of Platonic aesthetics. I respond to this novel, then, as an engaged leftist. I don't claim to be a revolutionary. I am not in search of a revolution, though if one were to come along, I hope I would choose the right side. In a sense, the revolution, some kind of revolution, is always there, waiting for us. There is always some situation that needs to be corrected, or at least ameliorated, and we don't have to wait for the Revolution in capital letters, to do what we can right now.

The ending also calls out for an aesthetic response. As an aesthetic principle, I suspect an ending that has to be printed in italics. The emphasis should be built into the shape of the story, not provided by typography. I fear that the author has not been able to imagine an ending adequate to the story he has told. Aesthetic questions may seem trivial when compared to the questions of public morality, but I think they are connected.

Some excellent novels have trouble with their endings. It may be that the greater the ambition of a novel, the more problematic the ending. The ending of *Catch-22,* for instance, seems to me to solve nothing (without solving *nothing,* to use our narrator's terms). Yossarian has a flash of insight, as our narrator has a flash of insight, but his insight does not really resolve the situation; desertion may (or may not) be Yossarian's best choice at the moment, but is not a viable way to live. The ending of *Huckleberry Finn* is notoriously unsatisfactory. There are various ways to state the problem— one is to note that the person who has been through Huck's experiences could not be the one who tells or who contrives this ending. Twain's problem, however, arose not just in the world of the novel but also in the world of the novelist. There was no place in the society of the shore for Huck and Jim. They were forced to return to the world of Tom Sawyer, who has not been through Huck's experiences and who probably could not have learned the lesson Huck learns. Twain's problem could not be solved until the Civil War, nor after the Civil War, and perhaps not yet. Twain could not solve or even clearly face this problem in *Huckleberry Finn;* perhaps he faced it at the end of *Pudd'nhead Wilson.*[14] I think similar criticisms can be brought to other ambitious novels, such as *Invisible Man, Crime and Punishment,* or *Kim. Moby-Dick* may escape simply by falling silent. Many novels—many great novels—succeed because they are less ambitious. It is not the task of every novel to solve the great problems or even to state them, and those that do may pay a price for their ambition.

But this political reading of the novel may miss the mark. The point of the story may be something deeper than ideology, and that is friendship. The narrator and his friends Bon and Man became blood brothers—"the three of us having sworn undying loyalty to one another by slicing our adolescent palms and mingling our blood in ritual handshakes" (10–11). This relationship endures even though the political commitments of the three diverge. As Man, the secret communist, tells Bon, the ardent anticommunist, "We're blood brothers, us three. We'll be blood brothers even if we lose this war, even if we lose our country. He looked at me and his eyes were damp. For us there is no end" (15; see also 16, 29).

> Like warriors of legend, we had sworn to die for one another, snared by the romance of schoolboy friendship, united by the eternal things we saw in each other: fidelity, honesty, conviction, the willingness to stand by friends and uphold beliefs. . . . I could not predict that Bon would one day join the Phoenix Program to avenge his murdered father, his task to assassinate the people whom Man and I considered comrades. And good-natured, sincere Bon did not know that Man and I would secretly come to believe that the only way to rescue our country was to become revolutionaries. All three of us followed our political beliefs, but only because of the reasons that led us to swear blood brotherhood in the first place. (35)

The narrator goes back to Vietnam with Bon because they are blood brothers. Man protects the narrator and Bon in the prison camp because they are blood brothers. And Man arranges for the narrator and Bon to leave the camp and go back to the U.S. because they are blood brothers.

The novel also explores the meaning of the self. At the beginning of chapter 21, as we have seen, the narrator starts to speak of himself in the third person (331); in chapter 22 he feels that his self has been divided (355); and in chapter 23, at the very end of novel, he speaks of himself in the plural:

> Besides a man with no face, only a man of two minds could get this joke, about how a revolution fought for independence and freedom

could make these things *worth less than nothing.* I was that man of two minds, me and myself. We had been through so much, me and myself. Everyone we met had tried to drive us apart from each other, wanted us to choose either one thing or another, except the commissar. He showed us his hand and we showed him ours, the red scars as indelible as they were in our youth. (376)

And this use of the plural continues to the very end of the book. The plural self is the same as the man with two minds, with two faces, the narrator we met in the first sentences of the novel. The ring composition invites the reader to see the ending in the beginning and the beginning in the ending.

Coda

The novel is a flexible genre, perhaps more flexible than any other literary form. There is no such thing as "the form" of the novel. To that extent G. K. Chesterton is right that the novel is "essentially formless," Thomas Pavel is right that there are "no written rules meant to govern prose narrative," and E. M. Forster is right that "principles and systems ... cannot be applicable" to the novel. But there is more to be said.

In this book and its companion volume, *How to Reread a Novel,* I explore some of the resources used by novelists (and other writers) to create and communicate meaning. *How to Reread a Novel* examines the narrative situation (the various roles of the narrator and the audience) and the language of narration (style and the figures of rhetoric). This volume describes some of the larger structures of the novel, from paragraphs to chapters and episodes up to the shapes of whole plots. These resources do not constitute principles and systems or a rule book that governs prose narrative; they are simply some of the tools used by novelists.

What is the form of a novel? What is the form of a piece of music? These questions are equally unanswerable because they are posed at the wrong level of analysis. There are many novel forms, just as there are many forms of musical composition, but there is no general form of a piece of music and no general form of the novel. We can, however, say something worthwhile about particular kinds of compositions, such as rondos or sonatas or the twelve-bar blues, and we can say something worthwhile about particular kinds of novels.

Many critics have noted that the action of a narrative generally begins with some instigating event, some event that creates some kind of instability in the world of the narrative; thus Phelan (2017, 10–11) says, "Plot dynamics typically develop through patterns of instability–complication–resolution. That is, an author generates a plot through introducing one or more characters in unstable situations, he advances the plot by complicating those instabilities, and he ends the plot by resolving those instabilities to one degree or another—or thematizing the impossibility of resolution." In chapter 4 of this book I have proposed that there are only a few types of such instigating events in common use; these are Birth, Death, Meeting, Arrival, Departure, and Lack (or its inverse, Gift). The ending of a novel may match the beginning to create a sense of closure: some typical endings are Departure, Return, Marriage, Death, Discovery, and Satisfaction.

The instigating events are the basis of a classification of subtypes of the novel. Not much can be said about the form of the novel as an overarching kind of literature, but quite a lot can be said about the various forms of the subtypes—novels that begin with a Birth, novels that begin with a Departure, and so on—as I have tried to demonstrate. There is no rule, however, that a novel must begin with one of these instigating events, or, indeed, with any specific instigating event at all, and no rule that the ending has to match the beginning.

This list of instigating events is derived from observation rather than from any prior principles. The list is not surprising, since these events are among the most important in the course of a life. Novels are not necessarily—and are never simply—representations of life, but neither are they unrelated to it.

More complex architectures can be fashioned through various transformations of the plot, especially—but not exclusively—through manipulation of the narrative chronology. The ending of a story may be brought forward to the beginning, as in C. S. Forester's *The General* or V. S. Naipaul's *A House for Mr. Biswas*. If a narrative begins *in medias res,* the situation before that beginning may be told in a retrospect; examples include Virgil's *Aeneid,* Vladimir Nabokov's *King, Queen, Knave,* and Willa Cather's *My Mortal Enemy*. The ending of a narrative may involve a revelation about events prior to the beginning, in a device I have called a Ghost from the Past, as in Henry James's *The American* or *The Portrait of a Lady*. The time of a narrative may be concentrated in a single day, as in Virginia Woolf's *Mrs. Dalloway* or John Barth's *The Floating Opera;* One-Day Novels usually include retrospects to fill in the story before the story. The action of a novel may take just a year, either exactly or approximately, as in Thomas Hardy's *The Return of the Native* or Jane Austen's *Emma*. Other kinds of complex forms include mirror plots, as in Anthony Burgess's *A Clockwork Orange* or

David Mitchell's *Cloud Atlas;* alternating chapters, as in Ursula K. Le Guin's *The Dispossesed;* or unnatural chronology, as in Alain Robbe-Grillet's *Jealousy* or Martin Amis's *Time's Arrow.* The history of this most flexible genre has been, and doubtless will continue to be, a history of innovation. The architecture of the novel is limited only by the imagination of novelists.

Notes

1. The Composition of *Emma* and *Mrs. Dalloway*

1. Spacing: 13, 30, 52, 62, 64, 104, 210; asterisks: 71, 185.
2. Other novels by Woolf do have explicit internal divisions; the chapter divisions in *The Years* are particularly interesting.
3. The book divisions in the Homeric epics were probably not made by the original composer, if there was such a person, but whoever made the divisions was generally sensitive to the episodic boundaries.
4. For other repetitions in an episode, see also "makintosh" at 139, 140, 141, 143; "sewing" at 158, 160, 161, 164, etc.
5. See also overlapping at 104–5, 114, and 156.
6. See also 12, 144, 157, 158, 163.
7. See 115, 116, 117, 118, 123.

2. Ring Composition

1. For references, see Whitman 1958, 253.
2. See Whitman 1958, Immerwahr 1966, Stanley 1993, and Douglas 2007.
3. See 139–49; 377–78; 402–3; and 538.
4. My analysis is indebted to Whitman 1958, 259 and MacLeod 1982, 16–35.

3. The Composition of *The Good Soldier* and *Catch-22*

1. See also 40, 42×2, 43, 44×3, 45×3, 46, 49, 61, 64, 72×2, 73, 74×3, 75×2, 76, 77, 78, 84, 89, 91×2, 92×2, 98, 101, 108, 109, 126, 144×2, 153, 154, 157×4, 158×2, 161, 166.
2. *Sentimental:* 29, 30, 49, 51, 63, 123, etc.; *intimacy:* 15, 29, 37, 47, 57, 94. etc.; *good people:* 34, 35, 37, 46, 55, 57, 59, etc.; *nice people:* 32, 33, 57, 116, etc.; *passion:* 29, 51, 52, 72, 77, 96, 97, etc.; *remorse:* 57, 64, 71, 72, 74, etc.; *sad:* 13, 30, 47, 182, 197, etc.; *hate:* 29, 60, 61, 111, 141, etc.

3. The anonymous peer reviewer for the Press notes that German "Kur" and French "cours" in this passage sound like "coeur" (heart).

4. See "profession" on page 44; "odd intimacy" on page 47; "Papists" on page 53; "terrible" on page 60; "trick" on page 63; "solid and serious virtues" on pages 69–70; and so on.

5. See also "sentiment," "sentimentalists," and "sentimental" on page 29; "nicer," "nice," "nice," and "nice" on pages 32–33; "good people" on pages 34–35; "flame" on pages 176–77; and so on.

6. I have found links from Chapters 1 to 2, 2 to 3, 3 to 4, 7 to 8, 8 to 10, 10 to 11, 11 to 12, 13 to 14, 14 to 15, 15 to 16, 16 to 17, 17 to 18, 19 to 20, 20 to 21, 21 to 22, 22 to 23, 26 to 27, 27 to 28, 28 to 29, 29 to 30, 30 to 31, 32 to 33, 33 to 34, 35 to 36, 36 to 37, 37 to 38, 39 to 40, and 40 to 41. I do not find links from Chapters 4 to 5, 5 to 6, 6 to 7, 8 to 9, 9 to 10, 12 to 13, 23 to 24, 24 to 25, 31 to 32, 34 to 35, 38 to 39, and 41 to 42.

7. See 66, 231–33, 239, 251–54, 256, 259, 263.

8. See also 104 to 124; 140 to 144; and so on.

4. Simple Plot Forms

1. See, for instance, Bal 1985, 5; Chatman 1978, 31; Genette 1980, 27; Rimmon-Kenan 1983, 3.

2. For an earlier discussion of these definitions, see Clark 2002.

3. See Dorfman 1969 for discussion of Insult in medieval epic narrative.

4. See Muir 1929, 62ff, for discussion of space in the character novel and time in the dramatic novel.

5. The anonymous peer reviewer for the Press notes that Dorothy Sayer's *The Nine Tailors* is an exception.

6. *La Peste* and *Blindness* may, however, be instances of a possible seventh category, General Catastrophe. Other examples might include M. P. Shiel's *The Purple Cloud,* Sir Arthur Conan Doyle's *The Poison Belt,* and Robert Heinlein's *The Puppet Masters.*

6. Complex Plot Forms, Part II

1. For discussion of *Emma* as a One-Year Novel, see Clark and Phelan 2020, 71.

2. For further discussion of unnatural chronology, see Richardson 2015, 30–32 and 101–110.

3. See Clark 2010, 142–46.

4. See 75, 78, 82, 87, 88, 90, 93, 102, 125, 127, 131–32, 133.

5. See 55, 56, 66–68, 123; there are many other references to her hair throughout the novel.

6. See 68, 69, 96–97, 104, 113, 114.

7. Viet Thanh Nguyen's *The Sympathizer*

1. In 2021 Nguyen published a sequel, *The Committed,* which I do not discuss here; this sequel resolves some, but not all, of the questions raised by *The Sympathizer* and adds new questions of its own. I will not be surprised to see the series continue with a third volume.

2. See also 113, 181, 248, 281, 290, 299, 304, 326, 344–45, 355, 358, 360, 365–66, 379.

3. See also 9, 15, 114, 175, 182, 186, 189, 190, 214, 218, 224, 232, 305, 306–7, 361.

4. See also 55, 92, 157, 173, 199, 361.

5. See 33, 38, 69, 70, 100, 104, 168, 238, 242, 258, 298–99, 353–54.

6. See also 158, 179, 192, 194, 189–90, 322, 328, 369, 373, 380.

7. This episode in the hospital and a later episode at the end of the narrator's reeducation both draw on the hospital episode in chapter 11 of Ellison's *Invisible Man*.

8. See also 53, 141, 207–8, 224, 291, 307, 314, 324, 341, 377.

9. There may be a reference here to St. Jerome's vision of Jesus, who charged him with being more Ciceronian than Christian.

10. The narrator of Ellison's *Invisible Man* is also nameless.

11. See also 76, 117, 153, 272, 273.

12. See also 300: "Somebody was screaming and it was not me. Somebody was cursing and it was not me."

13. See 3, 36, 57, 59, 61, 102, 103, 136, 145, 155, 195, 231, etc.

14. *Huckleberry Finn* was first published in 1884. One might say that the narrator, writing before the Civil War, could not find an adequate ending; nor could the author, writing after the Civil War.

References

Abel, Elizabeth. 1988. "Narrative Structure(s) and Female Development." In Bloom 1988: 103–25.
Agee, James. 2009 (1957). *A Death in the Family*. London: Penguin Classics.
Ambler, Eric. 1967 (1959). *Passage of Arms*. London: Fontana.
Amis, Martin. 1998 (1991). *Time's Arrow*. Toronto: Penguin Canada.
Apuleius. 1998. *The Golden Ass, or, Metamorphoses*. Translated with Introduction and Notes by E. J. Kenney. London: Penguin Books.
Armstrong, Paul. 1987. "Obscurity and Reflection in *The Good Soldier*." Chapter 5 in *The Challenge of Bewilderment: Understanding and Representation in James, Conrad, and Ford*, 189–224. Ithaca, NY: Cornell University Press.
Auerbach, Erich. 1957. *Mimesis: The Representation of Reality in Western Literature*. Translated by Willard Trask. New York: Doubleday & Company.
Austen, Jane. 2012 (1815). *Emma*. New York: W. W. Norton & Company.
———. 2003 (1818). *Persuasion*. London: Penguin Books.
———. 2001 (1813). *Pride and Prejudice*. New York: W. W. Norton & Company.
———. 2001 (1811). *Sense and Sensibility*. New York: The Modern Library (Random House).
Bal, Mieke. 1985. *Narratology: Introduction to the Theory of Narrative*. Translated by Christine van Boheemen. Toronto: University of Toronto Press.
Balzac, Honoré de. 1955 (1833). *Eugénie Grandet*. London: Penguin Classics.
Barth, John. 1988. *"The Floating Opera" and "The End of the Road."* New York: Anchor Books/Random House.
———. 1966. *Giles Goat-Boy*. Garden City, NY: Doubleday & Company.
———. 1960. *The Sot-Weed Factor*. New York: Grosset & Dunlap.
Baum, L. Frank. 2021 (1900). *The Wonderful Wizard of Oz*. Oxford: Benediction Classics.
Bellow, Saul. 2003 (1956). *Seize the Day*. London: Penguin Classics.
Benediktson, D. Thomas. 2013. "Ring Structures in Homeric Similes." *Quaderni Urbinati di Cultura Classica* 105, no. 3 (2013): 29–44.

Bennett, Arnold. 1983 (1908). *The Old Wives' Tale*. Harmondsworth: Penguin Books.

Bird, Robert Montgomery. 2008 (1836). *Sheppard Lee: Written by Himself*. New York: New York Review of Books.

Bloom, Harold, ed. 1988. *Virginia Woolf's "Mrs. Dalloway."* New York: Chelsea House Publishers.

Brontë, Charlotte. 2006 (1847). *Jane Eyre*. London: Penguin Classics.

Burgess, Anthony. 1986 (1962). *A Clockwork Orange*. New York: W. W. Norton.

Burroughs, Edgar Rice. 2007 (1917). *A Princess of Mars*. London: Penguin Classics.

Butler, Octavia E. 2004 (1979). *Kindred*. Boston: Beacon Press.

Camus, Albert. 1947. *La Peste*. Paris: Gallimard.

———. 1973. *The Plague* [*La Peste*]. Translated by Stuart Gilbert. Harmondsworth: Penguin.

Cather, Willa. 1972 (1923). *A Lost Lady*. New York: Vintage Books.

———. 1935. *Lucy Gayheart*. Toronto: Ryerson Press.

———. 1926. *My Mortal Enemy*. Toronto: Macmillan Co. of Canada.

———. 1950 (1922). *One of Ours*. New York: Random House.

———. 1971 (1931). *Shadows on the Rock*. New York: Vintage Books.

Chatman, Seymour. 1978. *Story and Discourse: Narrative Structure in Fiction and Film*. Ithaca, NY: Cornell University Press.

Chesterton, Gilbert Keith. 1911. *Appreciations and Criticism of the Works of Charles Dickens*. London: J. M. Dent and Sons.

Christie, Agatha. 2011 (1934). *Murder on the Orient Express*. New York: HarperCollins.

Clark, Matthew. 2002. *A Matter of Style: On Writing and Technique*. Toronto: Oxford University Press.

———. 2010. *Narrative Structures and the Language of the Self*. Columbus: Ohio State University Press.

Clark, Matthew, and James Phelan. 2020. *Debating Rhetorical Narratology: On the Synthetic, Mimetic, and Thematic Aspects of Narrative*. Columbus: Ohio State University Press.

Defoe, Daniel. 2011 (1722). *Moll Flanders*. Oxford: Oxford World Classics.

———. 2008 (1719). *Robinson Crusoe*. Oxford: Oxford World Classics.

———. 2008 (1724). *Roxana*. Oxford: Oxford World Classics.

Díaz, Junot. 2008 (2007). *The Brief Wondrous Life of Oscar Wao*. New York: Riverhead Books.

Dick, Philip K. 1992 (1975). *Confessions of a Crap Artist*. New York: Vintage Books.

———. 2007 (1968). *Do Androids Dream of Electric Sheep?* Oxford: Oxford University Press.

Dickens, Charles. 1990 (1850). *David Copperfield*. New York: W. W. Norton & Company.
———. 2002 (1848). *Dombey and Son*. London: Penguin Classics.
———. 1965 (1860–61). *Great Expectations*. Harmondsworth: Penguin Books.
———. 1980 (1855–57). *Little Dorrit*. London: Penguin Books.
———. 2009 (1839). *Nicholas Nickleby*. Oxford: Oxford World Classics.
———. 2003 (1838). *Oliver Twist*. London: Penguin Classics.
———. 1981 (1859). *A Tale of Two Cities*. New York: Bantam Books.
Dorfman, Eugene. 1969. *The Nareme in the Medieval Romance Epic: An Introduction to Narrative Structures*. Toronto: University of Toronto Press.
Dostoyevsky, Fyodor. 2009. *"Notes from Underground" and "The Double."* Translated by Ronald Wilks. London: Penguin Books.
Douglas, Mary. 2007. *Thinking in Circles: An Essay on Ring Composition*. New Haven, CT: Yale University Press.
Doyle, Sir Arthur Conan. 2001 (1913). *The Poison Belt*. Lincoln: University of Nebraska Press.
Eliot, George (Mary Ann Evans). 2016 (1876). *Daniel Deronda*. London: Vintage Classics.
———. 1956 (1871–72). *Middlemarch: A Study of Provincial Life*. Boston: Houghton Mifflin Company.
———. 1980 (1860). *The Mill on the Floss*. Harmondsworth: Penguin Books.
———. 1985 (1861). *Silas Marner*. London: Penguin Books.
Ellison, Ralph. 1980 (1952). *Invisible Man*. New York: Vintage International.
Erlich, Victor. 1965. *Russian Formalism: History, Doctrine*. The Hague: Mouton & Co.
Faulkner, William. 1991 (1930). *As I Lay Dying*. New York: Vintage Books.
———. 2012 (1932). *Light in August*. The Corrected Text. New York: Random House.
Fielding, Henry. 1950 (1749). *Tom Jones*. New York: Random House.
Finney, Charles G. 2001 (1935). *The Circus of Dr. Lao*. Lincoln: University of Nebraska Press.
Flaubert, Gustave. 2004 (1964). *Sentimental Education*. London: Penguin Classics.
Ford, Ford Madox. 1997 (1915). *The Good Soldier: A Tale of Passion*. New York: Penguin.
———. 2019 (1950). *Parade's End*. London: Penguin Classics.
Forester, C. S. 2017 (1936). *The General*. Glasgow: William Collins.
Forster, E. M. 1927. *Aspects of the Novel*. New York: Harcourt, Brace & World.
García Márquez, Gabriel. 1988 (1985). *Love in the Time of Cholera*. New York: Penguin.

Gaskell, Elizabeth. 1970 (1854–55). *North and South*. Harmondsworth: Penguin Books.
Genette, Gérard. 1982. *Figures of Literary Discourse*. Translated by Alan Sheridan. New York: Columbia University Press.
———. 1980. *Narrative Discourse: An Essay in Method*. Translated by Jane E. Lewin. Ithaca, NY: Cornell University Press.
Glasgow, Ellen. 1995 (1926). *The Romantic Comedians*. Charlotte: University of Virginia Press.
Gogol, Nikolai. 1987. "The Nose." In *Diary of a Madman and Other Stories*, 42–70. Translated by Ronald Wilks. London: Penguin Books.
Golding, William. 2011 (1954). *Lord of the Flies*. New York: Perigee (Penguin Group).
———. 2005 (1956). *Pincher Martin*. London: Faber & Faber.
Grass, Günter. 2010 (1959). *The Tin Drum*. New York: HarperCollins.
Graves, Robert. 1989 (1957). *They Hanged My Saintly Billy*. London: Xanadu Publications.
Greene, Graham. 1983 (1932). *Stamboul Train*. London: Penguin Books.
———. 2004 (1955). *The Quiet American*. New York: Vintage Classics.
Haggard, H. Rider. 1995 (1887). *Allan Quartermain*. Oxford: Oxford World Classics.
———. 2008 (1885). *King Solomon's Mines*. London: Penguin Classics.
Hardy, Thomas. 1968 (1895). *Jude the Obscure*. New York: St Martin's Press.
———. 1974 (1878). *The Return of the Native*. London: Macmillan.
Hartley, L. P. 2002 (1953). *The Go-Between*. New York: New York Review Press.
Harari, Yuval Noah. 2017. *Homo Deus: A Brief History of Tomorrow*. Toronto: McClelland & Stewart.
Heinlein, Robert A. 1976 (1959). "All You Zombies." In *The Unpleasant Profession of Jonathan Hoag*. New York: Berkley Publishing Corporation.
———. 1958. *Have Spacesuit, Will Travel*. New York: Ballantine Books.
———. 2003 (1951). *The Puppet Masters*. Riverdale, NY: Baen Publishing.
———. 2011 (1953). *Starman Jones*. Riverdale, NY: Baen Publishing.
———. 1956. *Time for the Stars*. New York: Ace Books.
———. 1955. *Tunnel in the Sky*. New York: Ace Books.
Heller, Joseph. 2011 (1961). *Catch-22*. New York: Simon & Schuster.
Hemingway, Ernest. 1997 (1929). *A Farewell to Arms*. New York: Scribner.
Homer. 1961. *The Iliad of Homer*. Translated by Richmond Lattimore. Chicago: University of Chicago Press.
———. 1991. *The Odyssey of Homer*. Translated by Richmond Lattimore. New York: HarperCollins.
Immerwahr, Henry R. 1966. *Form and Thought in Herodotus*. Cleveland, OH: Press of Western Reserve University.

Isherwood, Christopher. 2013 (1964). *A Single Man*. New York: Farrar, Straus & Giroux.
James, Henry. 1973 (1903). *The Ambassadors*. Harmondsworth: Penguin Books.
———. 1981 (1876–77). *The American*. London: Penguin Books.
———. 1964 (1880-81). *The Portrait of a Lady*. New York: New American Library.
———. 1965 (1875). *Roderick Hudson*. Harmondsworth: Penguin Books.
———. 2007 (1880). *Washington Square*. London: Penguin Classics.
———. 1964 (1902). *The Wings of the Dove*. New York: New American Library.
Joyce, James. 1964 (1916). *A Portrait of the Artist as a Young Man*. Harmondsworth: Penguin Modern Classics.
———. 2022 (1922). *Ulysses*. New York: Vintage Classics.
Kesey, Ken. 1962. *One Flew Over the Cuckoo's Nest*. New York: Viking Press.
Kipling, Rudyard. 1978 (1901). *Kim*. London: Pan Books.
Knowles, John. 2003 (1959). *A Separate Peace*. New York: Scribner.
Lanham, Richard. 1991. *A Handlist of Rhetorical Terms*. Second Edition. Berkeley: University of California Press.
Le Guin, Ursula K. 1985. *Always Coming Home*. New York: Harper & Row.
———. 2014 (1974). *The Dispossessed*. New York: HarperCollins.
Levenson, Michael. 1984. "Character in *The Good Soldier*," *Twentieth Century Literature* 30, no. 4 (Winter 1984): 373–87.
Longus. 1989. *Daphnis and Chloe*. In *Collected Ancient Greek Novels*. Edited by B. P. Reardon. Berkeley: University of California Press.
Lowry, Malcolm. 2007 (1947). *Under the Volcano*. New York: Harper Perennial Modern Classics.
MacLeod, Colin, ed. 1982. *Homer: "Iliad," Book XXIV*. Cambridge: Cambridge University Press.
Mann, Thomas. 1996 (1924). *The Magic Mountain*. New York: Vintage International.
Matheson, Richard. 2007 (1954). *I Am Legend*. New York: Tor Publishing.
———. 2016 (1956). *The Shrinking Man*. Studio City, CA: IDW Publishing.
Melville, Herman. 1954 (1857). *The Confidence-Man: His Masquerade*. New York: Signet Classic/New American Library.
———. 1972 (1851). *Moby-Dick; or, The Whale*. Harmondsworth: Penguin Books.
Miéville, China. 2018 (2016). *The Last Days of New Paris*. New York: Del Rey.
Millgate, Michael. 1987. "'A Novel: Not an Anecdote': Faulkner's *Light in August*." In Millgate, ed. 1987. *New Essays on "Light in August."* Cambridge: Cambridge University Press.
Morrison, Toni. 2007 (1970). *The Bluest Eye*. New York: Vintage International.
———. 2004 (1992). *Jazz*. New York: Random House.
Muir, Edwin. 1929. *The Structure of the Novel*. New York: Harcourt, Brace & World.

Nabokov, Vladimir. 1968 (1928). *King, Queen, Knave*. New York: McGraw Hill Book Company.

———. 1978 (1938). *Laughter in the Dark*. New York: New Directions.

———. 1984 (1955). *Lolita*. London: Weidenfeld & Nicolson.

———. 1985 (1957). *Pnin*. New York: Vintage Books

Naipaul, V. S. 1993 (1961). *A House for Mr. Biswas*. London: Penguin.

Nguyen, Viet Thanh. 2021. *The Committed*. New York: Grove Press.

———. 2015. *The Sympathizer*. New York: Grove Press.

O'Brien, Flann. 1999 (1967). *The Third Policeman*. Dallas, TX: Dalkey Archive Press.

Pavel, Thomas. 2013. *The Lives of the Novel: A History*. Princeton, NJ: Princeton University Press.

Phelan, James. 2007. *Experiencing Fiction: Judgments, Progressions, and the Rhetorical Theory of Narrative*. Columbus: Ohio State University Press.

———. 2017. *Somebody Telling Somebody Else: A Rhetorical Poetics of Narrative*. Columbus: Ohio State University Press.

Plato. 1961. *The Collected Dialogues of Plato*. Edited by Huntingon Cairns and Edith Hamilton. Princeton, NJ: Princeton University Press.

———. 1961. *Euthyphro*. In *The Collected Dialogues of Plato*, 169–185.

———. 1961. *The Republic*. In *The Collected Dialogues of Plato*, 575–844.

Porter, Katherine Anne. 1984 (1962). *Ship of Fools*. New York: Little, Brown & Company.

Prince, Gerald. 1987. *Dictionary of Narratology*. Lincoln: University of Nebraska Press.

Puig, Manuel. 1991 (1976). *Kiss of the Spider Woman*. New York: Vintage International.

Ray, Robert J. 1963. "Style in *The Good Soldier*." *Modern Fiction Studies* 9, no. 1 (Spring 1963): 61–66.

Richardson, Brian. 2015. *Unnatural Narrative: Theory, History, Practice*. Columbus: Ohio State University Press.

Rimmon-Kenan, Shlomith. 1983. *Narrative Fiction: Contemporary Poetics*. London: Methuen.

Robbe-Grillet, Alain. 1964. *The Erasers*. New York: Grove Press.

———. 1957. *La Jalousie*. Paris: Les Editions de Minuit.

———. 1965. *Two Novels by Robbe-Grillet: "Jealousy" and "In the Labyrinth."* Translated by Richard Howard. New York: Grove Press.

Roth, Henry. 1991 (1934). *Call It Sleep*. New York: Farrar, Straus & Giroux.

Roth, Philip. 1994 (1972). *The Breast*. New York: Vintage International.

Scholes, Robert. 1974. *Structuralism in Literature*. New Haven, CT: Yale University Press.

Schorer, Mark. 1948. "The Good Novelist in *The Good Soldier.*" *Princeton University Library Chronicle* 9, no. 3 (April 1948): 128–33.
Shiel, M. P. 2012 (1901). *The Purple Cloud.* London: Penguin Classics.
Stanley, Keith. 1993. *The Shield of Homer: Narrative Structure in the "Iliad."* Princeton, NJ: Princeton University Press.
Stein, Gertrude. 1990 (1909). *Three Lives.* London: Penguin Books.
Sternberg, Meir. 1987. *The Poetics of Biblical Narrative.* Bloomington: Indiana University Press.
Sterne, Laurence. 1964 (1759–1767). *The Life & Opinions of Tristram Shandy, Gent.* New York: Holt, Rinehart & Winston.
Stevenson, Robert Louis. 1994 (1886). *Kidnapped.* London: Penguin Classics.
———. 2008 (1886). *The Strange Case of Dr. Jekyll and Mr. Hyde.* Oxford: Oxford World Classics.
———. 1999 (1883). *Treasure Island.* London: Penguin Classics.
Stout, Rex. 1957. *Before Midnight.* New York: Bantam Books.
———. 1967 (1966). *Death of a Doxy.* New York: Bantam Books.
———. 1963 (1961). *The Final Deduction.* New York: Bantam Books.
———. 1959 (1957). *If Death Ever Slept.* New York: Bantam Books.
———. 1958 (1956). *Might As Well Be Dead.* New York: Bantam Books.
———. 1948 (1946). *The Silent Speaker.* New York: Bantam Books.
Thackeray, William Makepeace. 2003 (1847–48). *Vanity Fair.* London: Penguin Classics.
Tolkien, J. R. R. 1997 (1937). *The Hobbit.* Boston: Houghton Mifflin.
———. 2005 (1954–1955). *The Lord of the Rings.* Three Volumes. London: HarperCollins.
Trollope, Anthony. 1984 (1857). *Barchester Towers.* London: Penguin Classics.
———. 2004 (1858). *Doctor Thorne.* London: Penguin Books.
———. 2004 (1861). *Framley Parsonage.* London: Penguin Books.
Twain, Mark (Samuel Clemens). 1912 (1884). *The Adventures of Huckleberry Finn.* New York: P. F. Collier & Son.
———. 1997 (1881). *The Prince and the Pauper.* London: Penguin Classics.
Updike, John. 2012 (1959). *The Poorhouse Fair.* New York: Random House.
Virgil. 2008. *The Aeneid.* Translated by Sarah Ruden. New Haven, CT: Yale University Press.
Voltaire. 1961. *Romans de Voltaire.* Paris: Gallimard.
Vonnegut, Kurt. 1980 (1952). *Player Piano.* New York: Random House.
———. 2004 (1959). *The Sirens of Titan.* London: Orion Publishing Group.
Wallace, David Foster. 2016 (1996). *Infinite Jest.* New York: Back Bay Books.
Welty, Eudora. 2002 (1972). *The Optimist's Daughter.* New York: Random House.

Wharton, Edith. 1986 (1925). *The Mother's Recompense*. New York: Charles Scribner's Sons.
Whitman, Cedric. 1958. *Homer and the Heroic Tradition*. Cambridge, MA: Harvard University Press.
Woolf, Virginia. 1993 (1925). *Mrs. Dalloway*. New York: Alfred A. Knopf.
———. 1977 (1937). *The Years*. London: Granada Publishing.
Yates, Richard. 2008 (1961). *Revolutionary Road*. New York: Vintage Books.
Zola, Émile. 1954 (1885). *Germinal*. Translated by Leonard Tancock. London: Penguin.

Index

Abel, Elizabeth, 130
abrupt transitions, 20, 78
action(s): Arrival, 99, 191; Departure, 99; digressions, 35–36; Ghosts from the Past, 122–23; One-Day Novels, 130–33; plot rings, 44; rings in Nguyen's *Sympathizer*, 182; Second Chapter Retrospects, 119; segments and links in Austen's *Emma*, 16–17; unnatural chronology in Robbe-Grillet's *Jealousy* (*Jalousie*), 145–47. *See also* plots
Adventures of Huckleberry Finn (Twain), 94, 98, 187, 195n14
adverbs, 113, 126–28
Aeneid (Virgil), 37, 116–17, 191
aesthetic reading of Nguyen's *Sympathizer*, 187
Agee, James, 103
Alice's Adventures in Wonderland (Carroll), 47
Alice Through the Looking Glass (Carroll), 47
Allan Quartermain (Haggard), 97, 151
alliteration, 70, 160
allusions, 6, 157–58
"All You Zombies" (Heinlein), 143
alternating chapters, 136–41, 143, 192
Always Coming Home (Le Guin), 152
Ambassadors, The (James), 11
Ambler, Eric, 135

American, The (James), 92, 94, 110–11, 122–24, 191
Amis, Martin, 143–44, 192
anachronies, 47, 112–13, 130–31
anadiplosis, 13–15, 53, 65, 70, 123, 160
anagnorisis, 122
analepsis, 29–30, 126–27
anaphora, 13–15, 17, 53, 55, 70, 160, 162
Anna Karenina (Tolstoy), 92
antithesis, 70, 160–62
Apocalypse Now (film), 158
apodosis, 163
Apollonius of Rhodes, 95–96
apostrophe, 161
Apuleius, 109
archaeological time, 133
Argonautica (Apollonius of Rhodes), 95–96
Aristotle, 93, 122
Armstrong, Paul, 66
Arrival(s), 93–100; Dick's *Confessions of a Crap Artist*, 138; divisions of the whole narrative, 11; as instigating event, 191; Le Guin's *Dispossessed*, 137–38; Meeting, 107; Nguyen's *Sympathizer*, 154; Second Chapter Retrospects, 117–18; uncommon Beginnings, 109
As I Lay Dying (Faulkner), 103
asterisks, 9, 193n1
Astrophel and Stella (Sidney), 30

205

asyndeton, 160
Auerbach, Erich, 33
Austen, Jane: *Emma,* 11, 13–18, 125, 133, 191, 194n1; *Persuasion,* 99; *Pride and Prejudice,* 11, 92, 94, 97, 107, 125; *Sense and Sensibility,* 102, 107
autobiographies, 104

Balzac, Honoré de, 107, 160
Barchester Towers (Trollope), 102–3
Barth, John, 10, 131, 150, 191
Baum, L. Frank, 99–100
Before Midnight (Stout), 103
Beginning(s): Beginning, Middle, End, 92–95; Beginning with the Ending, 113–16, 132; common, 93–95, 100; Departure Beginning, 93–95, 117; Nguyen's *Sympathizer,* 156–59; uncommon, 109–11; zero beginnings and zero endings, 94–95. *See also* Ending(s); Middle(s)
Bellow, Saul, 131
Bennett, Arnold, 4, 11–12, 32
Bird, Robert Montgomery, 10, 101
Birth, 104–7
Blake, William, 158
Blindness (Saramago), 109, 194n6
Bluest Eye, The (Morrison), 133
book divisions, 10–12, 193n3
Breast, The (Roth), 109
Brief Wondrous Life of Oscar Wao, The (Díaz), 151
Brontë, Charlotte, 97, 124
Burgess, Anthony, 59, 134–35, 191
Burroughs, Edgar Rice, 97, 99–100, 151
Butler, Octavia E., 100

Cabell, James Branch, 47, 95
Call It Sleep (Roth), 30–31
Camus, Albert, 109, 182, 194n6
Candide (Voltaire), 98, 150

Canterbury Tales, The (Chaucer), 158
capitalization, 3
Carroll, Lewis, 47
Catch-22 (Heller), 69–89; characters, 71–73; Ending(s), 87–89, 187; fragmented narration, 82–85; inversions, 71–77, 85; links, 77–81, 194n6; paradoxes, 71–77, 85; reality and language, 75–76; repetitions in, 82–83, 85; rings, 85–89; style and rhetorical figures, 70–71, 85; unnatural chronology, 143
Cather, Willa, 10, 119–21, 133, 191
chapters: chapter anadiplosis, 15; chapter divisions in Woolf, 19, 193n2; chapter links in Austen's *Emma,* 15–16; chapter links in Heller's *Catch-22,* 79–81; chapter links in Nguyen's *Sympathizer,* 168, 173–75, 178; chapter links replaced by overlapping focalization, 20–21; chapter rings in Dickens's *Little Dorrit,* 37–38; chapter rings in Hardy's *Return of the Native,* 36; chapter titles, 9–13; chapter transitions in Austen's *Emma,* 18; chapter transitions in Heller's *Catch-22,* 80; chapter transitions in Le Guin's *Dispossessed,* 137–38; divisions of the whole narrative, 9–13; segmentation, 8
chapters, linked but not continuous, 7–8, 15–17, 66, 174
characters: complex rings, 39; Ghosts from the Past, 122; Heller's *Catch-22,* 71–73; Nguyen's *Sympathizer,* 155–56; plot rings, 44–45; readers' feelings about, 180–85; science-fiction stories, 99–100; Set-up, 94; Woolf's *Mrs. Dalloway,* 18, 20–21
Chatman, Seymour, 91
Chaucer, Geoffrey, 158

Chesterton, G. K., 1, 190
chiasmus, 29, 54, 161, 162
Christie, Agatha, 99
chronological progression. *See* progressive time
chronology: anachronies, 112–13; deviations from, 112–13, 114, 125–29, 191; fragmented narration, 83–85; inverted chronology, 143–44; manipulation of, 114, 191–92; plot time, 90–92; Second Chapter Retrospects, 94–95, 113, 116–22, 128, 143; underlying chronology, 91, 143; unnatural chronology, 143–49, 192, 194n2
Circus of Dr. Lao, The (Finney), 99, 131, 151–52
Civil War, 187, 195n14
clauses, 13, 163
climax, 69, 85, 88, 141, 169, 182
Clockwork Orange, A (Burgess), 59, 134–35, 191
Cloud Atlas (Mitchell), 136, 192
clusters, 14, 19, 56, 60–62, 64–65
Committed, The (Nguyen), 195n1
common Beginnings, 93–95, 100
comparison, 44, 47, 135, 157
complex plot forms, 112–29, 130–52; alternating chapters, 136–41; Beginning with the Ending, 113–16; Ghosts from the Past, 122–25; mirror plots, 134–36, 191–92; Multiple Retrospects, 113, 125–29; non-narrative elements in narrative, 149–52; One-Day Novels, 130–32; One-Year Novels, 132–33; Second Chapter Retrospects, 116–22; simultaneous narration, 141–43; unnatural chronology, 143–49, 192, 194n2
complex rings, 38–43
Confessions of a Crap Artist (Dick), 138–39
Confidence-Man, The (Melville), 130

congeries, 24–25, 70, 152, 161, 162–63, 174, 177
continuous narration, 7–9. *See also* chapters, linked but not continuous
Coppola, Francis Ford, 158
correctio, 59, 66–69, 160
correction, 51
Crime and Punishment (Dostoyevsky), 187
cross-references, 116
cyclical time, 47, 133

Daniel Deronda (Eliot), 11
Daphnis and Chloe (Longus), 104
David Copperfield (Dickens), 104–6
Death, 100–104
Death in the Family, A (Agee), 103
Death of a Doxy (Stout), 103
dedication, 92
Defoe, Daniel, 150
de Maupassant, Guy, 98
Departure, 98–99; Arrival, 100; Departure Beginning, 93–95, 117; Lack or Need, 95–97; Meeting, 107; Nguyen's *Sympathizer*, 154; Second Chapter Retrospects, 117–18; uncommon Beginnings, 109–10
deviations from chronology, 112–13, 114, 125–29
diacope, 30
dialogue, digressions in, 35
Díaz, Junot, 151
Dick, Philip K., 131, 138–39
Dickens, Charles: *David Copperfield*, 104–6; *Great Expectations*, 108; installments, 11; *Little Dorrit*, 32, 37–38; *Nicholas Nickleby*, 102–3; objects, 160; *Oliver Twist*, 102, 104; *A Tale of Two Cities*, 10
digressions: Dickens's *Little Dorrit*, 38; digressive rings, 33–36, 41; Homer's *Odyssey*, 33; intercalated digression,

Index 207

digressions (*continued*)
16; Second Chapter Retrospects, 117–18; Sterne's *Tristram Shandy*, 34–35; Trollope's *Doctor Thorne*, 39–40; Trollope's *Framley Parsonage*, 35–36
dinumeratio, 55–56
disclaimers, 150
Dispossessed, The (Le Guin), 136–38, 139, 143, 192
divisions of the whole narrative, 9–13
Do Androids Dream of Electric Sheep? (Dick), 131
Doctor Thorne (Trollope), 38–43, 96–97
Dombey and Son (Dickens), 102
Dostoyevsky, Fyodor, 157–59, 187
Douglas, Mary, 29
Doyle, Sir Arthur Conan, 194n6
dream rings, 47–49

"editorial authentication," 150
Eliot, George, 4, 10, 11, 97–98
Eliot, T. S., 158
Ellison, Ralph, 116, 157–59, 168, 187, 195n7, 195n10
Emerson, Ralph Waldo, 158
Emma (Austen): episodes, 11; Ghosts from the Past, 125; links, 13–18; One-Year Novels, 133, 191, 194n1; repetitions, 13–17; segmentation, 13–18
emotion, 54–55, 57–58, 85, 103, 160, 162–63
Ending(s): Beginning, Middle, End, 92–95, 191; Beginning with the Ending, 113–16, 132; Heller's *Catch-22*, 87–89, 187; Nguyen's *Sympathizer*, 185–89; zero beginnings and zero endings, 132
English novels, 97, 150
enlightenment, 95, 108, 178–79
epanalepsis, 29–30, 54
epics, 1, 11, 37, 95, 116–18, 186–87, 193n3, 194n3
epigraphs, 10, 12, 92

epilogues, 113–16, 132, 133
epimone, 59–60, 161, 163
episodes, 7; divisions of the whole narrative, 10–13, 98; repetitions in, 19, 193n4; rings, 23–24
epistrophe, 13–14, 54, 70, 160
epitheton, 56, 160, 171
epizeuxis, 53, 55, 160
equilibrium, 92–93
equivocation, 161, 169, 185
Erasers, The (Robbe-Grillet), 131
Eugénie Grandet (Balzac), 107
extended epizeuxis, 53, 160
external narration, 139

Fall, The (Camus), 182
fantasy, 89, 99–100
Farewell to Arms, A (Hemingway), 7–9
Faulkner, William, 45–47, 99, 103
"fictional authentications," 150
fictional biographies and autobiographies, 104
Fielding, Henry, 9–10, 11, 104
Final Deduction, The (Stout), 103
final repetition. *See* epistrophe
Finney, Charles G., 99, 131, 151–52
first-person narration, 138, 157, 174, 177
first sentences, 92
Fitzgerald, F. Scott, 181
flashbacks, 38, 41, 92
flashes of insight, 179, 187
Flaubert, Gustave, 108–9
flesh-and-blood reader, 159, 170
Floating Opera, The (Barth), 131, 191
focalization, 9, 18–28, 122, 132, 135, 141–43
footnotes, 150–51
Ford, Ford Madox, 10, 50–69, 131
Forester, C. S., 113, 143, 191
Forster, E. M., 1, 107, 190
fragmented narration, 50–51, 62–64, 71, 82–85

Framley Parsonage (Trollope), 35–36, 133
free indirect speech, 91, 124

García Márquez, Gabriel, 94
Gaskell, Elizabeth, 4–5, 96, 97, 109
General, The (Forester), 113, 143, 191
General Catastrophe, 194n6
Genette, Gérard, 47, 112
geographical time, 133
Germinal (Zola), 99
Ghosts from the Past, 113, 122–25, 128–29, 155–56, 177, 191
Gift plot, 96
Giles Goat-Boy (Barth), 150
Glasgow, Ellen, 133
Go-Between, The (Hartley), 114
Gogol, Nikolai, 109
Golden Ass, The (Apuleius), 109
Golding, William, 49, 100
Good Anna, The (Stein), 9, 35
Good Soldier, The (Ford), 10, 50–69; clusters, 60–62; correctio, 66–69; epimone, 59–60; epitheton, 56; fragmented narration, 62–64; key words, 56–59; links, 56, 64–66; repetitions, 50–51, 53–57, 59, 60–62; rhetorical figures, 50–69; rings, 56, 66; style and rhetorical figures, 50–69
gradatio, 55, 70
grammatical parallelism, 78
Grass, Günter, 106–7, 115–16
Graves, Robert, 139–41
Great Expectations (Dickens), 108
Great Gatsby, The (Fitzgerald), 181
Greene, Graham, 99, 158

Haggard, H. Rider, 96–97, 151
Harari, Yuval Noah, 30
Hardy, Thomas, 10, 36, 99, 132–33, 141–43, 191
Hartley, L. P., 114

Have Spacesuit, Will Travel (Heinlein), 98
Hegel, Georg Wilhelm Friedrich, 158, 169
Heinlein, Robert, 47–49, 98–100, 143, 194n6
Heller, Joseph, 69–89, 143, 194n6
Hemingway, Ernest, 7–9
High Place, The (Cabell), 47
Hilton, James, 97
Hobbit, The (Tolkien), 96
Homer/Homeric epics: book divisions, 193n3; episodes, 11; *Iliad*, 43–45, 95, 112; *Odyssey*, 11, 31–33, 37, 117–18; rings, 29, 33, 37
Homo Deus: A Brief History of Tomorrow (Harari), 30
homoioteleuton, 161
House for Mr. Biswas, A (Naipaul), 113, 191
How to Reread a Novel (Clark), 1–2, 30, 153, 190
hypotaxis, 4–5
hypothesis, 50–51

I Am Legend (Matheson), 109
If Death Ever Slept (Stout), 104
Iliad (Homer), 43–45, 95, 112
illusion, 150, 159
implied author, 10, 159, 161, 167, 181
implied reader, 159
incarceration novel. See *Sympathizer, The* (Nguyen)
indentation, 3
Infinite Jest (Wallace), 151
in medias res, 91, 117, 126, 191
instabilities, 92–95, 100, 102, 109, 111, 114, 190–91
installments, 11
instigating events, 190–91
Insult, 95, 168–69, 171, 194n3
internal divisions, 9, 193n2
internal reader, 159
inversions, 71–77, 85

inverted chronology, 143–44
Invisible Man (Ellison), 116, 157–59, 168, 187, 195n7, 195n10
Isherwood, Christopher, 131

James, Henry: *The Ambassadors*, 11; *The American*, 92, 94, 110–11, 122–24, 191; *The Portrait of a Lady*, 4, 96, 123–25, 143, 191; *Roderick Hudson*, 44–45; *Washington Square*, 107; *The Wings of the Dove*, 31, 94, 109–10
Jane Eyre (Brontë), 97, 124
Jason and the Golden Fleece. See *Argonautica* (Apollonius of Rhodes)
Jazz (Morrison), 9
Jealousy (*Jalousie*) (Robbe-Grillet), 109, 144–49, 192
Johnson, Samuel, 98
jokes, 10, 71–75, 85
Joyce, James, 130
Jude the Obscure (Hardy), 10
Jurgen (Cabell), 95

Kesey, Ken, 99
key words, 36, 56–59, 62, 64, 80, 153, 166–69, 173, 175, 181
Kidnapped (Stevenson), 96
Kim (Kipling), 95, 108, 187
Kindred (Butler), 100
King, Queen, Knave (Nabokov), 108–9, 118–19, 191
King Solomon's Mines (Haggard), 96–97, 151
Kipling, Rudyard, 95, 97, 108, 187
Kiss of the Spider Woman, The (Puig), 151
Knowles, John, 114–15

Lack or Need, 95–99
Land That Time Forgot, The (Burroughs), 97
Lanham, Richard, 30, 70

Last Days of New Paris, The (Miéville), 151
Last Post, The (Ford), 131
Laughter in the Dark (Nabokov), 121–22
Le Guin, Ursula K., 136–38, 139, 143, 152, 192
Levenson, Michael, 50, 59, 66
Light in August (Faulkner), 45–47, 99
links: Austen's *Emma*, 13–18; Ford's *Good Soldier*, 56, 64–66; Heller's *Catch-22*, 77–81, 194n6; repetition, 6–7
litotes, 161
Little Dorrit (Dickens), 32, 37–38
local palilogia, 160, 165
Lolita (Nabokov), 150
long chapter titles, 10
long paragraphs, 4–5
long-range palilogia, 165–66
Longus, 104
Lord of the Flies, The (Golding), 100
Lord of the Rings, The (Tolkien), 12–13, 96
Lost Horizon (Hilton), 97
Lost Lady, A (Cather), 10
"Lost World" genre, 96–97
Love in the Time of Cholera (García Márquez), 94
Lowry, Malcolm, 131–32
Lucy Gayheart (Cather), 133

Magic Mountain, The (Mann), 99
Mann, Thomas, 99
Man Who Would Be King, The (Kipling), 97
Marriage plot, 93–95, 96–97, 107–8, 109–10, 191
Matheson, Richard, 109
medium rings, 37–38
Meeting, 107–9, 117–18
Melanctha (Stein), 9
Melville, Herman, 99, 130, 151, 187
metaphors, 50, 161
Middlemarch (Eliot), 10

middle of the ring, 24, 29, 40, 114–16
Middle(s): Beginning, Middle, End, 92–95; Gift plot, 96; Meeting, 107. *See also* Beginning(s); Ending(s)
middle-sized rings, 86
Miéville, China, 151
Might As Well Be Dead (Stout), 103–4
Millgate, Michael, 46–47
Mill on the Floss, The (Eliot), 10
Milton, John, 91
Mimesis (Auerbach), 33
mirror plots, 134–36, 191–92
misuse of grammatical or logical forms, 73
Mitchell, David, 136, 192
Moby-Dick (Melville), 99, 151, 187
modernism, 112, 125
Moll Flanders (Defoe), 150
morality, 88–89, 156, 169, 181–82, 187
More, Sir Thomas, 99–100
Morrison, Toni, 9, 133
Mother's Recompense, The (Wharton), 102–3
Mrs. Dalloway (Woolf): chapter divisions, 9, 19; characters, 18, 20–21; One-Day Novels, 91, 109, 130–31, 191; repetition and focalization, 18–28; repetitions, 193n4; rings, 24–28; segmentation, 19–20, 28; themes, 18, 21–24; uncommon Beginnings, 109; verbal repetitions, 18–19, 21–22
Mr. Skeffington (von Arnim), 136
multiple narration, 139
Multiple Retrospects, 113, 125–29
murder mysteries, 100, 103–4
Murder on the Orient Express (Christie), 99
My Mortal Enemy (Cather), 119–21, 191

Nabokov, Vladimir, 11, 108–9, 118–19, 121–22, 150, 191
Naipaul, V. S., 113, 191
names and epithets, 171–73

narratee, 52, 159, 174
narrative units, 7, 29. *See also* chapters; episodes; paragraphs; rings; sections; sentences
narrative voice, 136, 138–41, 157, 167, 173, 174, 176–77, 188
negation, 44, 50–51
negative links, 16
nested narrative segments, 10–11, 136
Nguyen, Viet Thanh, 195n1; *The Sympathizer,* 153–89. See also *Sympathizer, The* (Nguyen)
Nicholas Nickleby (Dickens), 102–3
1984 (Orwell), 158
nonfiction memoirs, 150
non-narrative elements in narrative, 149–52
North and South (Gaskell), 4–5, 96, 97, 109
"Nose, The" (Gogol), 109
Notes from Underground (Dostoyevsky), 157–59
novellas, 9
novels, divisions of the whole narrative, 9–13
numbered sections, 12

objects, 160
O'Brien, Flann, 100–101, 151
obstacles, 92, 107, 184
Odyssey (Homer), 11, 31–33, 37, 117–18
Oedipus the King (Sophocles), 104, 122
Old Wives' Tale, The (Bennett), 4, 11–12, 32
Oliver Twist (Dickens), 102, 104
One-Day Novels, 91, 109, 130–32, 191
One Flew Over the Cuckoo's Nest (Kesey), 99
One of Ours (Cather), 10
One-Year Novels, 132–33, 194n1
Optimist's Daughter, The (Welty), 103

Index 211

oral technique, 32
Orwell, George, 158
Otterlo, W. A. A. Van, 29
overlapping focalization, 20–21, 28, 135, 193n5
overlapping rings, 29, 38–41
overlapping timelines, 143

palilogia, 160, 165–66
Paradise Lost (Milton), 91
paradoxes, 71–77, 85, 160
paragraphs: divisions of the whole narrative, 12; paragraph anadiplosis, 14–15, 65; paragraph anaphora, 15; paragraph links in Ford's *Good Soldier*, 64–65; paragraph links in Heller's *Catch-22*, 77–79; paragraph links in Nguyen's *Sympathizer*, 159, 173; paragraph links in Woolf's *Mrs. Dalloway*, 23–24; paragraph rings in James's *Wings of the Dove*, 31; paragraph rings in Roth's *Call It Sleep*, 30–31; paragraph transitions in Heller's *Catch-22*, 77–78; repetition in Woolf's *Mrs. Dalloway*, 18–19; segmentation, 3–8
parallelism, 50, 74, 78, 94, 110–11, 162, 177, 183
para prosdokian, 71–73
parataxis, 4–5
paronomasia, 70, 161
parts, 9–13, 37, 64–66, 130, 134–35, 152
Passage of Arms (Ambler), 135
passive voice, 183
past time of narrative, 129, 131
Pavel, Thomas, 1, 190
Persuasion (Austen), 99
Phelan, James, 92–93, 181, 190
Pincher Martin (Golding), 49
Plague, The (Camus), 109, 194n6
Player Piano (Vonnegut), 5–7

plot rings, 43–49, 175
plots: action of a narrative, 190–91; anachronies, 112–13; Beginning, Middle, End, 92–95; division of the whole narrative, 13; Gift plot, 96; Marriage plot, 93–95, 96–97, 107–8, 109–10, 191; plot time, 90–92; and stories, 90–92; transformations of, 191–92. *See also* complex plot forms; simple plot forms
pluperfect tenses, 118, 121, 126–28
plural self, 188–89
Pnin (Nabokov), 11
Poetics (Aristotle), 93, 122
Poison Belt, The (Doyle), 194n6
political reading of Nguyen's *Sympathizer*, 186–88
polyptoton, 13–14, 54, 70, 161
polysyndeton, 54, 160
Poorhouse Fair, The (Updike), 131
Porter, Katherine Anne, 12, 30, 99
Portrait of a Lady, The (James), 4, 96, 123–25, 143, 191
postmodern or metafictional effect, 150–51
pre-postmodern fiction, 150–51
present time of narrative, 119, 122, 126–28, 129, 131
Pride and Prejudice (Austen), 11, 92, 94, 97, 107, 125
primary narrators, 139–40
Prince, Gerald, 11
Prince and the Pauper, The (Twain), 109
Princess of Mars, A (Burroughs), 99–100, 151
progressive time, 47, 109, 112, 116, 129, 143, 149, 155
progress of human life, 133
prolepsis, 112, 127
prologue, 113–16
protasis, 163

Pudd'nhead Wilson (Twain), 187
Puig, Manuel, 151
punctuation, 3. *See also* quotation marks
Puppet Masters, The (Heinlein), 194n6
Purple Cloud, The (Shiel), 194n6
pysma, 161

Quest, 95–98
Quiet American, The (Greene), 158
quotation marks, 157

Rasselas (Johnson), 98
Ray, Robert, 50–51
readers' feelings about characters, 180–85
reality and language in Heller's *Catch-22*, 75–76
refrains, 56, 59, 71, 82–83
repetitions: Austen's *Emma*, 13–17; Burgess's *Clockwork Orange*, 134–35; clusters, 60–62; defined, 70; diacope, 30; digressive rings, 33; Ford's *Good Soldier*, 50–51, 53–57, 59, 60–62; Grass's *Tin Drum*, 116; Heller's *Catch-22*, 82–83, 85; Nabokov's *King, Queen, Knave*, 119; Nguyen's *Sympathizer*, 163–68; plot rings, 44–45, 47; rings, 29; Robbe-Grillet's *Jealousy* (*Jalousie*), 147–49; verbal rings, 31; Vonnegut's *Player Piano*, 6–7; Woolf's *Mrs. Dalloway*, 18–28, 193n4
representation in Nguyen's *Sympathizer*, 163–65
rereading, 153
Responsive Ring, 32
retrospects: deviations from chronology, 191; lives of the characters before the plot time, 92; Multiple Retrospects, 113, 125–29; Nyugen's *Sympathizer*, 155, 166, 175; Second Chapter Retrospects, 94–95, 113, 116–22, 128, 143. *See also* Ghosts from the Past

Return: Arrival, 99–100; Beginning, Middle, End, 93–95; Death, 102; Departure, 98; as Ending(s), 191; Lack or Need, 96; Le Guin's *Dispossessed*, 137–38; Nguyen's *Sympathizer*, 154
Return of the Native, The (Hardy), 36, 99, 132–33, 141–43, 191
Revenge of the Nephew plot, 96
Revolutionary Road (Yates), 125–29, 181
rhetorical figures in Ford's *Good Soldier*, 50–69
rhetorical figures in Heller's *Catch-22*, 70–71, 85
rhetorical figures in Nguyen's *Sympathizer*, 159–71
rhythm, 3
Rimmon-Kenan, Shlomith, 91
rings, 29–49; Ambler's *Passage of Arms*, 135; Beginning, Middle, End, 94; Beginning with the Ending, 113–16; Burgess's *Clockwork Orange*, 135; complex rings, 38–43; digressive rings, 33–36, 41; dream rings, 47–49; Ford's *Good Soldier*, 56, 66; Heller's *Catch-22*, 85–89; Le Guin's *Dispossessed*, 138; medium rings, 37–38; Nabokov's *Laughter in the Dark*, 122; Nabokov's *King, Queen, Knave*, 118–19; Nguyen's *Sympathizer*, 175, 182, 189; plot rings, 43–49, 175; small rings, 24–25, 29–36, 40–43, 46, 85, 175; Woolf's *Mrs. Dalloway*, 24–28
Robbe-Grillet, Alain, 109, 131, 144–49, 192
Robinson Crusoe (Defoe), 150
Roderick Hudson (James), 44–45
Romantic Comedians, The (Glasgow), 133
Room with a View, A (Forster), 107
Roth, Henry, 30–31
Roth, Philip, 109
Roxana (Defoe), 150

Ruden, Sarah, 37
Russian formalism, 90

Saramago, José, 109, 194n6
Scholes, Robert, 90–91
Schorer, Mark, 50
science-fiction stories, 98–100, 109
Scott, Sir Walter, 150
secondary narrators, 140
Second Chapter Retrospects, 94–95, 113, 116–22, 128, 143
section links, 63–65
sections, 7, 9, 12, 28
segmentation, 3–9; Austen's *Emma*, 13–18; divisions of the whole narrative, 10–11; Woolf's *Mrs. Dalloway*, 19–20, 28
Seize the Day (Bellow), 131
self, 188–89
semantic repetitions, 18–19
semantic rings, 31
Sense and Sensibility (Austen), 102, 107
sentences: segmentation, 3–9; sentence anadiplosis, 14–15; sentence epanalepsis, 29–30; sentence links in Austen's *Emma*, 13–17; sentence links in Ford's *Good Soldier*, 64
Sentimental Education (Flaubert), 108–9
Separate Peace, A (Knowles), 114–15
serial divisions, 11
Set-up, 94
Shadows on the Rock (Cather), 133
Sheppard Lee: Written by Himself (Bird), 10, 101
Shiel, M. P., 194n6
Ship of Fools (Porter), 12, 30, 99
short paragraphs, 5–7
short stories, 9
Shrinking Man, The (Matheson), 109
Sidney, Sir Philip, 30
Silas Marner (Eliot), 4, 97–98

Silent Speaker, The (Stout), 103
similes, 161
simple plot forms, 90–111; Arrival, 99–100, 191; Beginning, Middle, End, 92–95; Birth, 104–7; Death, 100–104; Lack or Need, 95–99; Meeting, 107–9; story and plot, 90–92; uncommon Beginnings, 109–11. *See also* Ending(s)
simultaneous narration, 141–43
Single Man, A (Isherwood), 131
Sirens of Titan, The (Vonnegut), 10, 150
small rings, 24–25, 29–36, 40–43, 46, 85, 175
Song of Roland, 95
Sophocles, 104, 122
Sot-Weed Factor, The (Barth), 10
spacing, 9, 193n1
Stamboul Train (Greene), 99
Starman Jones (Heinlein), 47–49, 98
Stein, Gertrude, 9, 35
Sterne, Laurence, 33–35
Stevenson, Robert Louis, 96, 109
St. Jerome's vision of Jesus, 195n9
story and plot, 90–92
Stout, Rex, 103–4
Strange Case of Dr. Jekyll and Mr. Hyde, The (Stevenson), 109
strata organization, 12
style in Ford's *Good Soldier*, 50–51
style in Heller's *Catch-22*, 70–71, 85
style in Nguyen's *Sympathizer*, 159–71
subsections, 10–11, 95
suspended or cyclic time, 149
Sympathizer, The (Nguyen), 153–89; Beginning(s), 156–59; chapter links, 173–75, 178; characters, 155–56; Ending(s), 185–89; names and epithets, 171–73; "nothing," 175–80, 185–86; overview, 154–56; political reading of, 186–88; readers' feelings about

characters, 180–85; rings, 175; style and rhetorical figures, 159–71
sympathy for characters, 180–85

Tale of Two Cities, A (Dickens), 10
temporal adverbs, 113, 126–28, 144
temporal experience of reading, 153–54
temporal shifts, 112–13, 114
Thackeray, William Makepeace, 98
They Hanged My Saintly Billy (Graves), 139–41
third-person narration, 138–39, 167, 173, 174, 176, 188
Third Policeman, The (O'Brien), 100–101, 151
Three Lives (Stein), 35
Time for the Stars (Heinlein), 98–99
Time's Arrow (Amis), 143–44, 192
time travel stories, 143–44
Tin Drum, The (Grass), 106–7, 115–16
titled chapters, 9–13
titles, 92, 150
Tolkien, J. R. R., 12–13, 96
Tolstoy, Leo, 92
Tom Jones (Fielding), 9–10, 11, 104
transitions, 4, 13, 15, 17–18, 20–21, 77–78, 80–81, 137–38, 142, 145
Treasure Island (Stevenson), 96
tricolon, 70, 160
Tristram Shandy (Sterne), 33–35
Trollope, Anthony, 35–36, 38–43, 96–97, 102–3, 133
Tunnel in the Sky (Heinlein), 100
Twain, Mark, 94, 98, 109, 187, 195n14

Ulysses (Joyce), 130
uncommon Beginnings, 109–11
underlying chronology, 91, 143
Under the Volcano (Lowry), 131–32
unequal parts, 12

unity/unified structure, 7, 11, 43, 44, 85–86
unnamed characters, 144, 171–73, 175, 195n10
unnatural chronology, 143–49, 192, 194n2
Updike, John, 131
Utopia (More), 99–100

Vanity Fair (Thackeray), 98
verbal links or clusters, 16–17, 63–64
verbal repetitions, 5–6, 18–19, 21–22
verbal rings, 31
Victorian novels, 11
Virgil, 37, 116–17, 191
Voltaire, 98, 150
volumes, 11–13
von Arnim, Elizabeth, 136
Vonnegut, Kurt, 5–7, 10, 150

Wallace, David Foster, 151
Washington Square (James), 107
Waste Land, The (Eliot), 158
Waverley (Scott), 150
Welty, Eudora, 103
Western canon, 158
Wharton, Edith, 102–3
Wings of the Dove, The (James), 31, 94, 109–10
Woman's Life, A (de Maupassant), 98
Wonderful Wizard of Oz, The (Baum), 99–100
Woolf, Virginia, 4, 109, 193n2. See also *Mrs. Dalloway* (Woolf)

Yates, Richard, 125–29, 181
Years, The (Woolf), 4, 109, 193n2

zero beginnings and zero endings, 94–95
zeugma, 73–74, 161
Zola, Émile, 99

www.ingramcontent.com/pod-product-compliance
Lightning Source LLC
Chambersburg PA
CBHW031812220426
43662CB00007B/618